CUCET

Central Universities Common Entrance Test

2022

DU | BHU | JNU | JMI | AMU

35

Practice Sets

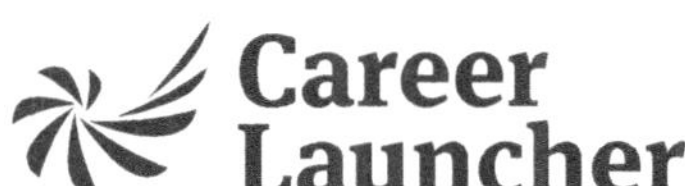

Title   : CUCET 2022 : 35 Practice Sets

Language   : English

Editor's Name   : Amitendra Kumar

Copyright ©   : 2022 CLIP

Typeset & Published by :

Career Launcher Infrastructure (P) Ltd.

A-45, Mohan Cooperative Industrial Area, Near Mohan Estate Metro Station, New Delhi - 110044

Marketed by :

G.K. Publications (P) Ltd.

Plot No. 9A, Sector-27A, Mathura Road, Faridabad, Haryana-121003

ISBN   : **978-93-92837-47-0**

Printer's Details : Made in India, New Delhi.

Contents

About CUCET

A year ago, it would have been unimaginable that cut-offs in Delhi University would skyrocket to 100% for some of the undergraduate courses! While DU has always been known for its high cut-offs, there are several other universities where the story is no different.

However, the National Education Policy 2020 (NEP) aims to do away with the tyranny of the ever-rising cut-offs by introducing a Common Entrance Test for all the Central Universities in the country. NEP not only proposes a holistic approach in evaluating the students by giving them the option to select subjects based on their interest, but it also aims to simplify the process of admission to higher-education institutes.

To start with, there would be a Common Entrance Test for all the Central Universities, which would be conducted twice a year from 2022. While this might sound like a new concept to many, the fact is, there is already a Central Universities Common Entrance Test (CUCET), which is conducted for the Central Universities established in or after 2009. As many as 14 of them already admit students based on their performance in the entrance test. The CUCET scores are also accepted by four state universities of the country.

The proposed CUCET aims to assess conceptual understanding and application of knowledge; and also, to lessen the burden of appearing in multiple tests.

CUCET Eligibility

Getting into a premier University is every student's dream. The brand value of the University not only facilitates securing a seat in a master's program in a national/international institute, but also helps in getting job offers through campus placements.

Entry to a Central University, in most cases earlier, was based on merit, i.e., marks secured in Class XII Board exams. However, from the academic year 2021, all Central Universities will also consider the CUCET score for admissions into their Undergraduate programs.

CUCET 2022: Eligibility Criteria

While the official criteria will be learnt once the CUCET 2021 notification is released, the stipulations are not expected to change much from those of previous years.

- A candidate must have passed Class XII (10+2) or equivalent from a recognized education Board.
- If the respective Board awards grades (or CGPA), the conversion factor given by the Board must be used to compute the percentage of marks.
- Candidates, who have completed their Class XII in 2021, and have passed the Board exams, will also be eligible to apply for CUCET 2022.

Eligibility: Class XII Students

While CUCET is for students who have passed the Class XII (or equivalent) Board exams, any student who is appearing for the Class XII Board exam in 2022 is also eligible to apply for CUCET 2021. The candidate would be required to produce the marksheets and relevant certificates as mandated by the participating Central University, and follow the timelines provided for admissions.

Key Points

- Each participating Central University is free to decide its own eligibility criteria for admissions.

- The weightages for CUCET and Class XII Board exam results(if, applicable) will be at the sole discretion of the Central University, to which admission is being sought.

- As of date, CUCET does not have an age limit. However, Central Universities can fix minimum & maximum age limit for admissions to all (or any) of the programs on offer.

Reservation of Seats

As CUCET is an entrance exam for admissions to Undergraduate courses at the Central Universities, which have been established under an Act of the Parliament, each Central University must follow the norms set by the Government of India, with respect to intake and reservation of seats.

Generally, the following break-up is followed:

Category	Reservation
Scheduled Castes	15%
Scheduled Tribes	7.5%
Other Backward Classes (Non-Creamy)	27%
Persons with Disability	5%

Some institutions might even have provisions for the Economically Weaker Sections, which can account for 10% of the total seats. These EWS seats are carved out from the Open Category.

To avail of the reservation benefit based on caste (or any other category as specified), a candidate must be able to produce valid documents/certificates to support such claims.

Conclusion

It is essential for every candidate to check the validity of their candidature for CUCET, as well as the Central University he/she is applying to. The candidate should be aware of the documents that might be required while applying for the exam, or during the admissions.

CUCET 2022 notification is expected in March 2022, and registration is also going to start then.

CUCET: Exam Pattern

Till 2021, the Central Universities—except for the 14 established in 2009 and after, and few others— have been admitting students to their undergraduate courses based on Class XII Board marks; resulting in tremendous mental pressure for students. With the ever-rising cut-offs, the best of the Central Universities (like the University of Delhi) was getting out of reach for many. Moreover, as there was no uniformity among the various examination Boards regarding syllabus and difficulty, students from some of the Boards got an undue advantage.

To overcome this issue, the Ministry of Education has decided that from the academic year 2022, CUCET will be a single entrance for admission to undergraduate courses offered by all the Central Universities.

CUCET 2022

CUCET 2022 is still in the discussion stages. The Ministry of Education has formed an expert Committee, which is working on the various aspects of the exam, including the pattern and weightages which need to be assigned to CUCET scores for admissions in the participating Central Universities.

However, CUCET 2022 is expected to be a General Ability Test with focus on:

- English Language, including Comprehension
- Numerical Ability
- Logical & Analytical Reasoning
- General Awareness, including Current Affairs

CUCET 2021

CUCET 2020 was conducted in online mode by 14 Central Universities and 4 State Universities. The paper was divided into two parts:

Part A: 25 MCQs covering Language, General Awareness, Mathematical Aptitude, and Analytical Skills. For certain courses, this section comprised 100 questions (No Part B in these cases)

Part B: 100 MCQs on Domain Knowledge across 4 sections. Each section had 25 questions. A candidate was required to answer any 3 sections (75 questions).

Every correct response entailed 3 marks, while there was a penalty of 1 mark for every incorrect response.

CUCET 2022: Marking Scheme

CUCET has a provision for negative marking. So, it is imperative that a candidate is careful about the risks involved, and refrain from making too many guesses.

The exact marking scheme for CUCET 2022 will be known once the official notification is released.

CUCET 2022: Importance

While CUCET 2021 was the gateway to 14 Central Universities, CUCET 2022 will open the doors for 41+ Central Universities in the country. Hence, it is important that students focus on preparing well for the exam, so as to ensure a seat in a program and university of their choice.

CUCET Syllabus

CUCET Syllabus

Before you start your preparation for any entrance exam, it is important to understand the syllabus. Otherwise, your prep will be directionless, and you might be left wondering where things might have gone wrong!

With more than 1.68 lakh seats on offer for the undergraduate courses at the 54 Central Universities, CUCET is one the most competitive examinations. For this very reason, while preparing for the exam, you will need to adopt a structured approach. And in doing that, understanding the syllabus is a critical step.

CUCET 2022 Overview

CUCET 2022 will be a Computer-Based Test (CBT), commonly referred to as an online exam. However, there is a difference between the two terms: CBT and online. In CBT, the questions are kept constant and simply presented in an online format; whereas in an Online Test, questions are stored as a bank, and the system decides which questions are to be presented to the candidate, based on a pre-defined logic.

CUCET 2022 is likely to be a General Ability Test, with focus on English Language, Numerical Ability, Logical & Analytical Reasoning, along with General Awareness and Current Affairs.

CUCET 2022 Syllabus

The CUCET 2022 exam pattern gives a good idea about what is in store for the candidate and how one needs to prepare for the exam.

- **English Language:** The questions in this section will test one's proficiency in the language, based on comprehension passages, fundamentals of grammar, and vocabulary. In the Comprehension section, candidates will be evaluated on their understanding of a passage and its central theme, meanings of words used therein, etc. The Grammar section entails correcting grammatically incorrect sentences, filling of blanks in sentences with appropriate words, etc. Questions on synonyms & antonyms will check one's command over English vocabulary.
- **Numerical Ability:** Questions on Numerical Ability will test the candidate's knowledge of elementary mathematics. Areas like arithmetic, number system, basics of algebra, and modern maths will be central to these types of questions.
- **Logical & Analytical Reasoning:** This section tests the candidate's ability to identify patterns & logical links, and rectify illogical arguments. It can include a variety of Logical Reasoning questions, such as those on syllogisms, logical sequences, analogies, etc., along with Analytical Reasoning questions on series, directions, clocks & calendars, arrangements, and puzzles to name a few.
- **General Awareness and Current Affairs:** The General Awareness section includes static general knowledge, while questions on Current Affairs will gauge a candidate's knowledge of national & international current affairs.

CUCET 2022 may or may not have a section on subject knowledge. Once the exam notification is out in March, there will be more clarity on this matter.

While there is no syllabus explicitly mentioned by CUCET, the broad idea is always presented. One must look at the previous years' papers and solve the sample papers available to form a basic understanding.

About University of Delhi

University of Delhi (commonly known as DU) was established in 1922 and is one of the largest Universities in the country. With 16 faculties, 86 academic departments, 90 colleges and 540 programs on offer, Delhi University is no doubt one of the sought-after University in the country.

With 1, 96,000 students enrolled in UG programs, Delhi University is a valued university and constantly ranked among the top in the country. DU bagged 11th Rank in NIRF 2020 and ranked 6th in QS India Rankings 2020. The University has two Campuses: North and South.

DU UG Programs

Delhi University offers several programs at the undergraduate level. With more than 60 constituent colleges, the Delhi University offers many undergraduate courses.

Please refer to the table below for the important undergraduate courses offered by the DU and the intake across each program.

Program	Intake
B. A (Pass)	11249
B. A (Hons) Geography	788
B. A (Hons) Economics	2754
B. A (Hons) History	2791
B. A (Hons) Political Science	3657
B. A (Hons) Sociology	596
B. A (Hons) Psychology	670
B. A (Hons) Applied Psychology	252
B. A (Hons) Social Work	133
B. A (Hons) Philosophy	783
B. A (Hons) English	2886
B. A (Hons) Hindi	2829
B. A (Hons) Sanskrit	1407
B. A (Hons) Punjabi	214
B. A (Hons) Urdu	207
BA(Hons) French	49

Program	Intake
BA(Hons) German	49
BA(Hons) Spanish	49
BA(Hons) Italian	49
B. Com (Hons)	7953
B.Com (Pass)	7854
Program	Intake
B.Sc. (H) Biomedical Science	162
B.Sc. (H) Botany	937
B.Sc. (H) Chemistry	1487
B.Sc. (H) Computer Science	1265
B.Sc. (H) Electronics	624
B.Sc. (H) Mathematics	2428
B.Sc. (H) Physics	1659
B.Sc. (H) Zoology	944
B.Sc. Life Sciences	1515
B.Sc. Physical Science with Chemistry	703
B.Sc. Physical Science with Computer Science	553
B.Sc. Physical Science with Electronics	247
B. Sc (Hons.) Statistics	476
B. Sc. (Prog.) Applied Physical Science Industrial Chemistry	96
B.Sc. (Hons.) Home Science	900
B. Sc. (Hons.) Psychology	57
B.Sc. (H) Food Technology	179
B.Sc. (H)Instrumentation	99
B.Sc. (H) Microbiology	238
B.Sc. (H) Polymer Science	59
B.SC. Mathematical Science	224
B.SC. (Hons.) Biochemistry	146
B.SC. Industrial Chemistry	78
B.Sc. (Prog.) Physical Science	940
B.SC. (Hons.) Geology	98

DU UG Programs Eligibility:

As the University offers multiple programs and separate intake for male and female candidates, it is important to check the university official website regularly to keep oneself updated about the eligibility for each program, which can change.

DU UG Admissions:

Until 2021, Delhi University admitted students on the basis of class XII marks. From the academic year 2022, admissions to UG programs offered Delhi University will be based on Central Universities Common Entrance Test (CUCET). CUCET will be a common entrance for admissions to UG programs offered by all the Central Universities in the country.

Delhi University UG Programs Reservation:

DU being a Central University offers reservations in admissions according to central government rules.

Schedule Caste (SC): 15% of the total seats are reserved for students who belong to SC category.

Schedule Tribe (ST): 7.5% of the total seats are reserved for students belonging to ST Category.

Other Backward Classes (OBC): 27% of the total intake is reserved for students from Other Backward Classes (OBC), excluding those from creamy layer.

Economically Weaker Section (EWS): The University has reserved 10% seats for EWS category, in accordance with the directive of Ministry of Education.

Persons with Disability (PWD): 5% of the seats are reserved on horizontal basis for students from PWD category.

About BHU

Banaras Hindu University (BHU), situated in the holy city of Varanasi, was founded by Pandit Madan Mohan Malviya in cooperation with Dr. Annie Besant, in 1916 under the act of Parliament-B.H.U Act, 1915. BHU, which is a Central University, comprises of 6 Institutes, 14 Faculties, 144 academic departments, and 4 Inter-disciplinary centers, spread over 1300 acres. The University consists of 15,000 students, 1700 teachers and 8000 non-teaching staff.

BHU was ranked 3rd among the Universities in India in 2020. According to university submissions for NIRF 2021, BHU has 10, 585 students pursuing UG programs, of which 236 students are foreign nationals.

BHU UG Programs

BHU offers a host of undergraduate programs including medical and engineering. Through its various faculties, BHU offers a range of programs which caters to students learning abilities. The University along with its main campus, also offers the undergraduate courses from the following colleges: Mahila Mahavidyalaya (MMV); Arya Mahila Post Graduate College (AMPGC), Vasant Kanya Mahavidyalaya (VKM); Vasanta College for Women (VCW); DAV Post Graduate College (DAVPGC) and Rajiv Gandhi South Campus (RGSC).

Please refer to the table below for the important undergraduate courses offered by BHU and the intake across each program/campuses.

Faculty of Arts				
Course	Campus	Intake	Status	Duration
B.A (Hons) Arts	Faculty of Arts	765	Co-Ed	3 Years
	Mahila Mahavidyalaya	286	Women	3 Years
	Arya Mahila Post Graduate College	383	Women	3 Years
	Vasant Kanya Mahavidyalaya	286	Women	3 Years
	Vasanta College for Women	412	Women	3 Years
	DAV Post Graduate College	309	Co-Ed	3 Years
Faculty of Social Sciences				
Course	Campus	Intake	Status	Duration
B.A (Hons) Social Sciences [incl. B. A (Hons) Economics]	Faculty of Social Sciences	573	Co-Ed	3 Years
	Mahila Mahavidyalaya	193	Women	3 Years
	Arya Mahila Post Graduate College	383	Women	3 Years
	Vasant Kanya Mahavidyalaya	249	Women	3 Years
	Vasanta College for Women	210	Women	3 Years
	DAV Post Graduate College	326	Co-Ed	3 Years

Faculty of Commerce				
Course	Campus	Intake	Status	Duration
B. Com (Hons)	Faculty of Commerce	286	Co-Ed	3 Years
	Vasant Kanya Mahavidyalaya	96	Women	3 Years
	Arya Mahila Post Graduate College	96	Women	3 Years
	DAV Post Graduate College	227	Co-Ed	3 Years
	Rajiv Gandhi South Campus, Mirzapur	114	Co-Ed	3 Years
B. Com (Hons) Financial Markets Management	Faculty of Commerce	62	Co-Ed	3 Years
	Rajiv Gandhi South Campus, Mirzapur	62	Co-Ed	3 Years
Institute of Science				
Course	Campus	Intake	Status	Duration
B.Sc (Hons) Maths Group	Faculty of Science	573	Co-Ed	3 Years
	Mahila Mahavidyalaya	96	Women	3 Years
B.Sc (Hons) Bio Group	Faculty of Science	383	Co-Ed	3 Years
	Mahila Mahavidyalaya	193	Women	3 Years

Faculty of Visual Arts				
Course	Campus	Intake	Status	Duration
B.F.A (Bachelor of Fine Arts)	Faculty of Visual Arts	96	Co-Ed	4 Years
Faculty of Arts				
Bachelor of Vocation (Retail and Logistics Management)	Rajiv Gandhi South Campus	62	Co-Ed	3 Years
Bachelor of Vocation (Hospitality & Tourism Management)	Rajiv Gandhi South Campus	62	Co-Ed	3 Years
Bachelor of Vocation (Fashion Designing and Event Management)	Rajiv Gandhi South Campus	62	Co-Ed	3 Years
Bachelor of Vocation (Modern Office Management)	Rajiv Gandhi South Campus	62	Co-Ed	3 Years
Bachelor of Vocation (Food Processing & Management)	Rajiv Gandhi South Campus	62	Co-Ed	3 Years
Bachelor of Vocation (Medical Lab. & Technology)	Rajiv Gandhi South Campus	62	Co-Ed	3 Years

BHU UG Programs Eligibility:

Each of the courses have different eligibility for admissions. To be eligible for admissions, one must fulfil all the criteria as laid down by the respective faculties of the University.

B.A (Hons) Arts/ B.A (Hons) Social Sciences: Candidate must not be more than 22 years of age and must have passed class XII or equivalent with minimum 50% marks in aggregate.

B.A (Hons) Economics: Candidate must not be more than 22 years of age and must have passed class XII or equivalent with minimum 50% marks in aggregate along with mathematics as one of the papers.

B. Com (Hons)/B. Com (Hons) Financial Markets Management: Candidate must not be more than 22 years of age and must have passed class XII or equivalent with minimum 50% marks in aggregate with Commerce/ Economics/Maths/Computer Science/Finance/Financial Markets Management as one of the subjects.

B. Sc (Hons) Maths Group: Candidate must not be more than 22 years of age and must have passed class XII or equivalent with minimum 50% marks in aggregate in the subjects Physics, Maths plus any one of the following: Chemistry, Statistics, Geology, Computer Science, Information Technology and Geography and must have passed in each of the concerned three subjects.

B. Sc (Hons) Bio Group: Candidate must not be more than 22 years of age and must have passed class XII or equivalent with minimum 50% marks in aggregate in the subjects Physics, Chemistry plus any one of the following: Biology, Geology and Geography and must have passed in each of the concerned three subjects.

B. F. A (Bachelor of Fine Arts): Candidate must not be more than 22 years of age and must have passed class XII or equivalent with minimum 50% marks in aggregate.

Bachelor of Vocation: Candidate must have passed class XII or equivalent in any stream (Science for Food Processing and Medical Lab Technology) or level 4 NSQF certificate.

BHU UG Admissions:

Until 2021, admissions to BHU UG courses were based on Undergraduate Entrance Test (UET) conducted by the University. From the academic year 2022, admissions to UG programs offered by BHU will be based on Central Universities Common Entrance Test (CUCET), which will replace the UET. CUCET will be a common entrance for admissions to UG programs offered by all the Central Universities in the country.

BHU UG Programs Reservation:

BHU being a Central University offers reservations in admissions according to central government rules.

Schedule Caste (SC): 15% of the total seats are reserved for students who belong to SC category.

Schedule Tribe (ST): 7.5% of the total seats are reserved for students belonging to ST Category.

Other Backward Classes (OBC): 27% of the total intake is reserved for students from Other Backward Classes (OBC), excluding those from creamy layer.

Economically Weaker Section (EWS): The University has reserved 10% seats for EWS category, in accordance with the directive of Ministry of Education.

Persons with Disability (PWD): 5% of the seats are reserved on horizontal basis for students from PWD category.

About JNU

Ever wondered which University, the cadets from National Defence Academy (NDA) graduate from? Yes. It is Jawaharlal Nehru University (JNU). JNU started in the year 1969, three years after the act of Parliament in 1966. With several academic centres of JNU declared "Centres of Excellence" by the University Grants Commission, JNU has been ranked No. 1 by National Assessment and Accreditation Council (NAAC). JNU has been ranked No. 2 by National Institutional Ranking Framework (NIRF) 2020 and has been awarded the Best University Award by the President of India in 2017. The European Commission has awarded the Jean Monnet Centre of Excellence for European Union Studies in India (CEEUSI) to Jawaharlal Nehru University in 2018. This is one of the highest international recognition for any European Studies programme.

JNU was the first University to start integrated five-year Master of Arts in Language Courses. JNU actively collaborates with National and International Universities for student and faculty exchange programs.

According to university submissions for NIRF 2020, JNU has 1,048 students pursuing UG programs, of which 46 are foreign nationals.

JNU UG Programs

JNU offers a limited program at the undergraduate level, unlike other universities. The focus at undergraduate has been largely on language courses. In 2018, JNU started two programs in engineering and plans to add a few more specializations in future.

Please refer to the table below for the important undergraduate courses offered by JNU and the intake across each program.

School	Program	Intake	Duration
School of Language, Literature and Cultural Studies	B. A (Hons) Pashto	19	3 Years
	B. A (Hons) Persian	39	3 Years
	B. A (Hons) Arabic	39	3 Years
	B. A (Hons) Japanese	48	3 Years
	B. A (Hons) Korean	39	3 Years
	B. A (Hons) Chinese	44	3 Years
	B. A (Hons) French	48	3 Years
	B. A (Hons) German	48	3 Years
	B. A (Hons) Russian	68	3 Years
	B. A (Hons) Spanish	39	3 Years

School of Sanskrit and Indic Studies	B. Sc - M. Sc Integrated Program in Ayurveda Biology	20	5 Years
School of Engineering	B. Tech in Computer Science and Engineering & MS/M. Tech in Social Sciences/Humanities/Science/Technology	25	5 Years
	B. Tech in Electronics and Communication Engineering & MS/M. Tech in Social Sciences/Humanities/Science/Technology	25	5 Years

JNU UG Programs Eligibility:

Each of the courses have different eligibility for admissions. To be eligible for admissions, one must fulfil all the criteria as laid down by the respective faculties of the University.

B.A (Hons) Language Courses: Candidate must not be less than 17 years of age and must have passed Senior School Certificate (10+2) or equivalent examination with minimum of 45% marks.

B. Sc - M. Sc Integrated Program in Ayurveda Biology: Candidate must not be less than 17 years of age and must have passed Senior School Certificate (10+2) or equivalent examination with minimum of 45% marks.

B. Tech-M. Tech: Based on JEE Mains

JNU UG Admissions:

Until 2021, admissions to JNU UG courses were based on JNU Entrance Examination (JNUEE) conducted by the National Testing Agency (NTA). From the academic year 2022, admissions to UG programs offered by JNU will be based on Central Universities Common Entrance Test (CUCET), which will replace the JNUEE. CUCET will be a common entrance for admissions to UG programs offered by all the Central Universities in the country.

JNU UG Programs Reservation:

JNU being a Central University offers reservations in admissions according to central government rules.

Schedule Caste (SC): 15% of the total seats are reserved for students who belong to SC category.

Schedule Tribe (ST): 7.5% of the total seats are reserved for students belonging to ST Category.

Other Backward Classes (OBC): 27% of the total intake is reserved for students from Other Backward Classes (OBC), excluding those from creamy layer. Also, Central List of Caste to be followed.

Economically Weaker Section (EWS): The University has reserved 10% seats for EWS category, in accordance with the directive of Ministry of Education.

Persons with Disability (PWD): 5% of the seats are reserved on horizontal basis for students from PWD category.

About Jamia Milia Islamia

Jamia Milia Islamia (JMI) was founded in 1920 in Aligarh and became a Central University in 1988 by the act of Parliament. Jamia in Urdu stands for University and Milia means National, making Jamia Milia Islamia a National University. Jamia Milia Islamia moved to Delhi in 1925 and shifted to its present campus in Okhla in 1935.

Jamia Milia Islamia is a NAAC accredited University with grade "A" and was placed 10th in NIRF Rankings 2020. According to submissions made by University for NIRF 2021, Jamia Milia Islamia has a total of 5,911 students pursuing undergraduate courses at the University, of which 105 are foreign nationals. The University also manage to place a total of 681 UG students with an average salary ranging 4.2 Lacs-6.0 Lacs.

JMI UG Programs

Jamia Milia Islamia (JMI) offers a host of undergraduate programs for students. Through its various faculties, JMI offers a range of programs which caters to students learning abilities.

Please refer to the table below for the important undergraduate courses offered by Jamia Milia Islamia and the intake across each program.

Faculty	Course	Intake	Duration
Faculty of Humanities and Language	B. A (Hons) English	60	3 Years
	B. A (Hons) Hindi	40	3 Years
	B. A (Hons) Mass Media-Hindi	40	3 Years
	B. A (Hons) History	60	3 Years
	Bachelor of Hotel Management (BHM)	40	3 Years
	Bachelor of Tourism and Travel Management	40	3 Years
	B. Voc (Food Production)	40	3 Years
Faculty of Social Sciences	Bachelor of Arts (B. A)	68	3 Years
	B. Com (Hons)	55	3 Years
	BBA (Bachelor of Business Administration)	44	3 Years
	B. A (Hons) Economics	53	3 Years
	B. A (Hons) Sociology	42	3 Years
	B. A (Hons) Political Science	42	3 Years
	B. A (Hons) Psychology	42	3 Years
Faculty of Natural Sciences	B. Sc (Bachelor of Science)	50	3 Years
	B. Sc Biosciences	40	3 Years
	B. Sc Biotechnology	35	3 Years
	B. Sc (Hons) Chemistry	40	3 Years
	B. A/B. Sc (Hons) Geography	60	3 Years
	B. Sc (Hons) Mathematics	45	3 Years
	B. Sc (Hons) Applied Mathematics	45	3 Years
	B. Sc (Hons) Physics	45	3 Years
Faculty of Fine Arts	Bachelor of Fine Arts (Applied Art)	30	4 Years
	Bachelor of Fine Arts (Art Education)	20	4 Years
	Bachelor of Fine Arts (Painting)	20	4 Years
	Bachelor of Fine Arts (Sculpture)	10	4 Years

JMI UG Programs Eligibility:

Each of the courses have different eligibility for admissions. To be eligible for admissions, one must fulfil all the criteria as laid down by the respective faculties of the University.

B. Com (Hons) /BBA /B. A (Hons) Economics: Candidate must have passed class XII or equivalent with a minimum of 50% marks in five subjects.

BHM/BTTM/B. Voc (Food Production): Candidate must have passed class XII or equivalent with a minimum of 45% marks in five subjects.

B. A (Hons) Mass Media/B. A (Hons) Hindi: Candidate must have passed class XII or equivalent with a minimum of 45% marks in five subjects.

B. Sc/B. Sc (Hons): Candidate must have passed class XII or equivalent with minimum 50% marks in each of the science subjects i.e. Physics, Chemistry and Mathematics and 50% marks in aggregate of best 5-subjects.

JMI UG Admissions:

Until 2021, admissions to JMI UG courses were based on Entrance Test (JMI-ET) conducted by the University. From the academic year 2022, admissions to UG programs offered by JMI will be based on Central Universities Common Entrance Test (CUCET), which will replace the JMI-ET. CUCET will be a common entrance for admissions to UG programs offered by all the Central Universities in the country.

JMI UG Programs Reservation:

JMI is a minority reservation-based University and accordingly, seats are reserved for candidates as per the norms laid down by the University.

Muslim Minority: 30% of the total seats are reserved for Muslim applicants; 10% of the total seats are reserved for women applicants who are Muslim; 10% of the total intake is for OBC-NC candidates who are Muslims.

Persons with Disability (PWD): 5% of the seats are reserved for students from PWD category.

Jamia Students: 5% seats in all Undergraduate Programs shall be filled by internal students of Jamia who have passed their qualifying examination of the concerned programme (X or XII) from Jamia Schools as regular students.

In addition, Jamia Milia Islamia has supernumerary seats for Kashmiri Migrants and students from Jammu and Kashmir.

About Aligarh Muslim University

Aligarh Muslim University also referred as AMU was established by Sir Syed Ahmad Khan in 1875. The University started as Muhammadan Anglo-Oriental College and became a University (AMU) in 1920. The university has been ranked 801–1000 in the QS World University Rankings of 2021 and 17 in India by the National Institutional Ranking Framework in 2020.

Aligarh Muslim University is institution of national importance, under the seventh schedule of the Constitution of India.

AMU UG Programs

Aligarh Muslim University offers several programs at the undergraduate level. With 7 constituent colleges, the Aligarh Muslim University offers many undergraduate courses.

Please refer to the table below for the important undergraduate courses offered by the AMU and the intake across each program.

Course	Intake	Duration
B. Sc (Hons) Home Science	30*	3 Years
B.Sc (Hons) Agriculture	40	4 Years
B. A (Hons) Arabic	20+10*	3 Years
B. A (Hons) Communicative English	15+20*	3 Years
B. A (Hons) English	40+35*	3 Years
B. A (Hons) Hindi	40+25*	3 Years
B. A (Hons) Geography	50+20*	3 Years
B. A (Hons) Linguistics	20+25*	3 Years
B. A (Hons) Persian	15+25*	3 Years
B. A (Hons) Philosophy	20+10*	3 Years
B. A (Hons) Quaranic Studies	10+10*	3 Years
B. A (Hons) Sanskrit	15+10*	3 Years
B. A (Hons) Urdu	40+50*	3 Years
Bachelor of Fine Arts	15+15*	3 Years
B. Com (Hons)	180+100*	3 Years
B. Voc Production Technology	50	3 Years
B Voc Polymer and Coating Technology	50	3 Years
B. Voc Fashion Design and Garment Technology	50	3 Years
B. A (Hons) Chinese	20	3 Years
B. A (Hons) French	20	3 Years
B. A (Hons) German	20	3 Years

B. A (Hons) Russian	20	3 Years
B. A (Hons) Spanish	20	3 Years
B. Sc (Hons) Biochemistry	30+30*	3 Years
B. Sc (Hons) Botany	60+40*	3 Years
B. Sc (Hons) Zoology	60+45*	3 Years
B. Sc (Hons) Physics	120+35*	3 Years
B. Sc (Hons) Chemistry	120+65*	3 Years
B. Sc (Hons) Mathematics	120+40*	3 Years
B. Sc (Hons) Geography	45+30*	3 Years
B. Sc (Hons) Geology	100+30*	3 Years
B. Sc (Hons) Statistics	60+30*	3 Years
B. Sc (Hons) Industrial Chemistry	20+10*	3 Years
B. Sc (Hons) Computer Applications	40+20*	3 Years

AMU UG Programs Eligibility:

As the University offers multiple programs and separate intake for male and female candidates, it is important to check the university official website regularly to keep oneself updated about the eligibility for each program, which can change.

AMU UG Admissions:

Until 2021, AMU conducted its own entrance test to admit students for the UG programs. From the academic year 2022, admissions to UG programs offered by Aligarh Muslim University will be based on Central Universities Common Entrance Test (CUCET). CUCET will be a common entrance for admissions to UG programs offered by all the Central Universities in the country.

University of Allahabad UG Programs Reservation:

Allahabad University being a Central University offers reservations in admissions according to central government rules. Kindly check the university website for further details.

QUANTITATIVE APTITUDE

1. How many natural numbers between 200 and 400 are there which are divisible by 4, 5, 8 or 10?
   - (a) 79
   - (b) 80
   - (c) 81
   - (d) None of these

2. In an examination, 80% marks are required to get scholarship. Abhi got 1,005 and failed to get the scholarship by 13% of the maximum marks. What was the maximum marks?
   - (a) 800
   - (b) 1,000
   - (c) 1,500
   - (d) 1,800

3. Cost of 3 balls is equal to the cost of 2 pads, cost of 3 pads is equal to the cost of 2 gloves. Cost of 3 gloves is equal to the cost of 2 bats. If the cost of bat is Rs. 54, what is the cost of the ball?
   - (a) Rs. 12
   - (b) Rs. 14
   - (c) Rs. 16
   - (d) Rs. 18

4. Fifteen men can harvest a field in 28 days. How long will it take to harvest this field if the number of men is reduced to 10?
   - (a) 40 days
   - (b) 36 days
   - (c) 38 days
   - (d) 42 days

5. A cistern can be filled by a supply pipe in 30 min and emptied by a waste pipe in $\frac{4}{5}$ hr. If both pipes are opened together, in what time will the cistern be filled?
   - (a) $\frac{1}{2}$ hr
   - (b) 1 hr
   - (c) $1\frac{1}{3}$ hr
   - (d) 2 hr

6. A cone has a height h and base radius r. The volume of the cone is bisected by a plane parallel to the base which is at a distance of k from the base. Then k is
   - (a) $\frac{1}{2}h$
   - (b) $\left(\frac{1}{2}\right)^{\frac{1}{2}}h$
   - (c) $\left(\frac{1}{2}\right)^{\frac{1}{3}}h$
   - (d) None of these

7. If $f(x, y) = 2x - y$, the value of $f(1, 1) + f\left(\frac{1}{4}, \frac{3}{4}\right) - f\left(\frac{1}{2}, \frac{1}{4}\right)$ is
   - (a) $\frac{1}{2}$
   - (b) $\frac{1}{3}$
   - (c) 0
   - (d) $\frac{1}{5}$

8. If two dice are thrown simultaneously, then what is the probability of getting the same number on both dice?
   - (a) $\frac{1}{12}$
   - (b) $\frac{1}{2}$
   - (c) $\frac{1}{6}$
   - (d) $\frac{1}{36}$

9. In a class of 200 students 70 play cricket, 60 play hockey and 80 play football. 30 play cricket and football, 30 play hockey and football, 40 play cricket and hockey. If 130 people play at least one game, find the number of people who play all the three games.
   - (a) 30
   - (b) 20
   - (c) 10
   - (d) None of these

10. Vijay and Shivku start simultaneously from the opposite ends of a pool which is 50 m long. They pass each other, reach the respective ends and immediately turn back. Now they meet at a distance of 15 m from where Vijay started 10 s after the start. Find the speed of Shivku.
    - (a) 6.5 m/sec
    - (b) 7.5 m/sec
    - (c) 8.5 m/sec
    - (d) 5 m/sec

11. Two numbers x and y are such that when divided by 6, they leave remainders 4 and 5 respectively. Find the remainder when $x^2 + y^2$ is divided by 6.
    - (a) 3
    - (b) 4
    - (c) 5
    - (d) None of these

12. Which of the following statements is true?

    (a) All the angles of a parallelogram can be acute.

    (b) If the diagonals of a quadrilateral are at right angles, it is a rhombus.

    (c) If the diagonals of a quadrilateral are at right angles, the figure formed by joining the mid-points of adjacent sides is a rectangle.

    (d) If one pair of opposite sides is parallel and the other pair of opposite sides is equal in a quadrilateral, then the quadrilateral is a parallelogram.

13. If $x^y + y^x = 17$ and $x + y = 5$, then $x - y$ $(x, y > 0)$ is

    (a) 1
    (b) −1
    (c) 1 or −1
    (d) None of these

14. How many odd integers from 1000 to 8000 (inclusive) have distinct digits?

    (a) 2520
    (b) 1736
    (c) 1680
    (d) 1920

15. In an apartment block there are 10 residents. The number of cars owned by the residents are 15. Four of the residents do not have any car, exactly 3 have one car each and one person has 4 cars. What may be the maximum number of cars owned by any resident?

    (a) 6
    (b) 7
    (c) 8
    (d) 5

16. There has been an increase in selling price of a car. If the increase is 20% of its final selling price, what is the increase as a percentage of original selling price?

    (a) 30%
    (b) 25%
    (c) 20%
    (d) None of these

17. Jane and Jill move towards each other from two towns that are 55 miles apart. Jane's speed is 12 miles per hr and Jill's speed is 10 miles per hr. After how much time will they be 11 miles apart?

    (a) 1 hr
    (b) 2 hr
    (c) 4 hr
    (d) 6 hr

18. Two horses were sold for Rs. 12,000 each, one at a loss of 20% and the other at a gain of 20%. The entire transaction resulted in

    (a) no loss no gain
    (b) loss of Rs. 1,000
    (c) gain of Rs. 1,000
    (d) None of these

19. What is the value of k if A (4, k) is the mid-point of (2, 3) and (6, 7)?

    (a) 4
    (b) 5
    (c) 6
    (d) 7

20. In how many ways can you select two odd numbers and two even numbers out of the first 128 whole numbers?

    (a) $^{64}C_2 \times {}^{64}C_2$
    (b) $^{64}C_2 \times {}^{63}C_2$
    (c) $^{63}C_2 \times {}^{63}C_2$
    (d) None of these

21. Two containers contain equal quantities of milk and water respectively. Half the contents of the first is poured in the second and then the same quantity is transferred back into the first container. This is done three times. What is the ratio of milk to water in the two containers at the end of the process?

    (a) 5 : 2, 2 : 5
    (b) 5 : 4, 4 : 5
    (c) 14 : 13, 13 : 14
    (d) None of these

22. A leak in the bottom of a tank can empty it in 6 hr. A pipe fills the tank at 4 litre per minutes. When the tank is full, the inlet is opened, but due to the leak the tank is emptied in 8 hr. What is the capacity of the tank?

    (a) 5,260 L
    (b) 5,760 L
    (c) 5,846 L
    (d) 6,970 L

23. A boat goes 14 km upsteram in 56 minutes. The speed of stream is 2 km/hr. The speed of boat in still water is

    (a) 6 km/hr
    (b) 15 km/hr
    (c) 14 km/hr
    (d) 17 km/hr

24. Chords AB, BC and CD subtend angles of 80°, 60° and 70° respectively at the centre O of a circle. Then the acute angle between AC and BD is

    (a) 60°
    (b) 75°
    (c) 65°
    (d) 80°

25. A cone circumscribes a sphere and its height is double the diameter of the sphere. The volume of the cone is K times the volume of the sphere. Then K is equal to

    (a) 3
    (b) 4
    (c) 2
    (d) 6

26. Find two consecutive even numbers such that 73 times their difference is equal to their sum.

    (a) 72, 74
    (b) 50, 52
    (c) 46, 48
    (d) 36, 38

27. The average marks obtained by 22 candidates in an examination is 50. The average of the first 10 candidates is 44, while that of the last eleven is 60. The marks obtained by the 11th candidate is
    (a) 50
    (b) 56
    (c) 0
    (d) 59

28. Karan sold his cycle at a profit of 20%. Had he bought it for 20% less and sold it for Rs. 20 less, he would have gained 25%. The cost price of cycle is.
    (a) Rs. 100/-
    (b) Rs. 125/-
    (c) Rs. 120/-
    (d) Rs. 80/-

29. Two isosceles triangles have equal angles and their areas are in ratio 25 : 49. Then the ratio of their corresponding heights is
    (a) 25 : 49
    (b) 3 : 5
    (c) 5 : 7
    (d) 7 : 9

30. In the given circle, OA = 4 cm and $\angle AOB = 112°$. What is $\angle ABO$?

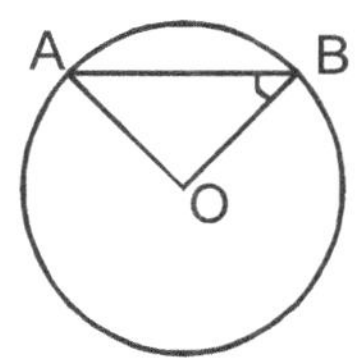

    (a) 22°
    (b) 34°
    (c) 44°
    (d) 45°

Answer Key

1. (a)	**2.** (c)	**3.** (c)	**4.** (d)	**5.** (c)	**6.** (d)	**7.** (c)	**8.** (c)	**9.** (b)	**10.** (a)
11. (c)	**12.** (c)	**13.** (c)	**14.** (b)	**15.** (a)	**16.** (b)	**17.** (b)	**18.** (b)	**19.** (b)	**20.** (b)
21. (c)	**22.** (b)	**23.** (d)	**24.** (b)	**25.** (c)	**26.** (a)	**27.** (c)	**28.** (a)	**29.** (c)	**30.** (b)

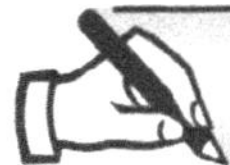

Explanations

1. a Here we just need to check that how many numbers are there between 200 and 400 that are divisible by 4 or 5, because that will take care of all the numbers in the range that are divisible by 8 or 10.

Number of numbers divisible by 4 in the given range = 49.

Number of numbers divisible by 5 in the given range = 39.

Number of numbers divisible by both 4 and 5 in the given range = 9.

∴ The required number of numbers = 49 + 39 − 9 = 79.

2. c Required marks = 80%; Obtained marks = 1005; Failed by 13%

∴ 1005 = (80 − 13)% of maximum marks = 67%;

Total marks = 1005 × 100/67 = 1500

3. c Cost of 1 glove = Cost of $\dfrac{2}{3}$ bat

Cost of 1 pad = Cost of $\dfrac{2}{3} \times \dfrac{2}{3}$ bat

Cost of 1 ball = Cost of $\dfrac{2}{3} \times \dfrac{2}{3} \times \dfrac{2}{3}$ bat

Hence, cost of 1 ball = $\dfrac{2}{3} \times \dfrac{2}{3} \times \dfrac{2}{3} \times 54 = $ Rs. 16.

4. d This is inverse variation

∴ Ratio of men × work = constant

Hence, 15 × 28 = 10 × x

∴ $X = \dfrac{15 \times 28}{10} = 42$ days

5. c Time required to fill the cistern = $\dfrac{1}{2 - \dfrac{5}{4}} = \dfrac{1}{\dfrac{3}{4}}$

$= \dfrac{4}{3}$ hr $= 1\dfrac{1}{3}$ hr

6. d

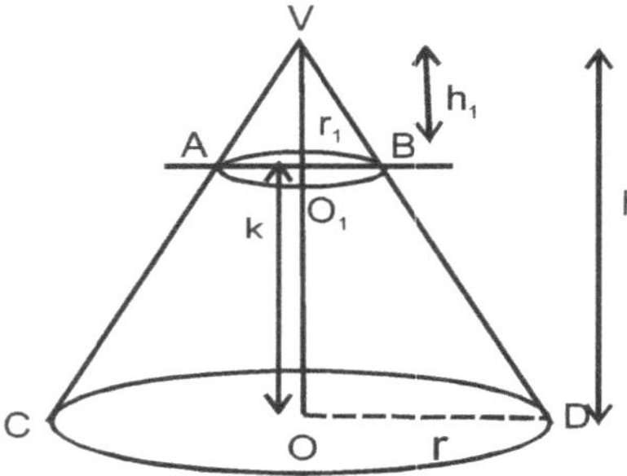

Let the radius of the cone VCD be r and the vertical height be h.

Volume of the cone = $\dfrac{1}{3}\pi r^2 h$

Let the radius of the cone VAB be r_1 and the vertical height be h_1.

Its volume = $\dfrac{1}{3}\pi r_1^2 h_1$ ∴ $\dfrac{1}{2}\left(\dfrac{1}{3}\pi r^2 h\right) = \dfrac{1}{3}\pi r_1^2 h_1$

∴ $h_1 = \dfrac{1}{2}\left(\dfrac{r}{r_1}\right)^2 h.$

ΔVO_1B and VOD are similar.

∴ $\dfrac{O_1B}{OD} = \dfrac{VO_1}{VO}$, i.e. $\dfrac{r_1}{r} = \dfrac{h_1}{h}$

Hence, $h_1 = \dfrac{1}{2}\left(\dfrac{h}{h_1}\right)^2 h$, i.e. $h_1 = \left(\dfrac{1}{2}\right)^{1/3} h$

Hence, $k = h - \left(\dfrac{1}{2}\right)^{\frac{1}{3}} h = h\left(1 - \dfrac{1}{2^{1/3}}\right).$

7. c Given that f(x, y) = 2x − y

So, $f(1,1) + f\left(\dfrac{1}{4}, \dfrac{3}{4}\right) - f\left(\dfrac{1}{2}, \dfrac{1}{4}\right)$

$= [2(1) - 1] + \left[2 \times \dfrac{1}{4} - \dfrac{3}{4}\right] - \left[2 \times \dfrac{1}{2} - \dfrac{1}{4}\right]$

$= 1 - \dfrac{1}{4} - \dfrac{3}{4} = 0$

8. c Total number of cases = 6 × 6 = 36

Number of cases when we get same number on both the dice = (1, 1), (2, 2), (3, 3), (4, 4), (5, 5) and (6, 6)

= 6 ways

Required probability = $\dfrac{6}{36} = \dfrac{1}{6}.$

9. b $n(A \cup B \cup C) = n(A) + n(B) + n(C) - n(A \cap B)$

$- n(B \cap C) - n(C \cap A) + n(A \cap B \cap C)$

130 = 70 + 60 + 80 − 30 − 30 − 40 + x

⇒ x = 20

10. a It is obvious that Shivku travels 50 + 15 = 65 m in 10 s

⇒ His speed is 6.5 m/s.

11. c Suppose x = $6k_1$ + 4 and y = $6k_2$ + 5

$x^2 + y^2 = (6k_1 + 4)^2 + (6k_2 + 5)^2$

$= 36k_1^2 + 48k_1 + 16 + 36k_2^2 + 60k_2 + 25$

$= 36k_1^2 + 48k_1 + 36k_2^2 + 60k_2 + 41$

Obviously, when this is divided by 6 the remainder will be 5.

12. c (a) If one angle is acute, the other angle is obtuse.

So, all the angles cannot be acute.

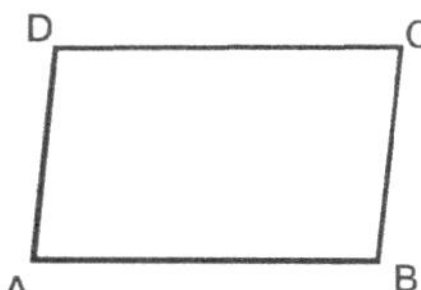

ABCD is a parallelogram.

$\angle A + \angle B = 180°$

(b) The diagonals should bisect each other at right angles, then only the quadrilateral is a rhombus.

(c)

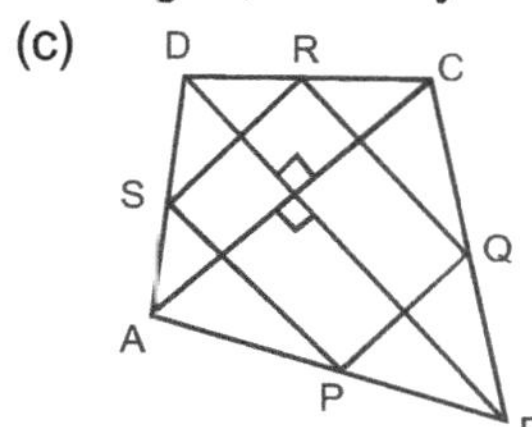

P is the mid-point of AB and Q is the mid-point of BC.

$\therefore PQ = \dfrac{1}{2}AC$ and PQ is parallel to AC.

Similarly, $SR = \dfrac{1}{2}AC$ and is parallel to AC.

$\therefore$ PQ = SR and PQ is parallel to SR.

$\therefore$ PQRS is a parallelogram.

RQ is parallel to BD.

$\therefore \angle SRQ = 90°$

$\therefore$ PQRS is a rectangle.

(d) An isosceles trapezium would also satisfy this condition as shown below:

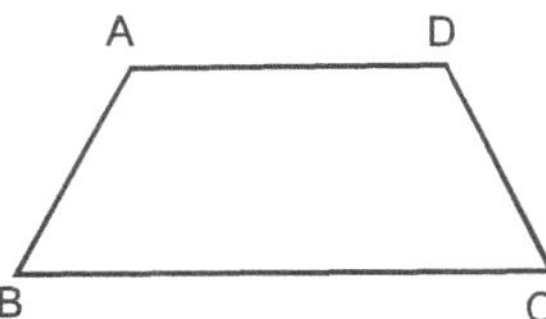

13. c Using choices, we have

(a) Let x – y = 1   … (i)

x + y = 5 (given)   … (ii)

Adding (i) and (ii), we get

$2x = 6 \Rightarrow x = 3$ and y = 2

Now substituting the values of x, y in

$x^y + y^x = 17$, we get

for x = 3, y = 2, $3^2 + 2^3 = 17$

(b) Let x – y = –1   … (i)

x + y = 5   (given)   … (ii)

Adding (i) and (ii), we get

$2x = 4 \Rightarrow x = 2$ and y = 3.

Now substituting the values of x, y in

$x^y + y^x = 17$, we get

for x = 2, y = 3, $2^3 + 3^2 = 17$

14. b Unit's place can be filled with any of the five digits 1, 3, 5, 7 or 9. When it is filled with 9, thousand's place can be filled in 7 ways (anything from 1 to 7) and remaining two places can be filled in 7 × 8 = 56 ways. So number of such numbers = 56 × 7 = 392.

When unit's place is filled with any of the four digits 1, 3, 5 or 7, the thousand's place can be filled in 7 – 1 = 6 ways and remaining two can be filled in 8 × 7 = 56 ways.

Number of such numbers = 56 × 6 × 4 = 1344.

$\therefore$ Total number of required numbers

= 1344 + 392 = 1736

15. a Four of the residents do not have any car, so 15 cars are owned by remaining 6 residents. One has 4 cars and exactly three have one car each, it means remaining 8 cars are owned by two people. Out of these two, one can own at least two and in that case the other will own 6 cars.

16. b Suppose, the final selling price is Rs. 100.

$\therefore$ The increase is Rs. 20 $\Rightarrow$ Original SP = Rs. 80.

$\therefore$ Increase is 25% of original SP.

17. b Distance covered in 1 hr = 12 + 10 = 22 miles. (Since they are moving in opposite directions)

In 2 hr, they will cover = 22 × 2 = 44

Difference = 55 – 44 = 11 miles

After 2 hr, they will be 11 miles apart

18. b Total selling price = Rs. 24,000 and in this type of transaction there is always loss.

Therefore, loss percentage = $\left(\dfrac{20}{100}\right)^2 = 4\%$

Now total cost price = $\dfrac{24000 \times 100}{96} = $ Rs. 25,000

Loss = 25000 – 24000 = Rs. 1,000

19. b Using mid-point formula

$x = \dfrac{x_1 + x_2}{2}$ and $y = \dfrac{y_1 + y_2}{2}$

$\therefore y_1 = 3, y_2 = 7$

$\therefore y = \dfrac{y_1 + y_2}{2} = \dfrac{3+7}{2} = 5$.

20. b First 128 whole numbers are 0, 1, 2, …, 126, 127. So, there are 64 odd numbers and 63 even numbers.

$\therefore$ Required number of ways is $^{64}C_2 \times {}^{63}C_2$.

21. c Start with a litre of milk in first container and a litre of water in second and proceed.

Consider two container I and II where we will consider the ratio of milk in these two containers

I(M)	II(M)
1	0
$\dfrac{1}{2}$	$\dfrac{1}{2}$
$\dfrac{2}{3}$	$\dfrac{1}{3}$
$\dfrac{1}{3}$	$\dfrac{2}{3}$
$\dfrac{5}{9}$	$\dfrac{4}{9}$
$\dfrac{5}{18}$	$\dfrac{13}{18}$
$\dfrac{14}{27}$	$\dfrac{13}{27}$

Thus, the ratio of milk and water in the two container is 14 : 13, 13 : 14.

22. b Fully filled tank is emptied in 6 hr when inlet is closed but when inlet is opened, it is emptied in 8 hr.

$\Rightarrow$ Total water poured by inlet pipe

$= 4 \times 8 \times 60 = 1920$ L

Emptied by leak in 2 hr = 960 litres per hour

Capacity of the tank $= 960 \times 6 = 5760$ L

23. d Let the speed of the boat in still water be x km/hr While going upstream

$14 = (x-2)\dfrac{56}{60} \Rightarrow x = 17$ km/hr

24. b

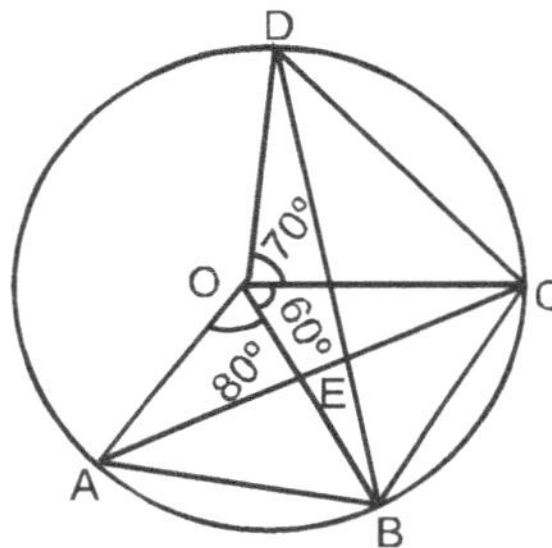

$\angle ACB = \dfrac{1}{2}\angle AOB = \dfrac{1}{2}(80°) = 40°$

$\angle DBC = \dfrac{1}{2}\angle DOC = \dfrac{1}{2}(70°) = 35°$

$\therefore \angle AEB = \angle ECB + \angle EBC = 40° + 35° = 75°$

25. c

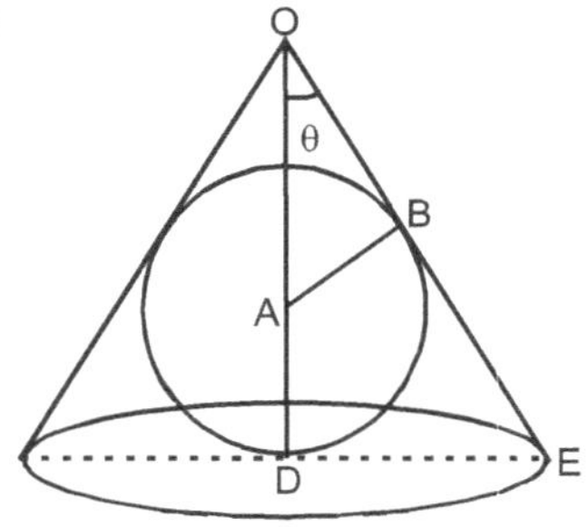

Here OD = 4r

$\therefore$ AO = 2r + r = 3r

Thus, $OB = \sqrt{(3r)^2 - r^2} = \sqrt{8}r$.

Now, $\dfrac{AB}{OB} = \dfrac{DE}{OD}$

$\Rightarrow DE = OD \times \dfrac{AB}{OB} = \dfrac{(4r) \times r}{\sqrt{8}r} = \dfrac{2r}{\sqrt{2}}$

Hence, the volume of the cone

$= \dfrac{1}{3} \times \pi \times \left(\dfrac{2r}{\sqrt{2}}\right)^2 \times (4r) = \pi r^3 \left(\dfrac{8}{3}\right)$

Volume of the sphere $= \dfrac{4}{3}\pi r^3$. Hence, K = 2.

26. a Let the two consecutive even numbers be x and x + 2

$\therefore$ x + x + 2 = 73 (x + 2 − x)

$\therefore$ 2x + 2 = 146

$\therefore$ 2x = 144

$\therefore$ x = 72

$\therefore$ The numbers are 72 and 74.

27. c Total marks obtained by 11th candidate

= 22 × 50 − 10 × 44 − 11 × 60 = 0

28. a Let the cost price of the cycle $=$ Rs. x.

In the 2nd case cost price = 0.8x.

Selling price $= 1.2x - 20$.

Profit $= 0.25(0.8x)$.

Hence, $0.8x(1 + 0.25) = 1.2x - 20$.

$\Rightarrow 1.25 \times 0.8x = 1.2x - 20. \Rightarrow x = \dfrac{20}{0.2} =$ Rs. 100

29. c $\dfrac{h_1}{h_2} = \sqrt{\dfrac{25}{49}} = \dfrac{5}{7}$

$\therefore h_1 : h_2 = 5 : 7$

30. b

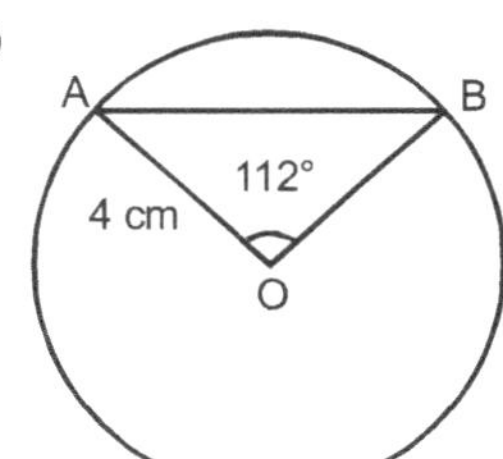

OA = OB (Radii of a circle)

$\therefore \angle BAO = \angle ABO$ (The angles opposite to equal sides are equal)

$\angle AOB + \angle ABO + \angle BAO = 180^0$

$\Rightarrow 2\angle ABO = 180° - 112°$

$\Rightarrow \angle ABO = \dfrac{68°}{2} = 34°$

Number of questions: 30   **Time Allowed: 30 mins.**

1. How many natural numbers between 200 and 400 are there which are divisible by 4, 5, 8 or 10?
   (a) 79
   (b) 80
   (c) 81
   (d) N

1. If the places of last two digits of a three-digit number are interchanged, a new number is obtained which is 27 less than the original number. Find the difference between the last two digits of the original number.
   (a) 6
   (b) 9
   (c) 3
   (d) Can't be determined

2. A candidate scoring 30% in an examination fails by 15 marks, while another candidate gets 60% which is 30 marks more than the minimum required for a pass. The minimum pass marks are
   (a) 75
   (b) 45
   (c) 60
   (d) 30

3. The pressure of a gas is directly proportional to its temperature and inversely proportional to its volume. The initial pressure, volume and temperature are 150 pascals, 20 cu.m. and 100° kelvin respectively. Find the final temperature if the final volume and pressure of the same gas are 8 cu. m. and 150 pascals respectively under same conditions.
   (a) 80° kelvin
   (b) 50° kelvin
   (c) 40° kelvin
   (d) None of these

4. The bisectors of the angles of a parallelogram enclose
   (a) another parallelogram
   (b) a rhombus
   (c) a rectangle
   (d) a trapezium

5. The parallel sides of a trapezium are 22 cm and 50 cm and the other sides are 26 cm and 30 cm. Its area is
   (a) 960 cm^2
   (b) 880 cm^2
   (c) 840 cm^2
   (d) 864 cm^2

6. If the price of coffee is raised by 25%, by what % must a houscholder reduce his consumption of coffee so as not increase his expenditure?
   (a) 20%
   (b) 25%
   (c) 33.33%
   (d) 40%

7. Three out of the following four expressions are exactly equal. Find the expression, which is not equal to the other three.
   (a) $12^2 \div 16 + 7 \times 3$
   (b) $16 \times 9 \div 12 + 9 \times 2$
   (c) $18^2 \div 12 + 3$
   (d) $16^2 \div 12 + 7 \times 2$

8. In a solution of 35 L, the ratio of milk to water is 4 : 1. If 7 L of water is added to the solution, then the ratio of milk to water in the resulting solution will be
   (a) 2 : 1
   (b) 3 : 1
   (c) 5 : 1
   (d) None of these

9. ABCD is a cyclic quadrilateral whose diagonals intersect at E. If $\angle BEC = 80°$, $\angle DBC = 60°$ and $\angle BDC = 40°$, which of the following statements is not true?
   (a) BD bisects $\angle ADC$
   (b) AB = BC
   (c) DA = DC
   (d) AC bisects $\angle BCD$

10. Two pipes can separately fill a cistern in 10 min and 15 min respectively. There is also pipe which is attached to the outlet of the cistern. When all the three pipes are kept open, the cistern is full in 18 min. How long will the outlet pipe take to empty the full cistern?
    (a) 7 min
    (b) 9 min
    (c) 12 min
    (d) 10 min

11. Rice is mixed in the ratio of 2 : 3 and sold at Rs. 22 per kg, resulting in a profit of 10%. If the smaller quantity be Rs. 14 per kg, then the cost per kg of the larger quantity is
    (a) Rs. 23
    (b) Rs. 24
    (c) Rs. 29
    (d) Rs. 30

12. In a race of 200 m, A beats B by 10 m and A beats C by 5 m. By how many metres would C beat B in a 200 m race?
    (a) 5.13 m
    (b) 10.5 m
    (c) 12 m
    (d) None of these

13. Which is the smallest number which when multiplied with 1944 will make it a perfect square?

    (a) 8 (b) 2

    (c) 4 (d) None of these

14. A tank, which has a leak in the bottom is filled in 15 hr. Had there been no leak, it would have been filled in 12 hr. If the tank is full, the leak can empty the tank in how many hours?

    (a) 60 hr (b) 3 hr

    (c) $\dfrac{20}{3}$ hr (d) None of these

15. Two concentric circles have radii 13 cm and 5 cm. If AB, the chord of the bigger circle, touches the smaller circle, then the length of AB is

    (a) 24 cm (b) 18 cm

    (c) 12 cm (d) 8 cm

16. What is the solution set for P if the roots of the equation $3x^2 + Px + 6 = 0$ are real and equal?

    (a) $\pm 2\sqrt{2}$ (b) $\pm 3\sqrt{2}$

    (c) $\pm 6\sqrt{2}$ (d) $\pm 2\sqrt{6}$

17. If 'm' is a prime number greater than 3, what will be the remainder when $(m^2 + 17)$ is divided by 12?

    (a) 1 (b) 5

    (c) 6 (d) None of these

18. Two equal amounts were distributed as loans, at the same rate, the first at a simple interest and the second at a compound interest. If the ratio of the interests at the end of the second year is 20 : 21, what is the rate of interest? Compound interest was being compounded annually.

    (a) 20% (b) 15%

    (c) 10% (d) None of these

19. Some person can complete a piece of work in 12 days. Twice the number of such persons can complete half of the same work in how many days?

    (a) 12 days (b) 6 days

    (c) 3 days (d) None of these

20. The sum of a two-digit number and its reverse is equal to 99. How many such two-digit numbers are there?

    (a) 6 (b) 9

    (c) 8 (d) None of these

21. A is thrice as fast as B, and therefore is able to finish a work in 60 days less than B. Find the time in which they can do it, working together.

    (a) 20 days (b) 10 days

    (c) 22.5 days (d) 40 days

22. The adjacent sides of a parallelogram are 18 cm and 25 cm and the included angle of the parallelogram is 150°. The area of the parallelogram is

    (a) 315 sq. cm (b) 450 sq. cm

    (c) 360 sq. cm (d) 225 sq. cm

23. Two pipes can fill a tank in 15 min and 20 min respectively. A third pipe at the bottom empties the tank in 30 min. Find the time required to fill a tank, which is already $\dfrac{1}{4}$ full?

    (a) 12 min (b) 9 min

    (c) 8 min (d) 7 min

24. Excluding stoppages the speed of a bus is 54 km/hr and including stoppages it is 45 km/hr. For how many minutes does the bus stop per hour?

    (a) 12 min (b) 10 min

    (c) 17 min (d) 15 min

25. The total cost of a trip is constant. The cost per head reduces from Rs. 25 to Rs. 20, when 20 more people join in. Find how much it would reduce further if 25 more join this new group.

    (a) Rs. 4 (b) Rs. 5

    (c) Rs. 8 (d) Rs. 6

26. A man bought a T.V. set priced at Rs. 1,600. He was given successive discounts of 20% and 10%. The price he paid was:

    (a) Rs. 1,200 (b) Rs. 1,224

    (c) Rs. 1,168 (d) Rs. 1,152

27. If no income tax is charged on the first Rs. 2,000 of the income, how much does a man pay as income tax at 3 paise per rupee, if his total income is Rs. 5,000?

    (a) Rs. 150 (b) Rs. 90

    (c) Rs. 9 (d) None of these

28. There are 3 copies of 4 different books. In how many ways can they be arranged on a shelf?

    (a) $4! \times 3!$ (b) $\dfrac{12!}{3! \times 3! \times 3! \times 3!}$

    (c) $\dfrac{12!}{13!}$ (d) $12! \times 3! \times 3! \times 3!$

29. Solve for x

$$\log_2 x + \log_4 x + \log_{16} x = \frac{2}{4}$$

(a) 2

(b) $\dfrac{1}{2}$

(c) 8

(d) 7

30. The price of an article was increased by p%. Later the new price was decreassed by p%. If the latest price was Re. 1, the original price was

(a) Re. 1

(b) Rs. $\left(\dfrac{1-p^2}{100}\right)$

(c) Rs. $\left(\dfrac{10000}{10000-p^2}\right)$

(d) Rs. $\dfrac{\sqrt{1-p^2}}{100}$

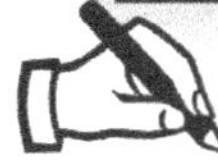

Answer Key

1. (c)	**2.** (c)	**3.** (c)	**4.** (c)	**5.** (d)	**6.** (a)	**7.** (d)	**8.** (a)	**9.** (c)	**10.** (b)
11. (b)	**12.** (a)	**13.** (d)	**4.** (a)	**15.** (a)	**16.** (c)	**17.** (c)	**18.** (c)	**19.** (c)	**20.** (b)
21. (c)	**22.** (d)	**23.** (b)	**24.** (b)	**25.** (a)	**26.** (d)	**27.** (b)	**28.** (b)	**29.** (c)	**30.** (c)

Explanations

1. c Let x, y and z be the digits at unit's place, ten's place and hundredth place, respectively. Then the number formed will be 100z + 10y + x.

   When the last two digits are interchanged, then the number so formed = 100z + 10x + y

   Now, according to the given problem

   100z + 10y + x − 27 = 100z + 10x + y

   9y − 9x = 27 or y − x = 3

   Thus, the difference between the last two digits will be 3.

2. c If P be the maximum marks, then

   $$\frac{30}{100}P + 15 = \frac{60}{100}P - 30$$

   Solving we get $\dfrac{30}{100}P = 45$ or $P = \dfrac{4500}{30} = 150$

   Hence, the pass marks $= \dfrac{30}{100} \times 150 + 15 = 60$

3. c We have $\dfrac{P_1 V_1}{T_1} = k = \dfrac{P_2 V_2}{T_2}$

   or $\dfrac{150 \times 20}{100} = \dfrac{150 \times 8}{T_2} \Rightarrow T_2 = 40°$ kelvin

4. c

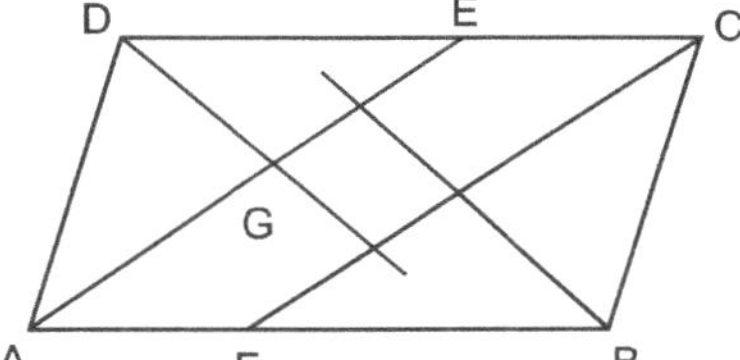

Let the bisector of ∠A be AE and ∠C be CF.

$$\angle DEA = \angle EAB = \frac{\angle A}{2}, \ \angle ECF = \frac{\angle C}{2}$$

But ∠A = ∠C

∴ ∠DEA = ∠ECF

∴ AE is parallel to CF.

Similarly, the bisectors of B and D are parallel.

Hence, the bisectors form a parallelogram.

$$\angle ADG = \frac{1}{2}\angle D, \ \angle DAG = \frac{1}{2}\angle A.$$

$$\therefore \angle ADG + \angle DAG = \frac{1}{2}(\angle D + \angle A) = \frac{1}{2} \times 180° = 90°$$

(Sum of two adjacent angles of a parallelogram is 180°)

∴ ∠DGA = 90°

Hence, the enclosed parallelogram is a rectangle.

5. d

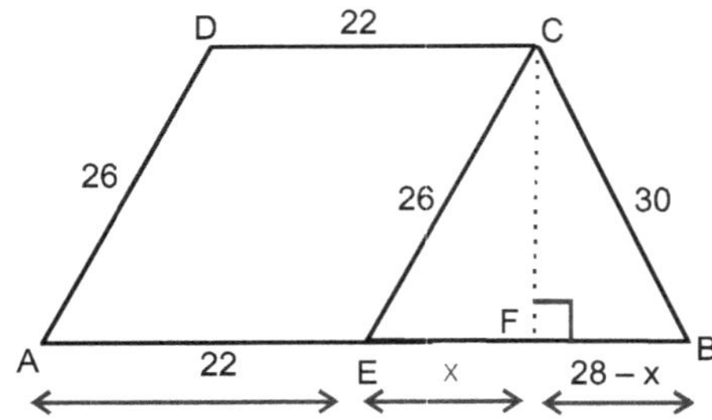

Draw CE parallel to DA.

Then CE = 26 cm. Draw CF perpendicular to BE.

Let EF be x.

AE = 22 cm

$\therefore$ BE = 28 cm. Hence, BF = 28 – x

$26^2 - x^2 = 30^2 - (28 - x)^2$ [Since each side is equal to CF^2.]

Solving this equation, we get x = 10 cm

Hence, $CF^2 = 26^2 - 10^2 = 576$

$\therefore$ CF = 24 cm

Area of the trapezium

$= \frac{1}{2}(22 + 50) \times 24$ sq. cm = 864 sq. cm

6. a Reduction in consumption $= \frac{25}{25 + 100} \times 100 = 20\%$

7. d Let us check each of the four options using BODMAS rule.

(a) $12^2 \div 16 + 7 \times 3 = 144 \div 16 + 7 \times 3 = 9 + 21 = 30$

(b) $16 \times 9 \div 12 + 9 \times 2 = 16 \times \frac{9}{12} + 9 \times 2 = 12 + 18 = 30$

(c) $18^2 \div 12 + 3 = 324 \div 12 + 3 = 27 + 3 = 30$

(d) $16^2 \div 12 + 7 \times 2 = 256 \div 12 + 14 = \frac{256}{12} + 14$

So, an option (d) is not equal to the other three.

8. a $\frac{M}{W} = \frac{\frac{4}{5} \times 35}{\frac{35}{5} + 7} = \frac{28}{14} = 2 : 1$

Hence, M : W = 2 : 1.

9. c

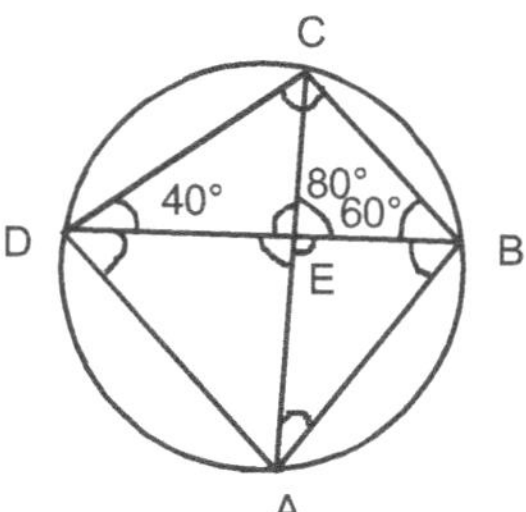

In $\triangle$ BEC, $\angle$BEC = 80° and $\angle$EBC = 60°

$\therefore \angle$ECB = 40°

$\angle$ADB = 40° = $\angle$ACB (Angles in the same segment)

Also $\angle$BDC = 40° (Given)

$\therefore$ BD bisects $\angle$ADC.

AB and BC subtend 40° at the circumference.

$\therefore$ AB = BC

DA subtends 40° at C

$(\because \angle$BEC = 80°, $\angle$EDC = 40°)

DC subtends 60° at A

$(\because \angle$DAC = $\angle$DBC = 60°)

$\therefore$ DA $\neq$ DC

$\angle$ACB = 40° and $\angle$DCA = 40°

$\therefore$ AC bisects $\angle$BCD.

10. b In 1 min first pipe fill $\frac{1}{10}$ of the cistern.

In 1 min second pipe will fill $\frac{1}{15}$ of the cistern.

Let the third pipe take x min to empty the cistern.

In 1 min third pipe will empty $\frac{1}{x}$ of the cistern.

Now, according to the problem

$\frac{1}{10} + \frac{1}{15} - \frac{1}{x} = \frac{1}{18}$

$\Rightarrow \frac{3x + 2x - 30}{30x} = \frac{1}{18} \Rightarrow 15x - 90 = 5x$

$\Rightarrow 10x = 90$

$\Rightarrow x = 9$ min.

11. b Cost price of the mixture per kilogram

$= \frac{22 \times 100}{110} = $ Rs. 20

Assume cost price of larger quantity per kilogram be x.

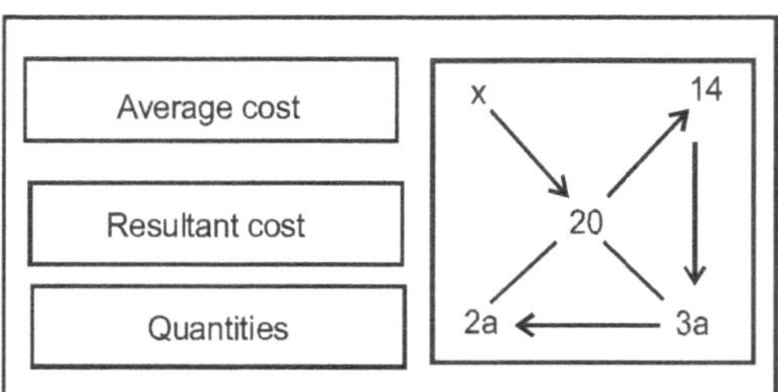

$\frac{x - 20}{20 - 14} = \frac{2a}{3a}$

$\Rightarrow \frac{6}{x - 20} = \frac{3}{2} \Rightarrow 3x = 72$

$\Rightarrow x = $ Rs. 24

Alternative method:

Let 2kg and 3kg of rice priced at Rs. 14 and Rs. x be mixed.

Cost price of Mixture = Rs. 20

Cost price of mixture = Rs. $\dfrac{3x + 28}{5}$

$\therefore \dfrac{3x + 28}{5} = 20 \Rightarrow 3x + 28 = 100$

$\Rightarrow 3x = 72 \Rightarrow x = $ Rs. 24

12. a When A covers 200 m, B covers 190 m and C covers 195 m. i.e. when C covers 195 m, B covers = 190 m, and when C covers 200 m, B covers = $\dfrac{190}{195} \times 200 = 194.87$ m

Hence, C would beat B by 200 – 194.87 = 5.13 m in a 200 m race.

Short cut:

In a race of L length, if Ist beats 3rd by x_1 distance, Ist beats 2nd by x_2 distance and 2nd beats 3rd by x_3 distance, then their relation is given by

$(L - x_2) x_3 = L (x_1 - x_2)$.

Using this, we get

$(200 - 5)x_3 = 200(10 - 5)$

$195 \times x_3 = 200 \times 5$

$x_3 = 5.13$ m.

13. d The factors of 1944 are

$2 \times 2 \times 2 \times 3 \times 3 \times 3 \times 3 \times 3$ or $2^2 \times 2 \times 3 \times 3^4$

So if one more 2 and 3 are multiplied, i.e. $2 \times 3 = 6$, then it make 1944 a perfect square.

14. a Without leak a tank can be filled in 12 hr.

In 1 hr a tank will be $\dfrac{1}{12}$ filled.

In 1 hr, a tank with a leak will be $\dfrac{1}{15}$ filled.

So, if the tank is full, then in 1 hr it will empty

$\dfrac{1}{12} - \dfrac{1}{15} = \dfrac{5 - 4}{60} = \dfrac{1}{60}$ of the tank.

Thus, in 60 hr, it will empty the whole tank.

15. a

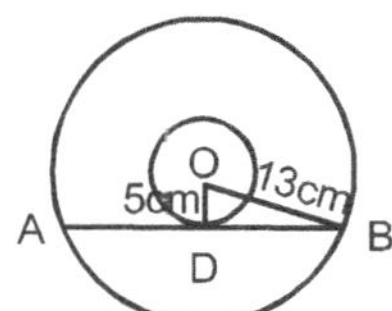

Let O be the centre of both the circles.

If AB touches the inner circle at D, then OD is perpendicular to AB and D is the mid-point of AB.

$\therefore BD^2 = OB^2 - OD^2 = 13^2 - 5^2 = 144$

Thus, BD = 12 cm. $\therefore$ AB = 24 cm.

16. c The roots are real and equal,

$b^2 - 4ac = P^2 - 4 (6) (3) = 0$,

i.e. $P = \pm\sqrt{72}$ or $\pm 6\sqrt{2}$.

17. c Let us check with the few prime numbers which are greater than 3, say, 5, 7, 11, 13...

Now $\dfrac{5^2 + 17}{12} = \dfrac{25 + 17}{12} = \dfrac{42}{12}$, remainder 6.

$\dfrac{7^2 + 17}{12} = \dfrac{49 + 17}{12} = \dfrac{66}{12}$, remainder 6.

$\dfrac{11^2 + 17}{12} = \dfrac{121 + 17}{12} = \dfrac{138}{12}$, remainder 6 and so on.

Thus, in each case, we have found that remainder is 6.

Alternative method:

Any prime number can be written as 6n – 1 or 6n + 1

Case I: Let m = 6n – 1

Then $m^2 + 17 = (6n - 1)^2 + 17 = 36n^2 - 12n + 18$

$= 12 (3n^2 - n + 1) + 6$ ... (i)

When (1) is divided by 12 we get 6 as the remainder.

Case II: Let m = 6n + 1

Then $m^2 + 17 = (6n - 1)^2 + 17 = 36n^2 + 12n + 18$

$= 12 \left(3n^2 + n + 1\right) + 6$ ... (ii)

When (ii) is divided by 12, we get 6 as the remainder.

18. c According to the problem, we have

$$\dfrac{20}{21} = \dfrac{\dfrac{P \times r \times t}{100}}{P\left[\left(1 + \dfrac{r}{100}\right)^t - 1\right]}$$

where P is the principal, r is the rate of interest, t is the duration.

Here, t = 2 years

Thus $\dfrac{20}{21} = \dfrac{\dfrac{r \times 2}{100}}{\left(1 + \dfrac{r}{100}\right)^2 - 1} = \dfrac{2r}{100} \times \dfrac{100^2}{r^2 + 200r}$

$\Rightarrow \dfrac{20}{21} = \dfrac{200}{r + 200} \Rightarrow r = 10\%$.

19. c Let number of persons who can complete the job in 12 days = x

Let the number of days taken by 2x persons to complete half the work = y.

Now

Persons	Work	Days	
x	1	12	
x	$\frac{1}{12}$	1	… (i)
2x	$\frac{1}{2}$	y	
2x	$\frac{1}{2} \times \frac{1}{y}$	1	… (ii)

Using relations (i) and (ii), we get

$x \times \frac{1}{2y} = \frac{2x}{12} \Rightarrow y = 3$ days.

20. b The numbers are 90, 81, 72, 63, 54, 45, 36, 27 and 18.

21. c A = 3B

A takes x days to do work alone.

B takes (x + 60) days to do work alone.

A's one day's work = $\frac{1}{x}$

B's one day's work = $\frac{1}{x+60}$ $\therefore \frac{1}{x} = \frac{3}{x+60}$

$x + 60 = 3x \Rightarrow 2x = 60 \Rightarrow x = 30$ days

A can do the work in 30 days.

B can do the work in 90 days.

In 1 day $\frac{1}{30} + \frac{1}{90} = \frac{4}{90} = \frac{2}{45}$ work is done.

$\therefore$ The work will take $\frac{45}{2}$ days = 22.5 days.

22. d

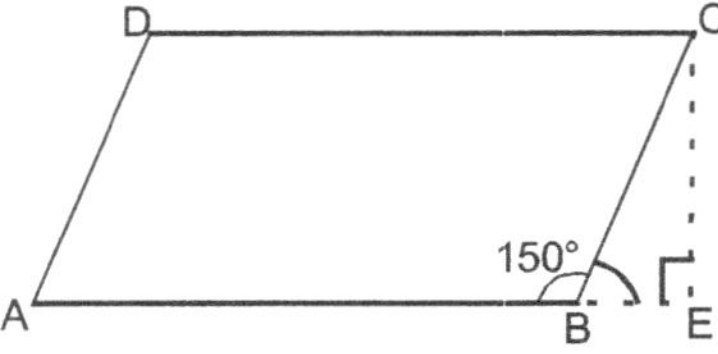

Let CE be the perpendicular from C to AB then
∠CBE = 30°

BC = 18 cm, AB = 25 cm

i.e. $\sin 30° = \frac{CE}{BC} = \frac{CE}{18}$

CE = 18 sin30° = 9 cm

Area of the parallelogram

= AB . EC = (25)9 sq. cm = 225 sq. cm

23. b In 1 min first pipe will fill $\frac{1}{15}$ of the tank.

In 1 min second pipe will fill $\frac{1}{20}$ of the tank.

In 1 min third pipe empty $\frac{1}{30}$ of the tank.

So, in 1 min when all the three pipes are active, they will fill $\frac{1}{15} + \frac{1}{20} - \frac{1}{30} = \frac{4+3-2}{60} = \frac{5}{60} = \frac{1}{12}$

Now in 1 min $\frac{1}{12}$ tank is filled, so remaining $\frac{3}{4}$ tank will be filled in $\frac{3}{4} \times 12 = 9$ min.

24. b Due to stoppages it covers 9 km less in 1 hr.

Time taken to cover 9 km = $\frac{9}{54} \times 60 = 10$ min.

Hence, on an average the bus stops for 10 min every hour.

25. a Suppose initially there were x people so we have 25x = 20(x + 20) or, x = 80. Therefore, total cost is 25 × 80 = Rs. 2,000. When there are 100 + 25 = 125 people, cost per head will be $\frac{2000}{125}$ = Rs. 16.

$\therefore$ There will be a further reduction of Rs. 4.

26. d 1600 × 0.8 × 0.9 = 1600 × 0.72

= Rs. 1,152

27. b Income tax to be paid on Rs. 3,000

= 0.03 × 3000 = Rs. 90

28. b Number of arrangements = $\frac{12!}{3! \times 3! \times 3! \times 3!}$

29. c $\log_2 x + \frac{\log_2 x}{\log_2 4} + \frac{\log_2 x}{\log_2 16} = \frac{21}{4}$

$\Rightarrow \log_2 x + \frac{\log_2 x}{2} + \frac{\log_2 x}{4} = \frac{21}{4} \Rightarrow 7\log_2 x = 21$

$\Rightarrow \log_2 x = 3 \Rightarrow 2^3 = x$

$\Rightarrow x = 8$

30. c Let the original price of the article be Rs. x

Then, $x \times \left(\frac{100+p}{100}\right) \times \left(\frac{100-p}{100}\right) = 1$

$x = \frac{100^2}{100^2 - p^2} = R\left(\frac{10000}{10000 - p^2}\right)$

Number of questions: 30   **Time Allowed: 30 mins.**

1. Rajesh covers two-thirds of a certain distance at 4 km/hr and the remaining at 5 km/hr. If he takes 42 min in all, what is the total distance covered by him?

   (a) 2.5 km   (b) 4 km

   (c) 3 km   (d) 4.6 km

2. The spring balance of a trader weighed 800 gm for 1 kg. What is the net result, is it a profit or a loss and by what per cent?

   (a) 25% loss   (b) 20% profit

   (c) 20% loss   (d) 25% profit

3. If a train 110 m long passes a telegraph pole in 3 s, then the time taken by it to cross a railway platform 165 m long is

   (a) $\dfrac{110}{3}$ sec   (b) 55 sec

   (c) 7.5 sec   (d) $\dfrac{55}{3}$ sec

4. The number 12 is divided into 3 parts which are in A.P. and the sum of their squares is 50. Find the smallest number.

   (a) 5   (b) 3

   (c) 4   (d) 6

5. How long will 20 men take to finish a certain job which 6 men complete in 10 days?

   (a) 3.5 days   (b) 3.5 days

   (c) 3 days   (d) 5 days

6. Ranjit went to the market carrying Rs. 100 in his purse. If he buys three pens and six pencils he uses up all his money. On the other hand, if he buys three pencils and six pens he would fall short by 20%. If he wants to buy equal number of pens and pencils, how many pencils can he buy?

   (a) 5   (b) 25

   (c) 4   (d) 10

7. A and B are racing on a circular track in the same direction with speeds 20 m/s and 25 m/s respectively. Find the length of the track if they meet 20 sec after they start.

   (a) 100 m   (b) 200 m

   (c) 300 m   (d) 400 m

8. A vendor sells 30% of his fruit and throws away 40% of the remainder. Next day he sells 50% of the remainder and throws away the rest. What per cent of the fruit does the vendor throw?

   (a) 51%   (b) 49%

   (c) 63%   (d) 72%

9. An orchard has 48 apple trees, 60 mango trees and 96 banana trees. These have to be arranged in rows such that each row has the same number of trees and of the same type. Find the minimum number of such rows that can be formed.

   (a) 12   (b) 34

   (c) 17   (d) 11

10. The cross section of a canal is trapezium in shape. The canal is 12 m wide at the top and 8 m wide at the bottom. If the area of the cross section is 840 sq. m, find the depth of the canal.

    (a) 42 m   (b) 63 m

    (c) 84 m   (d) None of these

11. Which parts contain the fractions in ascending order?

    (a) $\dfrac{11}{14}, \dfrac{16}{19}, \dfrac{19}{21}$ (b) $\dfrac{16}{19}, \dfrac{11}{14}, \dfrac{19}{21}$

    (c) $\dfrac{19}{21}, \dfrac{11}{14}, \dfrac{16}{19}$ (d) $\dfrac{16}{19}, \dfrac{19}{21}, \dfrac{11}{14}$

12. S and L are the smallest and the largest n-digit natural numbers respectively. L − S is always divisible by

    (a) 9   (b) 10

    (c) 9 and 10   (d) None of these

13. A train 360 m long is running at a speed of 15 m/sec. Find the time taken by the train to cross a tunnel 390 m long?

    (a) 60 sec   (b) 26 sec

    (c) 24 sec   (d) 50 sec

14. The difference between the CI and SI on a certain sum of money at 5% per annum for 2 years is Rs. 1.50. Find the sum.

    (a) Rs. 613   (b) Rs. 603

    (c) Rs. 600   (d) Rs. 620

15. If all the sides of a cuboid increase by 20%, then by what percent does its volume increases?

    (a) 20% (b) 44%

    (c) 60% (d) 72.8%

16. Divide Rs. 2,700 into three parts such that 12 times the first is equal to 5 times the second and 6 times the third.

    (a) Rs. 500, Rs. 1,200, Rs. 1,000

    (b) Rs. 500, Rs. 1,500, Rs. 700

    (c) Rs. 900, Rs. 800, Rs. 1,000

    (d) Rs. 1,100, Rs. 1,200, Rs. 400

17. The sum of two numbers is five times their difference. If their product is 24, the numbers are

    (a) 2, 12 (b) 3, 8

    (c) 6, 4 (d) 1, 24

18. Which of the following numbers is exactly divisible by 99?

    (a) 3572403 (b) 913464

    (c) 114345 (d) None of these

19. Arrange the following fractions in descending order

    $$\frac{28}{25}, \frac{32}{29}, \frac{8}{11}, \frac{19}{16}.$$

    (a) $\frac{28}{25}, \frac{32}{29}, \frac{8}{11}, \frac{41}{44}$

    (b) $\frac{28}{25}, \frac{19}{16}, \frac{32}{29}, \frac{8}{11}$

    (c) $\frac{19}{16}, \frac{32}{29}, \frac{28}{25}, \frac{8}{11}$

    (d) $\frac{19}{16}, \frac{28}{25}, \frac{32}{29}, \frac{8}{11}$

20. 'a' and 'b' are the roots of the equation, $x^2 - x - 3 = 0$. Form the equation whose roots are $(3a + 1)$ and $(3b + 1)$.

    (a) $x^2 - 5x - 23 = 0$

    (b) $x^2 + 5x - 23 = 0$

    (c) $x^2 - (3a + 1)x - (3b + 1) = 0$

    (d) Cannot be determined

21. Gopi gives Rs. 90 as salary to his servant for one year plus one turban. The servant leaves after 9 months and receives Rs. 65 and the turban. Find the price of the turban.

    (a) Rs. 10 (b) Rs. 15

    (c) Rs. 25 (d) Rs. 20

22. Find the greatest number which will divide 12288, 28421, 44333 so as to leave the same remainder in each case.

    (a) 221 (b) 120

    (c) 272 (d) 431

23. In a science course, all students are offered at least one of the subjects, namely mathematics, physics and chemistry. 54 students took mathematics, 51 took physics, 66 took chemistry: 33 took mathematics and physics, 30 took physics and chemistry, 39 took mathematics and chemistry and 24 took all the three subjects. Find how many took only mathematics, how many took only physics and how many took only chemistry?

    (a) 6, 12, 21

    (b) 9, 15, 6

    (c) 15, 24, 6

    (d) None of these

24. Two pipes X and Y can fill a tank in 20 min and 30 min respectively. A third pipe Z can empty the tank in 40 min. Pipes X and Y are kept open initially. After 5 min, pipe Z is also opened. In how much time the tank is full?

    (a) 10 min

    (b) 25 min

    (c) 12 min

    (d) $7\frac{1}{7}$ min

25. A man bought some bananas at the rate of 5 for Rs. 4 and sold all of them at the rate of 4 for Rs. 5. The gain/loss in percentage is.

    (a) 36% gain

    (b) 56.25% gain

    (c) 56.25% loss

    (d) 25% loss.

26. Hari has a piece of cake 60 cm long. He gives Raja half of it. He then gives Gopal $\frac{1}{4}$ th of what is left. After giving a piece to Sahil, he is left with $\frac{1}{10}$ th of the original. How much did he give to Sahil?

    (a) 21. 5 cm

    (b) 16. 5 cm

    (c) 1.5 cm

    (d) 11. 5 cm

27. Three man rent a pasture for Rs. 660. The first man uses it for 50 sheep for 4 months, the 2nd man for 40 sheep for 3 months and the 3rd man for 46 sheep for 5 months. How much should the 1st man pay?

    (a) Rs. 220   (b) Rs. 235

    (c) Rs. 240   (d) Rs. 276

28. The average income of a person for the first 6 days is Rs. 29, for the next 6 days it is Rs. 24, for the next 10 days it is Rs. 32 and for the remaining days of the month November it is Rs. 30. Find the average income per day:

    (a) Rs. 31.64

    (b) Rs. 30.64

    (c) Rs. 29.26

    (d) Can't be determined

29. A loan was repaid in two annual instalments of Rs. 121 each. If the rate of interest be 10% p.a, compounded annually, the sum borrowed was:

    (a) Rs. 200   (b) Rs. 210

    (c) Rs. 217.80   (d) Rs. 216

30. The distance between two stations A and B is 220 km. A train leaves A towards B at an average speed of 80 km/hr. After half an hour another train leaves B towards A at an average speed of 100 km/hr. Find the distance from A to the point where the two trains meet:

    (a) 180 km

    (b) 120 km

    (c) 160 km

    (d) 80 km

✎ Answer Key

1. (c)	**2.** (d)	**3.** (c)	**4.** (b)	**5.** (c)	**6.** (c)	**7.** (a)	**8.** (b)	**9.** (c)	**10.** (c)
11. (a)	**12.** (d)	**13.** (d)	**14.** (c)	**15.** (d)	**16.** (a)	**17.** (c)	**18.** (c)	**19.** (d)	**20.** (a)
21. (a)	**22.** (a)	**23.** (a)	**24.** (a)	**25.** (b)	**26.** (b)	**27.** (c)	**28.** (c)	**29.** (b)	**30.** (b)

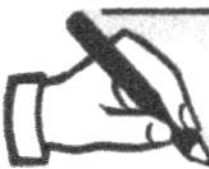# Explanations

1. c Let the total distance covered by Rajesh be x km.

$$\frac{2}{3}x \qquad\qquad \frac{1}{3}x$$

$$\text{4 km/hr} \qquad\qquad \text{5 km/hr}$$

Total time taken by Rajesh to cover x km is 42 min.

Thus, $\dfrac{42}{60} = \dfrac{\frac{2}{3}x}{4} + \dfrac{\frac{1}{3}x}{5}$

$\Rightarrow 42 = 14x \Rightarrow x = 3$ km.

2. d Trader has net profit $= \dfrac{200}{800} \times 100 = 25\%$.

3. c Speed of the train while passing through a telegraph pole $= \dfrac{110}{3}$ m/s.

Now to cross a 165 m long platform time taken by 110 m long train $= \dfrac{110 + 165}{110} \times 3$

$= \dfrac{275}{110} \times 3 = 2.5 \times 3 = 7.5$ sec

4. b Very easy way is to go through the answer choices , we see that the numbers are 3, 4 and 5 as $3^2 + 4^2 + 5^2 = 50$ and $3 + 4 + 5 = 12$

5. c $20 \times X = 6 \times 10$

$X = \dfrac{6 \times 10}{20} = 3$ days

6. c Let the cost of pen be Rs. x and the cost of pencil be Rs. y.

Then according to the question

$3x + 6y = 100$ … (i)

$6x + 3y = 125$ … (ii)

Solving (i) and (ii), we get

$y = \dfrac{25}{3}$ and $x = \dfrac{50}{3}$

Let n be the quantity of equal number of pens and pencils.

$\therefore n(x + y) = 100 \Rightarrow n = \dfrac{100 \times 3}{75} = 4$

7. a Relative speed of B with respect to A $= 25 - 20 = 5$ m/s. When they meet, B must have taken a lead of exactly one round.

Lead = Relative speed × Time = 5 m/s × 20 s = 100 m

8. b Base 100 (original number of fruits)

Day - I

Sells 30% = 30% of 100 = 30

Throws 40% of 70 = 28

Remainder = 42

Day - II

Sells 50% of 42 = 21

Throws 50% of 42 = 21

Total thrown = 49%.

9. c Since all these trees have to be arranged in rows such that each row has the same number of trees and of the same type. As all the three group of trees are multipes of 12. Thus, the minimum number of such rows where each row consist of 12 trees are 4 + 5 + 8 = 17.

Alternative method:

The HCF of 48, 60 and 96 is 12.

∴ 12 Trees will be arranged in each row.

Number of rows $= \dfrac{48 + 60 + 96}{12} = 17$.

10. c 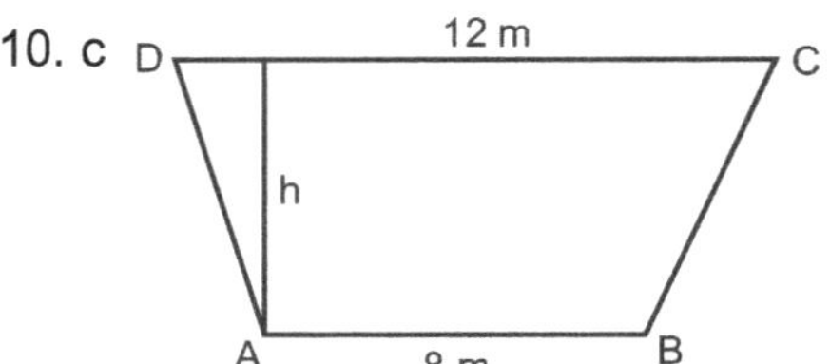

Let the depth of the canal be h m.

Now area of trapezium $= \dfrac{1}{2}h$ (Sum of parallel sides)

$840 = \dfrac{1}{2} \times h \times (12 + 8)$

$\Rightarrow h = \dfrac{840 \times 2}{20} = 84$ m

11. a Take LCM of 14, 19 and 21 which comes out to be 798 and make the denominator of all the fractions as 798.

Now, the fractions are $\dfrac{11}{14} = \dfrac{627}{798}$

Similarly, $\dfrac{16}{19} = \dfrac{672}{798}$ and $\dfrac{19}{21} = \dfrac{722}{798}$

$\Rightarrow \dfrac{627}{798} < \dfrac{672}{798} < \dfrac{722}{798}$

12. d When n = 1, L – S = 8; when n = 2, L – S = 89, etc. Thus, we see that L – S is never divisible by 9 or 10.

13. d Time taken by 360 m train to cross 390 m long tunnel running with a speed of 15 m/s.

$= \dfrac{360 + 390}{15} = \dfrac{750}{15} = 50$ sec

14. c $SI = x \times \dfrac{5}{100} \times 2 = \dfrac{10}{100}x$ (where x = sum of money)

Amount $= x\left(1+\dfrac{r}{100}\right)^{n}$

$CI = x\left(1+\dfrac{5}{100}\right)^{2} - x = \dfrac{11025\,x}{10000} - x = \left(\dfrac{1025}{10000}\right)x$

Difference $= \dfrac{1025}{10000}x - \dfrac{10}{100}x = 1.5$

or $\dfrac{25}{10000}x = 1.5$ or x = Rs. 600

Short cut:

$\Rightarrow$ Difference in interest $= CI_2 - SI_2 = x \times \left(\dfrac{r}{100}\right)^{2}$

(Only when difference of CI and SI in 2 years)

Sum $= \dfrac{1.50 \times 100 \times 100}{5 \times 5}$ = Rs. 600

15. d Suppose initially the sides are x, y and z.

Initial volume $= xyz$

After the change the sides will be $1.2x$, $1.2y$ and $1.2z$.

New volume $= 1.728(xyz)$

$\therefore$ Increase in volume is 72.8%.

16. a $12A = 5B = 6C = k$ (Say) $\Rightarrow A = \dfrac{k}{12}, B = \dfrac{k}{5}, C = \dfrac{k}{6}$

Similarly, $A : B : C \Rightarrow \dfrac{k}{12} : \dfrac{k}{5} : \dfrac{k}{6} \Rightarrow 5 : 12 : 10$

A's share $= \dfrac{5}{27} \times 2700 = $ Rs. 500

B's share $= \dfrac{12}{27} \times 2700 = $ Rs. 1,200.

C's share = Rs. 1,000.

17. c Let the two numbers be x and y.

Then according to the question,

$x + y = 5(x - y)$

$\Rightarrow 4x - 6y = 0$

$\Rightarrow x = \dfrac{3}{2}y$ ... (i)

and $xy = 24$ ... (ii)

Using (i) in (ii), we get

$\dfrac{3}{2}y \cdot y = 24$; $y^2 = 16 \Rightarrow y = 4$

So, $x = 6$.

18. c The number is divisible by 99, if it is divisible by 9 as well as 11. Using the divisibility rule of 9 and 11, we have found that 114345 is divisible by 99.

19. d Changing the fractions in decimal form, we have found that

$\dfrac{28}{25} = 1.12$ (approximately)

$\dfrac{32}{29} = 1.103$ (approximately)

$\dfrac{8}{11} = 0.72$ (approximately)

$\dfrac{19}{16} = 1.1875$ (approximately)

Thus the descending order is

$\dfrac{19}{16} > \dfrac{28}{25} > \dfrac{32}{29} > \dfrac{8}{11}$.

Alternative method:

$\dfrac{28}{25}, \dfrac{32}{29}, \dfrac{8}{11}, \dfrac{19}{16}$ or $1\dfrac{3}{25}, 1\dfrac{3}{29}, \dfrac{8}{11}, 1\dfrac{3}{16}$

$\dfrac{8}{11}$ is the smallest.

Numerator in the other fraction is same.

The number with the smallest denominator will be greatest

$\therefore 1\dfrac{3}{16} > 1\dfrac{3}{25} > 1\dfrac{3}{29} > \dfrac{8}{11}$ or $\dfrac{19}{16} > \dfrac{28}{25} > \dfrac{32}{29} > \dfrac{8}{11}$

20. a An equation $x^2 - x - 3 = 0$ has real and distinct roots as we can see discriminant $D = b^2 - 4ac > 0$.

Thus, $x = \dfrac{1 \pm \sqrt{1+12}}{2} = \dfrac{1 \pm \sqrt{13}}{2}$

So, the two roots a and b are $a = \dfrac{1+\sqrt{13}}{2}, b = \dfrac{1-\sqrt{13}}{2}$

Now $3a + 1 = \dfrac{3\left(1+\sqrt{13}\right)}{2} + 1 = \dfrac{5+3\sqrt{13}}{2}$

and $3b + 1 = \dfrac{3\left(1-\sqrt{13}\right)}{2} + 1 = \dfrac{5-3\sqrt{13}}{2}$

Since $3a + 1$ and $3b + 1$ are the roots of the equation.

$\therefore$ Sum of the roots $= (3a + 1) + (3b + 1)$

$= \dfrac{5+3\sqrt{3}}{2} + \dfrac{5-3\sqrt{3}}{2} = 5$

and product of the roots $= (3a + 1)(3b + 1)$

$= \left(\dfrac{5+3\sqrt{13}}{2}\right)\left(\dfrac{5-3\sqrt{13}}{2}\right)$

$= \dfrac{25 - 9 \times 13}{4} = \dfrac{25 - 117}{4} = \dfrac{-92}{4} = -23$

$\therefore$ The equation is $x^2 - 5x - 23 = 0$.

Alternative method:

If a and b are roots $x^2 - x - 3 = 0$

then sum of the roots $= a + b = 1$ ... (i)

and products of the roots $= ab = -3$ ... (ii)

An equation with roots 3a + 1 and 3b + 1 will be

[x – (3a + 1)] [x – (3b + 1)] = 0

$\Rightarrow x^2 - [3(a + b) + 2] \times + (3a + 1)(3b + 1) = 0$

$\Rightarrow x^2 - [3(a + b) + 2] \times + 9ab + 3(a + b) + 1 = 0$

Putting values of a + b and ab from (i) and (ii),

we get $x^2 - 5x - 23 = 0$

21. a Gopi's servant receives Rs. 90 in a year and a turban.

Thus for one month, he will receive Rs. 7.5.

Thus in 9 months the servant has received

Rs. 7.5 × 9 = Rs. 67.5

But he has given servant Rs. 65 and a turban after 9 months when he had left.

The cost of turban deducted for 3 months = Rs. (67.5 – 65) = Rs. 2.5.

Cost of turban = 2.5 × 4 = Rs. 10

Alternative method:

$\left(\dfrac{90 + T}{12}\right) \times 9 = 65 + T \Rightarrow 270 + 3t = 260 + 4T$

$\Rightarrow T = Rs. 10$

22. a 28421 – 12288 = 16133

So, divisible number should be odd so two choices are out. Now taking first choice, we get the answer.

23. a

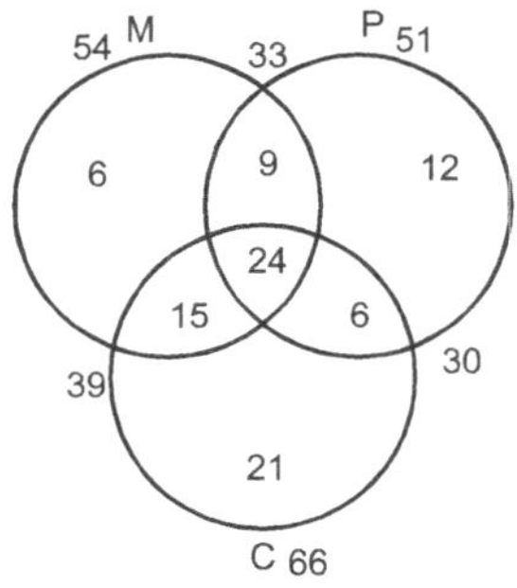

Thus, 6 students have only mathematics, 12 students have only physics, 21 students have only chemistry.

24. a In 1 min two pipes X and Y can fill

$\dfrac{1}{20} + \dfrac{1}{30} = \dfrac{1}{12}$ tank

In 1 min when all the three pipes are active can fill

$\dfrac{1}{20} + \dfrac{1}{30} - \dfrac{1}{40} = \dfrac{7}{120}$ tank.

In 5 min, two pipes can fill $\dfrac{5}{12}$ tank.

So, the remaining tank $\dfrac{7}{12}$ can be filled

$\dfrac{7}{12} \times \dfrac{120}{7} = 10$ min.

25. b L.C.M of 5 and 4 = 20.

Cost price of 20 bananas $= 20 \times \dfrac{4}{5} = Rs. 16$.

Selling price of 20 bananas $= 20 \times \dfrac{5}{4} = Rs. 25$.

Gain $= 25 - 16 = 9$.

Gain percentage $= \dfrac{9}{16} \times 100 = 56.25\%$ gain.

26. b Total length = 60 cm

Raja's share = 30 cm

Gopal's share $= \dfrac{30}{4} = 7.5$ cm

Sahil's share = x

Hari's share = 6

$\therefore 30 + \dfrac{15}{2} + x + 6 = 60$

60 + 15 + 2x + 12 = 120

$\therefore 2x = 33 \Rightarrow x = 16.5$ cm.

27. c The ratio of the share of their expenses

= (50 × 4) : (40 × 3) : (46 × 5)

= 200   : 120 : 230

= 20   : 12 : 23

$\therefore$ Share of the 1st $= \dfrac{20}{55} \times 660 = Rs. 240$

28. c Total income for the month

(29 × 6 + 24 × 6 + 32 × 10 + 30 × 8) = Rs. 878

$\therefore$ average income per day $= \dfrac{878}{30} = Rs. 29.26$

29. b Principal = (Present worth of Rs. 121 due 1 year hence) + (Present worth of Rs. 121 due 2 year hence)

$= \dfrac{121}{\left(1 + \dfrac{10}{100}\right)} + \dfrac{121}{\left(1 + \dfrac{10}{100}\right)^2} = \dfrac{121}{1.1} + \dfrac{121}{1.1 \times 1.1}$

= Rs. 210

30. b Distance travelled by the train moving from A in $\dfrac{1}{2}$ hour = 40 km

Now, the distance of (220 – 40) = 180 km will be covered by a relative speed of (80 + 100) = 180 km/hr.

Hence, time taken in meeting between points A and B $= \dfrac{180}{180} = 1$ hr

Now, distance travelled by the first train in 1 hr = 80 km

Total distance moved by this train before both the train meet = (40 + 80) = 120 km

Number of questions: 30 **Time Allowed: 30 mins.**

1. Anuva takes 20 min less to reach her office if her speed increases by 5 km/hr and takes 30 min more if her speed decreases by 5 km/hr, what is her original speed?
   - (a) 20 km/hr
   - (b) 30 km/hr
   - (c) 25 km/hr
   - (d) None of these

2. Three light signals change after every 24 sec, 30 sec and 42 sec respectively. If they all change simultaneously at 1 : 30 : 00 hour, then at what time they again change simultaneously?
   - (a) 1 : 45 : 00
   - (b) 1 : 44 : 00
   - (c) 1 : 44 : 30
   - (d) 1 : 45 : 30

3. The adjacent sides of a parallelogram are a and b and the perpendicular distance between the parallel sides of length a is d. The perpendicular distance between the parallel sides of length b is equal to
   - (a) $\dfrac{ab}{d}$
   - (b) $\dfrac{ad}{b}$
   - (c) $\dfrac{bd}{a}$
   - (d) None of these

4. The length of the shadow of a tree extends by 20 m when the angle of elevation of the sun with respect to the top of the tree decreases from 45° to 30°. Find the height of the tree.
   - (a) 20 m
   - (b) 26.39 m
   - (c) 27.32 m
   - (d) None of these

5. In how many ways, can five-digits even numbers be formed using the digits 3, 2, 5, 7, 6 exactly once and also when repetition of digits is allowed?
   - (a) 48, 256
   - (b) 48, 1250
   - (c) 24, 256
   - (d) 24, 512

6. $11^2 + \left(\dfrac{11^4}{11^3}\right) - 11 + \left(\dfrac{1}{2}\right) \times 11^2 = ?$
   - (a) 302.5
   - (b) 281.5
   - (c) 1211
   - (d) 181.5

7. Find the roots of the quadratic equation, $x^2 - 7x + 12 = 0$.
   - (a) 3, 4
   - (b) 2, 3
   - (c) 6, 2
   - (d) 1, 12

8. Lata has the same number of sisters as she has brothers, but her brother, Shyam has twice as many sisters as he has brothers. How many children are there in the family?
   - (a) 7
   - (b) 8
   - (c) 5
   - (d) 6

9. What is the smallest three-digit number which when divided by 6 leaves a remainder of 5 and when divided by 5 leaves a remainder of 3?
   - (a) 125
   - (b) 209
   - (c) 137
   - (d) 113

10. What is the value of 397 × 397 + 104 × 104 + 397 × 208?
    - (a) 2,50,001
    - (b) 2,51,001
    - (c) 2,60,101
    - (d) None of these

11. A boat takes 20 min and 30 min to cover a particular distance downstream and upstream respectively. If the speed of the boat in still water is 20 m/s, find the speed of the stream.
    - (a) 4 km/hr
    - (b) 8 m/s
    - (c) 12 m/s
    - (d) 4 m/s

12. An equilateral triangle has side 8 cm. The mid-points of the sides of this triangle are joined to form another triangle. Then, the mid-points of that triangle are joined to form yet another triangle. This process is repeated infinite number of times. Find the sum of the perimeters and that of the areas of all such triangles formed.
    - (a) 48 cm, $\dfrac{64}{\sqrt{3}}$ cm^2
    - (b) 24 cm, $\dfrac{48}{\sqrt{3}}$ cm^2
    - (c) 48 cm, $\dfrac{48}{\sqrt{3}}$ cm^2
    - (d) None of these

13. Five men take as much time to do a job as 10 women take. If 6 men take 10 days to complete a job working 4 hours per day, how much time would 10 women take to do a job twice as much as the former working 6 hr a day?
    - (a) 12 days
    - (b) 14 days
    - (c) 16 days
    - (d) 18 days

14. A and B can do a piece of work in 45 days and 40 days respectively. They began to do the work together but A leaves after some days and then B completed the remaining work in 23 days. Find the number of days after which A left the work.
    (a) 6 days
    (b) 8 days
    (c) 3 days
    (d) 9 days

15. If 3 men, or 4 boys, or 6 women take 10 days to do a job, how much time would they take to complete the same job working together?
    (a) $\dfrac{10}{3}$ days
    (b) 4 days
    (c) $\dfrac{11}{3}$ days
    (d) None of these

16. The third term of an arithmetic progression (AP) is 11 and the sixth term is 23. What is the 12th term? Find the sum of all the 12 terms.
    (a) 250
    (b) 300
    (c) 354
    (d) 350

17. If $\sec\theta + \tan\theta = 2$, then which of the following is true?
    (a) $5\cos^2\theta - 4\cos\theta = 0$
    (b) $4\cos^2\theta = 5\cos\theta$
    (c) $5\cos\theta = 4\sin\theta$
    (d) None of these

18. If (x + 2) is a factor of $x^4 - 4x^2 + 2ax + 3$, what is the value of a?
    (a) $-\dfrac{4}{3}$
    (b) $-\dfrac{3}{4}$
    (c) $\dfrac{4}{3}$
    (d) $\dfrac{3}{4}$

19. If 3 men or 5 women or 8 boys can finish a work in 38 days, then the number of days taken by 6 men, 10 women and 6 boys to finish the work is
    (a) 70 days
    (b) 20 days
    (c) 10 days
    (d) 8 days

20. The given figure is a plane of a field and the angles at B, C and D are all right angles.

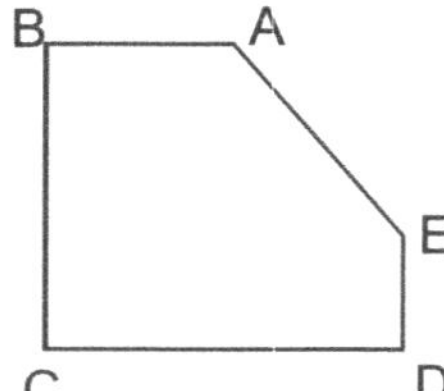

If AB = 15 m, BC = 30 m, CD = 22 m and DE = 6 m, the perimeter of the field is
    (a) 89 m
    (b) 98 m
    (c) 102 m
    (d) 80 m

21. After a conditioning camp of the Indian Cricket team, the final team of 11 players out of a total of 15 players is to be decided such that two players — Sehwag and Dravid are always chosen. Find the total number of ways the final team can be selected.
    (a) 312
    (b) 1365
    (c) 715
    (d) 1005

22. Six strings of a violin start vibrating simultaneously and they vibrate at 3, 4, 5, 6, 10 and 12 times in a minute. After how much time will all six of them vibrate together? How many times will they vibrate together in 30 min?
    (a) 60 min, 31 times
    (b) 60 sec, 31 times
    (c) 60 sec, 30 times
    (d) 120 sec, 31 times

23. P is any point on a circle whose centre is O. A chord which is parallel to the tangent at P bisects OP. If the length of the chord is 12 cm, the radius of the circle is
    (a) 4 cm
    (b) $4\sqrt{3}$ cm
    (c) 3 cm
    (d) $2\sqrt{5}$ cm

24. A can complete a task in 10 days while B can complete it in 15 days. If they work together for 6 days, what fraction of the work will be left?
    (a) $\dfrac{3}{5}$ th
    (b) $\dfrac{2}{5}$ th
    (c) $\dfrac{1}{6}$ th
    (d) Work is completed

25. Sam can row 18 km travelling downstream in 4 hr. His return journey takes 12 hr. What is the speed of the current?
    (a) 1.5 km/hr
    (b) 3 km/hr
    (c) 5 km/hr
    (d) 6 km/hr

26. The radii of two cylinders are in the ratio of 2 : 3 and their heights are in the ratio of 5 : 3. Find the ratio of their volumes.
    (a) 10 : 9
    (b) 3 : 7
    (c) 4 : 9
    (d) 20 : 27

27. There are 5 boys and 3 girls. In how many ways can they be seated in a row so that all the three girls don't sit together?

(a) $8! \times 3! \times 2!$ (b) $6! \times 50!$

(c) $49 \times 50!$ (d) $50 \times 6!$

28. A merchant has 100 kg of sugar, part of which he sells at 7% profit and the rest at 17% profit. He gains 10% on the whole. How much is sold at 17% profit?

(a) 70 kg   (b) 50 kg

(c) 35 kg   (d) 30 kg

29. Mohan Kumar is 8 km ahead of Ram chand. The speeds of Mohan Kumar and Ram Chand are 4 km/hr and 6 km/hr respectively. Ram Chand will overtake Mohan Kumar in:

(a) 2 hrs   (b) 1 hr 20 min

(c) 4 hrs   (d) 48 min

30. At an election in which there are only 2 candidates, a candidate, who gets 62% of the total votes polled, is elected by a majority of 288 votes. The total number of votes is:

(a) 456 votes   (b) 744 votes

(c) 912 votes   (d) 1200 votes

Answer Key

1. (c)	**2.** (b)	**3.** (b)	**4.** (c)	**5.** (b)	**6.** (d)	**7.** (a)	**8.** (a)	**9.** (d)	**10.** (b)
11. (d)	**12.** (a)	**13.** (c)	**14.** (d)	**15.** (a)	**16.** (b)	**17.** (a)	**18.** (d)	**19.** (d)	**20.** (b)
21. (c)	**22.** (b)	**23.** (b)	**24.** (d)	**25.** (a)	**26.** (d)	**27.** (d)	**28.** (d)	**29.** (c)	**30.** (d)

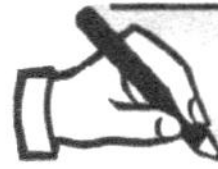

Explanations

1. c Since the distance remains constant, therefore we have

$$D = ST \qquad \text{... (i)}$$

$$D = (S + 5)\left(T - \frac{1}{3}\right) \qquad \text{... (ii)}$$

and $D = (S - 5)\left(T + \frac{1}{2}\right) \qquad \text{... (iii)}$

(Where D is distance, S is original speed and T is original time.)

Solving them, we get S = 25 km/hr.

2. b The light signals will change after (LCM of 24, 30 and 42) or 840 seconds or 14 minutes after 1:30 or 1:44.

3. b

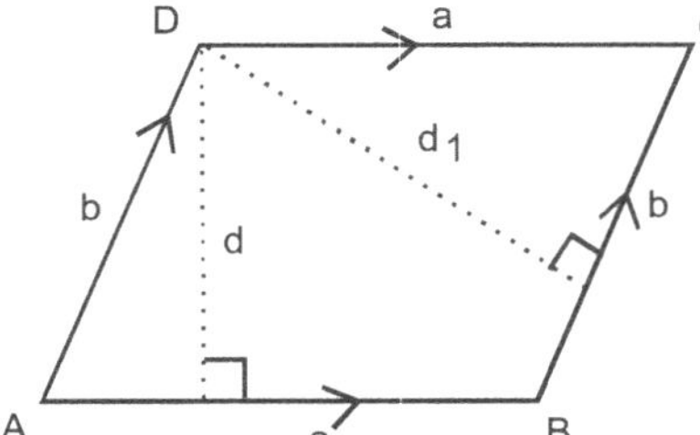

Area of the paralleogram = ad = bd_1

$$\therefore d_1 = \frac{ad}{b}$$

4. c

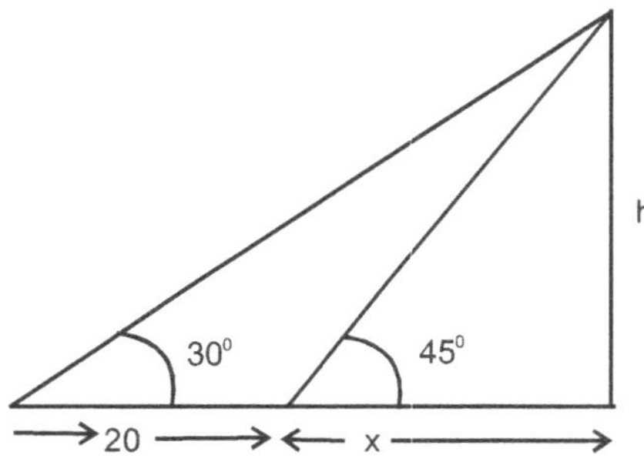

We have

$$\tan 30° = \frac{h}{20 + x} \quad \text{or} \quad (20 + x)\frac{1}{\sqrt{3}} = h$$

and $\tan 45° = \dfrac{h}{x}$ or h = x

$$\therefore (20 + h)\frac{1}{\sqrt{3}} = h$$

$$\therefore h = 27.32 \text{ m}$$

5. b Since five-digit number is an even number, therefore unit place can be filled with any of the two numbers 2 or 6 and rest of the places can be filled in the manner 4 × 3 × 2 × 1

Thus, a five-digit even number using digits 3, 2, 5, 7, 6 exactly once can be formed in 2 × 4 × 3 × 2 × 1 = 48 ways.

And when repetition is allowed again unit place can be filled in two ways and rest of the places in 5 × 5 × 5 × 5.

Thus, with repetition, it can be formed in 5 × 5 × 5 × 5 × 2 = 1250 ways.

6. d Using BODMAS rule in the given expression

$$11^2 + \left(\frac{11^4}{11^3}\right) - 11 + \left(\frac{1}{2}\right) \times 11^2, \text{ we have}$$

$$= 11^2 + 11 - 11 + \frac{1}{2} \times 11^2$$

$$= 121 + \frac{1}{2} \times 121 = 121\left(1 + \frac{1}{2}\right) = 121 \times \frac{3}{2}$$

$$= \frac{363}{2} = 181.5$$

7. a Given quadratic equation is

$$x^2 - 7x + 12 = 0$$
$$\Rightarrow x^2 - 3x - 4x + 12 = 0$$
$$\Rightarrow x(x - 3) - 4(x - 3) = 0$$
$$\Rightarrow (x - 4)(x - 3) = 0 \Rightarrow x = 4 \text{ or } 3$$

8. a Let there be b brothers and s sisters in the family.

Lata has b brothers and (s – 1) sisters.

$$\therefore b = s - 1$$
$$\Rightarrow s = b + 1 \qquad \text{... (i)}$$

Her brother Shyam has (b – 1) brothers and s sisters.

$$\therefore 2(b-1) = s$$
$$\text{or } 2b - 2 = s \qquad \text{... (ii)}$$

Solving (i) and (ii), we get

$$\Rightarrow b + 1 = 2b - 2 \Rightarrow b = 3$$

and s = 3 + 1 = 4

Children in the family = 3 + 4 = 7

9. d When 5 divides a number it leaves a remainder of 3, last digit of the number has to be 8 or 3. Only one option has three as unit digit.

10. b The given expression of the form

$$(397)^2 + (104)^2 + 2 \times 104 \times 397$$

which is the formula of $(a + b)^2$.

Thus, the given expression

$$= (397 + 104)^2 = (501)^2 = 251,001.$$

11. d Here, we have $\dfrac{20+v}{20-v}=\dfrac{30}{20}$

(where v is speed of the stream)

or 40 + 2v = 60 − 3v

or v = 4 m/s.

12. a The required figure is shown below:

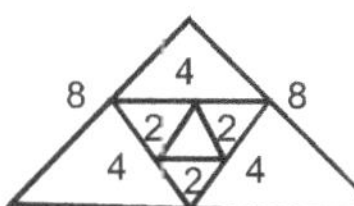

Perimeter of all the triangles are 24, 12, 6, 3, ... and so on. We have that the series so obtained is in GP with common ratio $\dfrac{1}{2}$. Thus sum of the perimeter upto infinity = $\dfrac{24}{1-\dfrac{1}{2}}=48$ cm .

Areas of all the equilateral triangles so formed

$\dfrac{\sqrt{3}}{4}\times 64,\ \dfrac{\sqrt{3}}{4}\times 16,\ \dfrac{\sqrt{3}}{4}\times 4$ ... and so on.

i.e. $16\sqrt{3},\ 4\sqrt{3},\ \sqrt{3},$ ... and so on, which is again a series in GP with common ratio $\dfrac{1}{4}$.

Thus the sum of areas of all the triangles upto infinity

$=\dfrac{a}{1-r}=\dfrac{16\sqrt{3}}{1-\dfrac{1}{4}}=\dfrac{64\sqrt{3}}{3}=\dfrac{64}{\sqrt{3}}$ cm^2

13. c 6 men = 12 women

Number of women-hours of first job = 12 × 10 × 4 = 480

Number of women-hours of second job = 480 × 2 = 960

∴ Time taken by 10 women working 6 hr a day to finish the second job = $\dfrac{960}{10\times 6}=16$ days .

14. d A's one day work $=\dfrac{1}{45}$

B's one day work $=\dfrac{1}{40}$

Together they will do $=\dfrac{1}{40}+\dfrac{1}{45}=\dfrac{17}{360}$ work in one day

Let them work together for x days, then

the work done $=\dfrac{17}{360}\times x$

So, the remaining work $=1-\dfrac{17x}{360}=\dfrac{360-17x}{360}$.

Now B completes the remaining work in 23 days.

Thus, by convention, we have

23 days $\longrightarrow \dfrac{360-17x}{360}$

1 day $\longrightarrow \dfrac{1}{40}$

$\therefore \dfrac{23}{40}=\dfrac{360-17x}{360}$

$\Rightarrow 23\times 9=360-17x \Rightarrow x=9$ days.

15. a Three men can do the work in 10 days.

Four boys can also do the work in 10 days.

Six women can do the work in 10 days.

Hence, if all three groups work together, they will finish the work in $\dfrac{10}{3}$ days.

16. b Let a be the first term and d be the common difference of an AP.

Thus, third term is a + 2d = 11   … (i)

and sixth term is a + 5d = 23   … (ii)

Subtracting (i) from (ii), we get

3d = 12 $\Rightarrow$ d = 4

∴ a = 3

Now, 12th term = a + 11d = 3 + 44 = 47

Sum = $S_n=\dfrac{12}{2}(6+11\times 4)=6\times 50=300$.

17. a $\dfrac{1+\sin\theta}{\cos\theta}=2$

∴ $1+\sin\theta=2\cos\theta$ or $\sin\theta=2\cos\theta-1$

∴ $\sin^2\theta=4\cos^2\theta-4\cos\theta+1$

or $1-\cos^2\theta=4\cos^2\theta-4\cos\theta+1$

or $5\cos^2\theta-4\cos\theta=0$.

18. d $a=\dfrac{3}{4}$. Using the remainder theorem,

$f(-2)=0\Rightarrow 16-16-4a+3=0\Rightarrow a=\dfrac{3}{4}$

19. d If 3 men can finish the job in 38 days,

then 1 man in 1 day can do $\dfrac{1}{3\times 38}$ work.

Similarly, 1 woman in 1 day can do $\dfrac{1}{5\times 38}$ work

and 1 boy in 1 day can do $\dfrac{1}{8\times 38}$ work.

Now 6 men, 10 women and 6 boys finish the work

in 1 day = $\dfrac{6\times 1}{3\times 38}+\dfrac{10\times 1}{5\times 38}+\dfrac{6\times 1}{8\times 38}=\dfrac{1}{8}$

∴ In 8 days they will finish the work.

20. b

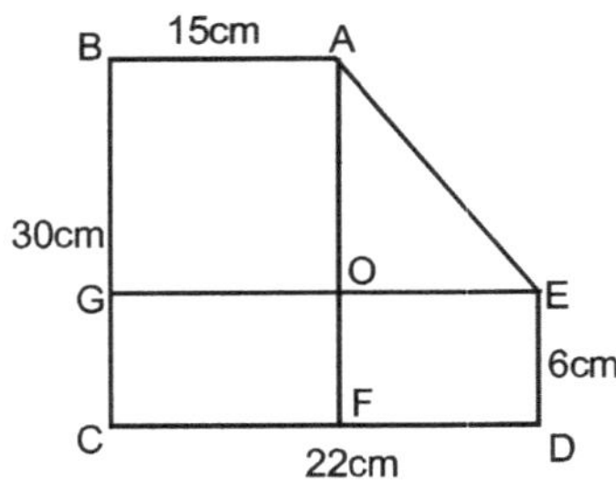

Draw AF perpendicular to CD and EG perpendicular to BC meeting at O. Then AO = 24 m and EO = 7 m

$\therefore AE^2 = AO^2 + EO^2 = 24^2 + 7^2 = 625$

$\therefore AE = 25$ m.

Hence, the perimeter of the field is

= (15 + 30 + 22 + 6 + 25) m = 98 m.

21. c 11 players out of 15 are to be chosen. But 2 of them are fixed — Sehwag and Dravid.

$\therefore$ Total number of ways = $^{15-2}C_{11-2} = {}^{13}C_9 = 715$.

22. b Six strings vibrate 3, 4, 5, 6, 10 and 12 times in a minute.

$\therefore$ These six strings vibrate every 20s, 15s, 12s, 10s, 6s and 5s.

LCM of 20, 15, 12, 10, 6 and 5 is 60.

$\therefore$ Every 60 sec they vibrate together and they will vibrate together 31 times in 30 minutes.

23. b

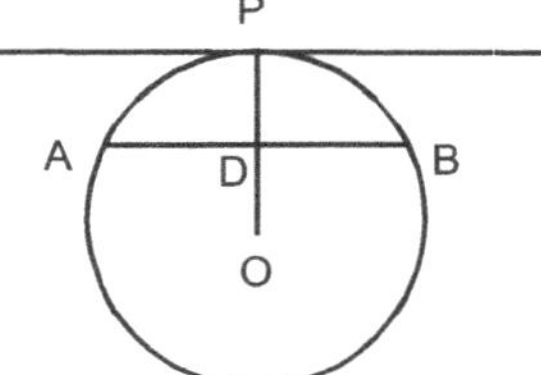

Let r be the radius of the circle.

Then OD = $\dfrac{r}{2}$

$OB^2 = BD^2 + OD^2$

$r^2 = (6)^2 + \left(\dfrac{r}{2}\right)^2$, i.e. $\dfrac{3}{4}r^2 = 36$

$\therefore r^2 = 48$ or $r = 4\sqrt{3}$ cm.

24. d $\dfrac{1}{A} = \dfrac{1}{10}$ and $\dfrac{1}{B} = \dfrac{1}{15}$

In 1 day, part completed working together

$= \dfrac{1}{A} + \dfrac{1}{B} = \dfrac{1}{10} + \dfrac{1}{15} = \dfrac{3+2}{30} = \dfrac{5}{30} = \dfrac{1}{6}$

$\therefore$ In 6 days they will finish $6 \times \dfrac{1}{6} = 1$, i.e. whole work.

25. a Speed downstream = $\dfrac{18}{4}$ km/hr

Speed upstream = $\dfrac{18}{12}$ km/hr

Speed of the current

$= \dfrac{1}{2}$ (Speed downstream – Speed upstream)

$= \dfrac{1}{2}\left(\dfrac{18}{4} - \dfrac{18}{12}\right) = 1.5$ km / hr.

26. d The ratio of the volume of two cylinders

$= \dfrac{\pi(2r)^2\,5h}{\pi(3r^2)3h} = \dfrac{4 \times 5}{9 \times 3} = \dfrac{20}{27}$.

27. d When there is no restriction 8 persons can be seated in 8! ways. But when all three girls sit together.

Consider the three girls as one, we have only 5 + 1 = 6 persons.

These 6 persons can be seated in 6! ways.

But there three girls can be arranged among themselves in 3! ways.

$\therefore$ Required number of ways in which all the three girls don't sit together = 8! – 6! × 3! = 6! (56 – 6) = 50 × 6!

28. d Let x be the quantity sold at 17% profit

By alligation,

$\dfrac{\text{Quantity sold at 7\% gain}}{\text{Quantity sold at 17\% gain}} =$

$\dfrac{\text{Price of sugar at 17\% – mean price}}{\text{Mean price – Price of sugar at 7\% gain}}$

$\dfrac{100 - x}{x} = \dfrac{17 - 10}{10 - 7}$

$\therefore x = 30$ kg

29. c Distance to be covered = 8 km

Relative speed = 6 – 4 = 2km/hr

Time taken = $\dfrac{8}{2}$ = 4 hrs.

30. d Let the total votes polled be x.

$\dfrac{62x}{100} - \dfrac{38x}{100} = 288$

$\dfrac{24x}{100} = 288$

$\therefore \quad x = \dfrac{288}{24} \times 100 = 1200$ votes

Number of questions: 30   **Time Allowed: 30 mins.**

1. Find the 100th term of the following given series, 1, 2, 4, 7, 11, 16, 22, 29, 37, 46 ....
   (a) 5050
   (b) 5051
   (c) 4951
   (d) 4950

2. If $x : y = 4 : 5$, find the value of $\dfrac{(11x+13y)}{(11x-13y)}$.
   (a) $-\dfrac{109}{21}$
   (b) $\dfrac{104}{21}$
   (c) $\dfrac{109}{21}$
   (d) None of these

3. The L.C.M. of 2 numbers of three digits each is 1740 and the H.C.F. is 290. The two numbers are
   (a) 290, 870
   (b) 290, 580
   (c) 580, 870
   (d) 290, 1160

4. The ratio between the length and breadth of a rectangular field is 5 : 4. If the breadth is 20 m less than the length, find the perimeter of the field.
   (a) 260 m
   (b) 360 m
   (c) 280 m
   (d) 180 m

5. $f(x)$ is defined as
$$f(x) = x+1 \quad 0 < x < 4$$
$$= 2x+1 \quad 4 \le x < 8$$
$$= x^2 +1 \quad 8 \le x < \infty$$
   Find $f(f(x))$ for $x = 5$.
   (a) 120
   (b) 122
   (c) 125
   (d) None of these

6. A sum of money is divided among A, B and C such that, for each two rupee, A gets one rupee, B gets 65 paise and C gets 35 paise. If C's share is Rs. 560, the sum is
   (a) Rs. 2,400
   (b) Rs. 2,800
   (c) Rs. 3,200
   (d) Rs. 3,600

7. Two trains 200 km apart start from opposite directions at the same time. They cross each other at a distance of 110 km from one of the stations. What is the ratio of their speeds?
   (a) 11 : 20
   (b) 9 : 20
   (c) 11 : 9
   (d) 10 : 11

8. The second term of a geometric progression (GP) is 27 and the third term is 9. Find the sixth term and the sum of all the six terms.
   (a) $\dfrac{1}{3}$, 121
   (b) $\dfrac{1}{3}$, $\dfrac{364}{3}$
   (c) $\dfrac{1}{9}$, $\dfrac{364}{3}$
   (d) $\dfrac{1}{9}$, 121

9. Walking at $\dfrac{6}{7}$ of his usual speed, Shyam is 25 min late. What is his usual time?
   (a) $1\dfrac{1}{2}$ hr
   (b) $2\dfrac{1}{2}$ hr
   (c) $1\dfrac{6}{7}$ hr
   (d) 3 hr

10. A bag contains 25 paisa, 10 paisa and 5 paisa coins in the ratio of 1 : 2 : 3. If their total value is Rs. 45, the number of 10 paisa coins is
    (a) 75
    (b) 150
    (c) 200
    (d) 225

11. If a boy walks from his house to his school at the rate of 4 km/hr, he reaches the school 10 min earlier than the scheduled time. However, if he walks at the rate of 3 km/hr, he reaches the school 10 min late. Find the distance of the school from his house.
    (a) 6 km
    (b) 4.5 km
    (c) 4 km
    (d) None of these

12. A television survey gives the following data for TV channel viewing: 60% watch *Zee*, 50% watch *Sony*, 50% watch *Star Plus*; 30% watch *Zee* and *Sony*, 20% watch *Sony* and *Star Plus*, 30% watch *Star Plus* and *Zee*. 10% do not view any channels. Find out what per cent view *Zee*, *Sony* and *Star Plus*, what per cent view exactly two channels and what per cent watch only channel *Zee*.
    (a) 10%, 50%, 20%
    (b) 10%, 10%, 10%
    (c) 10%, 50%, 10%
    (d) None of these

13. Identify the correct relation :

    (a) $\cos 2\theta = \dfrac{2\tan\theta}{1-\tan^2\theta}$

    (b) $\cos 2\theta = \dfrac{2\tan\theta}{1+\tan^2\theta}$

    (c) $\cos 2\theta = \dfrac{1+\tan^2\theta}{1-\tan^2\theta}$

    (d) $\cos 2\theta = \dfrac{1-\tan^2\theta}{1+\tan^2\theta}$

14. The present cost of Bajaj Motorcycle is Rs. 50,000. What will be its value after 3 years if the cost increases every year by 10%?

    (a) Rs. 65,000   (b) Rs. 60,000

    (c) Rs. 66,550   (d) Rs. 66,650

15. A ball is thrown up from a height of 5 m. It reaches a height of 20 m from the ground and returns to the ground. Every bounce reduces the subsequent height reached by 25%. Find the total distance covered by the ball before it finally comes to rest

    (a) 150 m   (b) 155 m

    (c) $167\dfrac{2}{3}$ m   (d) 180 m

16. The ages of A and B are in the ratio $9 : 4$. Seven years hence the ratio will be $5 : 3$. The present ages of A and B respectively be

    (a) 9 years, 4 years

    (b) 18 years, 8 years

    (c) 27 years, 12 years

    (d) None of these

17. Walking at $\dfrac{3}{4}$ of his usual speed, a man is late by 2.5 hr only. Find his usual time.

    (a) $7\dfrac{1}{2}$ hr   (b) $3\dfrac{1}{2}$ hr

    (c) $3\dfrac{1}{4}$ hr   (d) $\dfrac{7}{8}$ hr

18. If $x = 2 + 2^{2/3} + 2^{1/3}$, then what is the value of $x^3 - 6x^2 + 6x$?

    (a) 6   (b) 12

    (c) 4   (d) 2

19. A 200 L solution of alcohol and water contains $\dfrac{1}{4}$th of alcohol. Find the new percentage of alcohol, if 50 L of the original solution is replaced by 50 L of alcohol.

    (a) 43.75%   (b) 50%

    (c) 66.66%   (d) 80%

20. If $x : y = 2 : 5$, then $(3x + 4y) : (4x + 5) = ?$

    (a) $16 : 23$

    (b) $26 : 33$

    (c) $33 : 26$

    (d) Can't be determined

21. In a class of 200 students 70 played cricket, 60 played hockey and 80 played football, 30 played cricket and football, 30 played hockey and football, 40 played cricket and hockey. Then find the maximum number of people playing all the three games and minimum number of people playing at least one game.

    (a) 200, 100   (b) 30, 110

    (c) 30, 120   (d) None of these

22. The entrance fee of a museum was reduced by 25%, but the daily turn out increased by 30%. What was the effect of this on the daily revenue?

    (a) 2% increase   (b) 2% decrease

    (c) 2.5% increase   (d) 2.5% decrease

23. If a solid sphere of radius 10 cm is moulded into 8 spherical solid balls of equal radius, then what is the radius of each such ball?

    (a) 5 cm   (b) 2.5 cm

    (c) 3.75 cm   (d) 10 cm

24. What is the least number which when divided by 18, 27 and 36 leaves the remainders 5, 14 and 23?

    (a) 108   (b) 113

    (c) 149   (d) 95

25. A train 108 m long moving at a speed of 50 km/hr crosses another train 112 m long coming from opposite direction in 6 sec. What is the speed of the second train?

    (a) 82 km/hr   (b) 48 km/hr

    (c) 66 km/hr   (d) 54 km/hr

26. A four-digit number is formed writing four of the five digits 0, 1, 2, 3 and 4. What is the probability that this number is not divisible by 3?

    (a) $\dfrac{2}{7}$ (b) $\dfrac{1}{3}$

    (c) $\dfrac{3}{8}$ (d) $\dfrac{5}{8}$

27. There are 13 couples, 5 single men and 7 single ladies in a party. Every man greets every lady once but no one greets his wife. How many greetings took place in the party?

    (a) 247   (b) 347

    (c) 360   (d) 191

28. If $\left[3^{m^2} \div \left(3^m\right)^2\right]^{\frac{1}{m}} = 81$, what is the value of m?

    (a) 3   (b) 6

    (c) −6   (d) −3

29. If 18 men and 10 boys can do in a day as much work as 10 men and 22 boys; how much should a man be paid a day if a boy is to get Rs. 5 a day?

    (a) Rs. 6   (b) Rs. $6\frac{1}{2}$

    (c) Rs. $7\frac{1}{2}$ (d) Rs. 8

30. A cask contains 3 parts wine and one part water. What part of the mixture must be drawn off and substituted by water so that the resulting mixture may be half wine and half water?

    (a) $\frac{1}{2}$

    (b) $\frac{5}{2}$

    (c) $\frac{1}{3}$

    (d) $\frac{3}{2}$

Answer Key

1. (c)	2. (a)	3. (c)	4. (b)	5. (b)	6. (c)	7. (c)	8. (b)	9. (b)	10. (b)
11. (c)	12. (c)	13. (d)	14. (c)	15. (b)	16. (b)	17. (a)	18. (d)	19. (a)	20. (d)
21. (c)	22. (d)	23. (a)	24. (d)	25. (a)	26. (d)	27. (b)	28. (b)	29. (c)	30. (c)

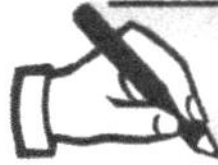

Explanations

1. c $t_1 = 1$

$t_2 = 1 + 1$

$t_3 = 1 + 1 + 2$

$t_4 = 1 + 1 + 2 + 3$

$\therefore t_n = 1 + \sum\limits_{i=0}^{n-1} i$

$\therefore t_{100} = 1 + \sum\limits_{i=0}^{99} i = 1 + \dfrac{99 \times 100}{2} = 4951$

2. a Given that $\dfrac{x}{y} = \dfrac{4}{5}$

Now $\dfrac{11x + 3y}{11x - 13y} = \dfrac{11\left(\dfrac{x}{y}\right) + 13}{11\left(\dfrac{x}{y}\right) - 13} = \dfrac{11 \times \dfrac{4}{5} + 13}{11 \times \dfrac{4}{5} - 13}$

$= \dfrac{44 + 65}{44 - 65} = -\dfrac{109}{21}$.

3. c All the options have 290 as H.C.F, but only option (c) has 1740 as L.C.M.

4. b Let the length and breadth of a rectangular field be 5x and 4x. Also $4x = 5x - 20 \Rightarrow x = 20$ m

$\therefore$ Length $= 5 \times 20 = 100$ m

Breadth $= 4 \times 20 = 80$ m

Thus the perimeter of the field $= 2(100 + 80) = 360$ m.

5. b $f(5) = 2 \times 5 + 1 = 11$

$f(11) = 11^2 + 1 = 122$

6. c Assume that the sum be x.

The ratio's of A, B and C $= 100 : 65 : 35 = 20 : 13 : 7$

Then,

$x \times \dfrac{7}{40} = 560 \Rightarrow x = \dfrac{560 \times 40}{7} = 80 \times 40 = $ Rs. 3,200

7. c Let the time $= t$

Speed of the first train $= \dfrac{110}{t}$ km/hr

Speed of the second train $= \dfrac{90}{t}$ km/hr

Ratio of speeds $= \dfrac{\dfrac{110}{t}}{\dfrac{90}{t}} = 11 : 9$.

8. b Let a be the first term and r be the common ratio of GP.

Then second term is $ar = 27$ ... (i)

and the third term is $ar^2 = 9$ ... (ii)

Using (i), in (ii), we get $ar.r = 9 \Rightarrow 27.r = 9$

$\Rightarrow r = \dfrac{1}{3}$ and $ar = 27 \Rightarrow a = 81$

Now, the sixth term $= ar^5 = 81 \times \dfrac{1}{3^5} = \dfrac{1}{3}$

Sum of six terms $= \dfrac{a(1 - r^n)}{1 - r} = \dfrac{81\left(1 - \dfrac{1}{3^6}\right)}{1 - \dfrac{1}{3}}$

$= \dfrac{728}{6} = \dfrac{364}{3}$.

9. b Let the usual speed be x km/hr and usual time be t hr.

Distance travelled $= xt$

According to the question, we have

$xt = \dfrac{6}{7}x\left(t + \dfrac{25}{60}\right) \Rightarrow 7t = 6t + \dfrac{25}{10}$

$\Rightarrow t = \dfrac{5}{2} = 2.5$ hr .

10. b If the number of coins is x, 2x and 3x, then the value of the coins, is

$x \times 25 + 2x \times 10 + 3x \times 5 = 4500$

$$60x = 4500$$
$$x = 75$$
$$2x = 150$$

Hence, the number of 10 paisa coins is 150.

11. c Let t be the usual time taken by a boy to reach school.

Now according to the question

$4\left(t - \dfrac{10}{60}\right) = 3\left(t + \dfrac{10}{60}\right)$

$4t - \dfrac{4}{6} = 3t + \dfrac{3}{6}$; $t = \dfrac{7}{6}$

Now distance travelled $= 4\left(\dfrac{7}{6} - \dfrac{1}{6}\right) = 4$ km

12. c Using Venn diagram, we have found that

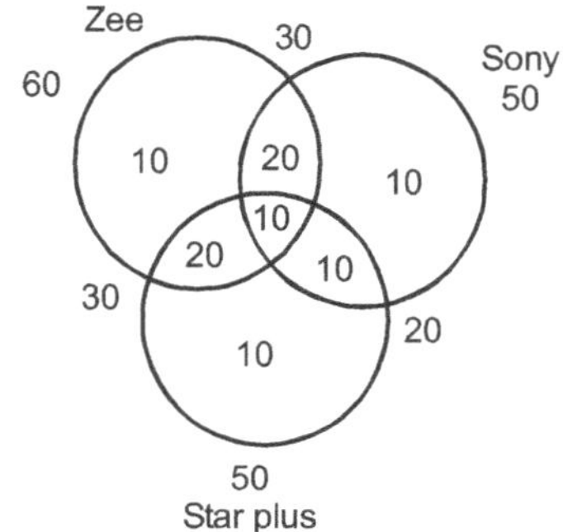

Since 10% do not watch any channel which means, 90% watch all the channels.

∴ Using $n(A \cup B \cup C) = n(A) + n(B) + n(C) - n(A \cap B)$
$$-n(A \cap C) - n(C \cap A) + n(A \cap B \cap C)$$

$90 = 60 + 50 + 50 - 30 - 30 - 20 + n(A \cap B \cap C)$

$\Rightarrow n(A \cap B \cap C) = 10$.

13. d The correct relation is

$$\cos 2\theta = \frac{1 - \tan^2 \theta}{1 + \tan^2 \theta}$$

14. c The value of Bajaj Motorcycle after 3 years is

$$= \text{Rs. } 50,000 \left(1 + \frac{10}{100}\right)^3$$

$$= \text{Rs. } 50,000 \left(\frac{11}{10}\right)^3 = \text{Rs. } 66,550.$$

15. b $-5 + 20 + 20 + 15 + 15 + 11.25 + 11.25 + ...$

$= -5 + 2 \{20 + 15 + 11.25 + ...\}$

[∵ It reduces by 25%, hence common ratio of the infinite GP series = 0.75]

$$= -5 + 2 \times \frac{20}{1 - 0.75} = 155 \text{ m}$$

16. b $\dfrac{9x + 7}{4x + 7} = \dfrac{5}{3}$

$\Rightarrow 27x + 21 = 20x + 35 \Rightarrow 7x = 14$

$\Rightarrow x = 2$

Hence, their present ages are 18 years and 8 years.

17. a Let the usual speed of a man be x km/hr and the time taken be t hours.

Since distance travelled = Speed × Time.

Now, according to the question, we have

$$xt = \frac{3}{4}x(t + 2.5) \Rightarrow 4t = 3t + 7.5 \Rightarrow t = 7.5 \text{ hr.}$$

18. d Given that

$x = 2 + 2^{\frac{2}{3}} + 2^{\frac{1}{3}}$, and we need to find the value of $x^3 - 6x^2 + 6x$.

Consider $x = 2 + 2^{\frac{2}{3}} + 2^{\frac{1}{3}}$

$\Rightarrow x - 2 = 2^{\frac{2}{3}} + 2^{\frac{1}{3}}$

Taking cube to both sides, we get

$$(x - 2)^3 = \left(2^{\frac{2}{3}} + 2^{\frac{1}{3}}\right)^3$$

$\Rightarrow x^3 - 6x^2 + 12x - 8 = 2^2 + 3 \cdot 2^{\frac{4}{3}} \cdot 2^{\frac{1}{3}} + 3 \cdot 2^{\frac{2}{3}} \cdot 2^{\frac{2}{3}} + 2$

$\Rightarrow x^3 - 6x^2 + 12x - 14 = 6\left(2^{\frac{2}{3}} + 2^{\frac{1}{3}}\right)$

$\Rightarrow x^3 - 6x^2 + 12x - 14 = 6(x - 2)$

$\Rightarrow x^3 - 6x^2 + 6x = 2$.

19. a Alcohol = 50 L, water = 150 L

Alcohol taken out $= \dfrac{50}{4} = 12.5 \text{L}$

New alcohol = 50 − 12.5 + 50 = 87.5 L

Final alcohol percentage $= \dfrac{87.5}{200} \times 100 = 43.75\%$

20. d Given that $\dfrac{x}{y} = \dfrac{2}{5}$ and $\dfrac{3x + 4y}{4x + 5}$, from the given fraction we cannot determine the value of fraction, as when we divide with y, we do not have $\dfrac{x}{y}$ form in the denominator.

21. c For maximizing

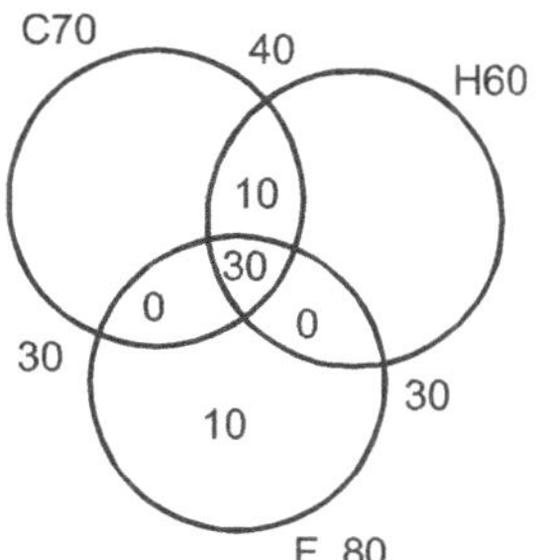

For minimizing

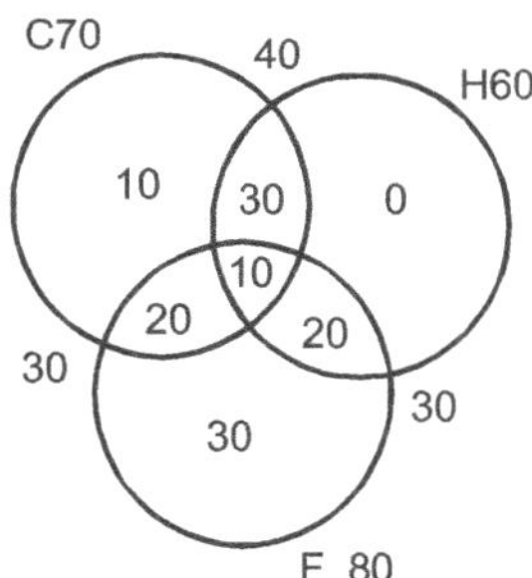

Maximum number of people playing three games = 30

Minimum number of people playing at least one game = 120.

22. d Let the entrance fee be Rs. x and daily turn out be y. Now if entrance fee is reduced by 25%, then the resultant price be $\dfrac{3x}{4}$ and if daily turn out is increase by 30%, then the resultant effect will be

$$y + \frac{30y}{100} = \frac{13y}{10}$$

So, the net effect on the daily receipts

$$= \frac{xy - \frac{3}{4} \times \left(\frac{13y}{10}\right) \times 100}{xy}$$

$$= \frac{40 - 39}{40} \times 100 = 2.5\% \text{ decrease .}$$

23. a Volume of given solid sphere with radius 10 cm

$$= \frac{4}{3}\pi(10)^3$$

and volume of 8 moulded spherical balls of equal

radius, say, r = $8 \times \frac{4}{3}\pi r^3$

Now, according to the question, we have

$$\frac{4}{3}\pi(10)^3 = 8 \times \frac{4}{3}\pi r^3$$

$$\Rightarrow \frac{10^3}{8} = r^3 \Rightarrow \frac{10^3}{2^3} = r^3$$

$$\Rightarrow \frac{10}{2} = r \Rightarrow r = 5\,\text{cm} \; .$$

24. d Going with the options we have found that 95 is the number.

25. a Let the speed of the train be x km/hr.

Now, using the concept of relative speed, we have

$$\frac{\frac{108}{1000} + \frac{112}{1000}}{50 + x} = \frac{6}{3600}$$

$$\Rightarrow \frac{220}{(50 + x)1000} = \frac{1}{600}$$

$$\Rightarrow 132 = 50 + x \Rightarrow x = 82\,\text{km/hr.}$$

26. d We make a four-digit number with 0, 1, 2 and 3.

Number of such numbers is 3 × 3 × 2 = 18.

When we formed a four-digit number with 0, 2, 3 and 4.

Number of such number is 3 × 3 × 2 = 18.

It means 18 + 18 = 36 out of those 96 numbers will be divisible by 3.

$\Rightarrow$ 96 − 36 = 60 numbers will not be divisible by 3

$\therefore$ The required probability = $\frac{60}{96} = \frac{5}{8}$

27. b Any single man will have 13 + 7 = 20 options.

$\therefore$ Total number of greetings by single males

= 5 × 20 = 100

Any married man will have 12 + 7 = 19 options.

$\therefore$ Total number of greetings by married men

= 19 × 13 = 247

$\therefore$ Total number of greetings = 247 + 100 = 347

28. b $\left[3^{m^2} \div \left(3^m\right)^2\right]^{\frac{1}{m}} = 81$

$$\Rightarrow \left(3^{m^2 - 2m}\right)^{1/m} = 3^4$$

$$\Rightarrow 3^{m(m-2)\frac{1}{m}} = 3^4 \quad \Rightarrow m - 2 = 4 \Rightarrow m = 6$$

29. c 18 men + 10 boys = 10 men + 22 boys

$\therefore$ 12 boys = 8 men

Money earned by 12 boys = Rs. 60 = Money earned by 8 men

$\therefore$ 1 man should be paid = $\frac{60}{8} = \text{Rs. } 7\frac{1}{2}$ a day

30. c Let the cask contain x L of mixture

Amount of wine = $\frac{3x}{4}$ and amount of water $\frac{x}{4}$

Let y L. of mixture be drawn off and replaced with water.

Wine left = $\frac{3x}{4} - \frac{3y}{4} = \frac{3}{4}(x - y)$

and water = $\frac{1}{4}x - \frac{1}{4}y + y = \frac{1}{4}x + \frac{3}{4}y$

$$= \frac{1}{4}(x + 3y)$$

$$\therefore \frac{3}{4}(x - y) = \frac{1}{4}(x + 3y)$$

$$\Rightarrow 3x - 3y = x + 3y$$

$$\Rightarrow 2x = 6y$$

$$\Rightarrow y = \frac{1}{3}x$$

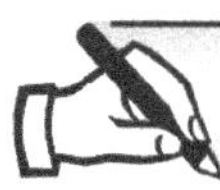

Practice Test-6

Number of questions: 30 **Time Allowed: 30 mins.**

1. The cost of cultivating a square field at the rate of Rs. 135 per hectare is Rs. 1,215. What is the cost of fencing the same field if the rate of fencing is 75 paise per metre?

   (Given: 1 hectare = 10,000 sq. m)

   (a) Rs. 810 (b) Rs. 900

   (c) Rs. 1,800 (d) None of these

2. Two trains start from A and B, and head towards B and A respectively. Train from A starts at 11 p.m. and reaches B at 5 p.m. next day. Train from B starts at 10 p.m. the same day and reaches A at 6 a.m. the next day. At what time (approximately) will they cross each other?

   (a) 4 a.m. (b) 3.51 a.m.

   (c) 2 a.m. (d) 1.30 a.m.

3. The area of a parallelogram ABCD is A sq. cm. The distance between AB and DC is d_1 cm and the distance between BC and AD is d_2 cm. Then the perimeter of the parallelogram is

   (a) $\dfrac{2A\left(d_1+d_2\right)}{d_1 d_2}$ (b) $\dfrac{2A\left(d_1 d_2\right)}{d_1+d_2}$

   (c) $\dfrac{A d_1 d_2}{d_1+d_2}$ (d) $\dfrac{A\left(d_1+d_2\right)}{d_1 d_2}$

4. Two cars are driven by A and B respectively. They are 580 miles apart and they drive towards each other. A's car had travelled 20 miles an hour, 4 hours per day for 5 days, when it had met B's car. If B had driven 3 hr a day for 5 days, what was B's speed?

   (a) 8 miles/hr (b) 9 miles/hr

   (c) 10 miles/hr (d) 12 miles/hr

5. Sujay alone can finish a project in 10 days while Vijay alone can finish it in 15 days. If they work together and finish the project then, how much amount will Sujay get out of total wages of Rs. 225?

   (a) Rs. 135

   (b) Rs. 112.5

   (c) Rs. 150

   (d) Rs. 90

6. There are 10 points arranged in a line. There are 15 points arranged in parallel below these 10 points. How many possible triangles can be formed?

   (a) 1050 (b) 675

   (c) 1725 (d) 375

7. A man goes uphill at 24 km/hr and comes down at 36 km/hr. What is his average speed?

   (a) 30 km/hr (b) 35.8 km/hr

   (c) 32.6 km/hr (d) 28.8 km/hr

8. Find the area of a rhombus one side of which measures 20 cm and one diagonal 24 cm.

   (a) 240 cm^2 (b) 120 cm^2

   (c) 300 cm^2 (d) 384 cm^2

9. If the price of a commodity increases first by 10%, then by 20% and subsequently decreases by 20%, what is the net percentage increase/decrease in the price?

   (a) 10% increase (b) 20% decrease

   (c) 5.6% decrease (d) None of these

10. A bag contains one rupee, 50 paise and 25 paise coins in the ratio 5 : 6 : 7. If the total amount is Rs. 390, find the number of 25 paise coins in the bag.

    (a) 140

    (b) 390

    (c) 240

    (d) 280

11. Azhar, Jadeja and Mongia rent a piece of pasture for a month. Azhar puts in 27 cattle for 19 days. Jadeja puts in 21 cattle for 17 days and Mongia puts in 24 cattle for 23 days. If at the end of the month the rent amounts to Rs. 237, how much should Mongia pay?

    (a) Rs. 102

    (b) Rs. 137

    (c) Rs. 92

    (d) Rs. 90

12. AB = AC, DB = DC, $\angle ABC = \dfrac{1}{2}\angle DBC$ and $\angle D$ = 70°. What is the measure of angle A?

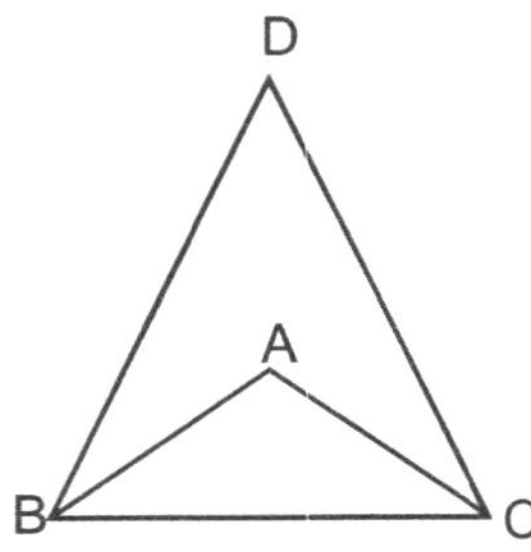

   (a) 125°   (b) 105°
   (c) 70°   (d) 55°

13. If you travel 39 km at a speed of 26 km/hr, another 39 km at a speed of 39 km/hr and next 39 km at a speed of 52 km/hr, what is your average speed for the entire journey?

   (a) 39 km/hr   (b) 37.6 km/hr
   (c) 33.33 km/hr   (d) None of these

14. Two years ago Ram was 6 times as old as his son. After 18 years, he will be twice as old as his son. Find the present ages of Ram and his son.

   (a) 34 years, 9 years

   (b) 36 years, 11 years

   (c) 32 years, 7 years

   (d) 30 years, 10 years

15. The cost of manufacturing a commodity increased by 20%. A trader who did not revise the selling price noted that there was a drop of Rs. 20 in his profit. What is the original cost price?

   (a) Rs. 100   (b) Rs. 200
   (c) Rs. 500   (d) None of these

16. Mangesh writes first hundred whole numbers. How many times does he write zero? Also find out how many times will the number '9' occur in the set of first hundred whole numbers?

   (a) 12, 19   (b) 10, 20
   (c) 11, 19   (d) 12, 20

17. A car is running at a speed of 72 km/hr. How much time will it take to cover a distance of 100 m?

   (a) 5 sec

   (b) 72 sec

   (c) 10 sec

   (d) 5 hr

18. The average weight of 2 men A and B is 84 kg. Another man C joins the group and the average weight decreases by 4 kg. If another man D, whose weight is 3 kg more than that of C, replaces A, then the average weight of B, C and D becomes 79 kg. The weight of A (in kg) is

   (a) 82   (b) 78
   (c) 75   (d) 79

19. A man travels 20 miles at 4 miles per hour and another 60 miles at 6 miles per hour. What is his average speed for the entire trip?

   (a) $12\dfrac{1}{3}$ miles/h   (b) $8\dfrac{2}{7}$ miles/h

   (c) $7\dfrac{3}{11}$ miles/h   (d) $5\dfrac{1}{3}$ miles/h

20. The incomes of Asha and Brinda are in the ratio 3 : 2 and their expenditures in the ratio 5 : 3. If both of them save Rs.1,500 each, then how much is Brinda's income?

   (a) Rs. 3,000   (b) Rs. 6,000
   (c) Rs. 4,500   (d) Rs. 5,000

21. If $(2^{x+4}) - (2^{x+2}) = 3$, then what is the value of 'x'?

   (a) 0   (b) – 2
   (c) – 1   (d) 2

22. If 18 pumps can raise 2,170 tonnes of water in 10 days working 7 hr a day, in how many days will 16 pumps raise 1,736 tonnes working 9 hr a day?

   (a) 5 days   (b) 6 days
   (c) 8 days   (d) 7 days

23. How many three-digit numbers would you find, which when divided by 3, 4, 5, 6 and 7 leave the remainders 1, 2, 3, 4 and 5 respectively?

   (a) 4   (b) 3
   (c) 1   (d) 2

24. The daily Madhubani - Delhi express starts from Madhubani at 6 a.m. and reaches Delhi at 6 p.m. the next day. The corresponding Delhi - Madhubani express departs from Delhi at 9 p.m. and reaches Madhubani in 36 hr. Both the trains take same route. Find the number of trains from Madhubani to Delhi that a train from Delhi to Madhubani will cross.

   (a) 1

   (b) 2

   (c) 3

   (d) None of these

25. Tangents at A and B of a circle intersect at C. D is any point on the minor arc AB.

    If $\angle ACB = 40°$, then $\angle ADB$ is

    (a) 140° (b) 130°
    (c) 110° (d) 120°

26. A battalion of 4000 men has provisions for 40 days, if after 10 days another 1000 men join, how long will the food last?

    (a) 30 days (b) 20 days
    (c) 22 days (d) 24 days

27. The cost of making an article is divided between materials, labour and overheads in the ratio 3 : 4 : 1. If the materials cost Rs. 22.50, find the cost of the article.

    (a) Rs. 62 (b) Rs. 52.50
    (c) Rs. 70 (d) Rs. 60

28. $$\dfrac{2 + \dfrac{1}{3 + \dfrac{4}{5}}}{2 + \dfrac{1}{3 + \dfrac{1}{1 + \dfrac{1}{4}}}} = ?$$

    (a) 1 (b) $\dfrac{3}{7}$

    (c) $\dfrac{1}{7}$ (d) $\dfrac{8}{7}$

29. A number N when divided by 5 leaves the remainder 1, and when divided by 6 leaves the remainder 5. The smallest positive N is:

    (a) 14
    (b) 11
    (c) 41
    (d) 22

30. In this figure, the area of the shaded part is

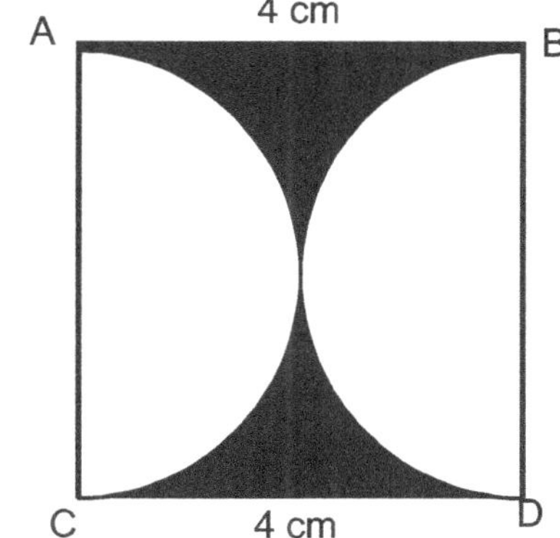

    (a) 3.44 cm²
    (b) 3.2 cm²
    (c) 2.5 cm²
    (d) 4 cm²

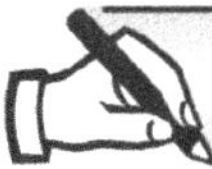 ## Answer Key

1. (b)	2. (b)	3. (a)	4. (d)	5. (a)	6. (c)	7. (d)	8. (d)	9. (d)	10. (d)
11. (c)	12. (a)	13. (d)	14. (c)	15. (a)	16. (b)	17. (a)	18. (b)	19. (d)	20. (b)
21. (b)	22. (d)	23. (d)	24. (c)	25. (c)	26. (d)	27. (d)	28. (a)	29. (b)	30. (a)

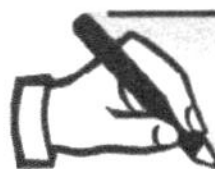

Explanations

1. b Area of the square field $= \dfrac{1215}{135}$

$= 9$ hectare

$= 90{,}000$ sq. m

Thus, the side of a square $= \sqrt{90{,}000} = 300$ m

Now cost of fencing the same field

$= 4 \times 300 \times \dfrac{75}{100} = 12 \times 75 = $ Rs. 900 .

2. b We see that the trains take 18 hr and 8 hr respectively to complete its journeys.

Let the distance between the stations be LCM (18, 8), i.e. 72 km.

$\therefore$ Speed of the first train = 4 km/hr

Speed of the second train = 9 km/hr

By the time the train from A starts, train from B has already travelled 9 km in 1 hr.

Now the distance between the trains = 72 – 9 = 63 km

Relative speed of the trains = 9 + 4 = 13 km/hr

$\therefore$ They will meet $\dfrac{63}{13}$ hr after 11 p.m. i.e. 3.51 a.m.

3. a $AB \cdot d_1 = A$ and $AD \cdot d_2 = A$

$\therefore AB = \dfrac{A}{d_1}$ and $AD = \dfrac{A}{d_2}$

The perimeter of the parallelogram

$= 2(AB + AD) = 2\left(\dfrac{A}{d_1} + \dfrac{A}{d_2}\right) = 2A\left(\dfrac{d_1 + d_2}{d_1 d_2}\right)$

4. d

20 miles/hr	580 miles	x miles/hr
4 hrs/day		3 hrs/day
5 days		5 days

Distance travelled by A = 20 × 4 × 5 miles = 400 miles.

So the remaining distance = 580 – 400 = 180 miles has to covered by B in order to meet A.

$\therefore$ Speed of B $= \dfrac{180}{15} = 12$ miles / hr.

5. a Sujay's one day's work $= \dfrac{1}{10}$

Vijay's one day's work $= \dfrac{1}{15}$

If they work together they will complete

$= \dfrac{1}{10} + \dfrac{1}{15} = \dfrac{1}{6}$ th work .

Thus, to complete whole work they will take 6 days.

So, Sujay will get an amount $= 6 \times \dfrac{1}{10} \times 225$

$= \dfrac{3}{5} \times 225 = $ Rs. 135

6. c The number possible triangles that can be formed

$= {}^{10}C_1 \times {}^{15}C_2 + {}^{10}C_2 \times {}^{15}C_1$

$= 10 \times 105 + 45 \times 15 = 1725$

7. d Average speed $= \dfrac{2}{\dfrac{1}{24} + \dfrac{1}{36}} = 28.8 \, km / hr$

8. d

In right-angled triangle AOB, we have

$OB^2 = 400 - 144 = 256$

$\Rightarrow OB = 16$ $\therefore$ BD = 32 cm

Now area of rhombus $= \dfrac{1}{2} \times d_1 \times d_2 = \dfrac{1}{2} \times 32 \times 24$

$= 16 \times 24 = 384 \, cm^2$

9. d Suppose the initial price is y.

Final price = y × 1.1 × 1.2 × 0.8 = 1.056y.

$\therefore$ There is 5.6% increase.

10. d Let one Rupee, 50 paise and 25 paise coins be 5x, 6x and 7x

$\therefore$ According to the question, we have

$5x + \dfrac{1}{2} \times 6x + \dfrac{1}{4} \times 7x = 390$

$\Rightarrow 20x + 12x + 7x = 1560$

$\Rightarrow 39x = 1560 \Rightarrow x = \dfrac{1560}{39} = 40$

So, the number of 25-paisa coin = 7 × 40 = 280 coins.

11. c Let Rs. x be the common amount which each of them has to pay.

Now, according to the question,

$27 \times \dfrac{19}{30}x + 21 \times \dfrac{17}{30}x + 24 \times \dfrac{23}{30}x = 237$

$3x[9 \times 19 + 7 \times 17 + 8 \times 23]$

$= 237 \times 30$

$\Rightarrow 474x = 2370 \Rightarrow x = 5$

$\therefore$ Mongia has to pay $24 \times \dfrac{23}{30} \times 5 = \text{Rs. } 92$

12. a Since DB = DC

Therefore, triangle is an isosceles triangle.

Thus $\angle DBC = \angle DCB$

As the sum of the angles of the triangle is 180°.

$\therefore 2 \angle DBC + 70° = 180°$

$\Rightarrow \angle DBC = 55°$

Again AB = AC

$\therefore \angle ABC = \angle ACB$

$\Rightarrow \dfrac{1}{2} \angle DBC = \angle ACB$

$\Rightarrow \angle BAC = 180° - 2\angle ABC = 180° - 55° = 125°$

13. d Average speed is $\dfrac{3 \times 26 \times 39 \times 52}{26 \times 39 + 39 \times 52 + 52 \times 26}$.

$= \dfrac{13^3 (3 \times 2 \times 3 \times 4)}{13^2 (2 \times 3 + 3 \times 4 + 4 \times 2)} = \dfrac{13 \times 72}{26} = 36 \text{ km / hr}$

Alternative method:

Assume distance for each different speed = x

Total distance = 3x

Total time = $\dfrac{x}{26} + \dfrac{x}{39} + \dfrac{x}{52} = \dfrac{169x}{39 \times 52}$

Hence, average speed = $\dfrac{3x}{\dfrac{169x}{39 \times 52}} = 36 \text{ km/hr}$.

14. c Let the age of Ram's son 2 years ago be x years.

Then the age of Ram be 6x (2 years ago).

After 18 years, or from two years ago, i.e 20 years after, son's age will be (x + 20) years

and Ram's age will be 6x + 20 years.

Now according to the question, we have

$2(x + 20) = 6x + 20$.

$\Rightarrow 2x + 40 = 6x + 20$

$\Rightarrow 4x = 20 \Rightarrow x = 5$

$\therefore$ Their present ages are x + 2 = 5 + 2 = 7 years, 6x + 2 = 30 + 2 = 32 years.

15. a Suppose initial cost price was Rs. x and the selling price is Rs. y.

Initial profit = y − x

After the increase cost price = 1.2x

Now profit = y − 1.2x (Selling price does not change)

Now it is given that $(y - x) - (y - 1.2x) = 20$

or $y - x - y + 1.2x = 20$

or $0.2x = 20$

or x = Rs. 100

16. b The first hundred whole numbers begin from 0 to 99.

Thus, number of zero's Mangesh has to write = 0, 10, 20, 30, 40, 50, 60, 70, 80, 90, i.e. 10 times

And number of 9's in the set of hundred whole numbers = 9, 19, 29, 39, 49, 59, 69, 79, 89, 90, 91, ... 99, i.e. 20 times.

17. a Time = $\dfrac{\text{Distance}}{\text{Speed}} = \dfrac{100 \times 3600}{1000 \times 72} = 5 \text{ sec}$

18. b Given A + B = 84 × 2 = 168 kg

A + B + C = 80 × 3 = 240 kg

Hence C = 240 − 168 = 72 kg

D = 72 + 3 = 75 kg

Given B + C + D = 79 × 3 = 237 kg

Hence, A = (A + B) + C + D − (B + C + D)

= 168 + 147 − 237 = 315 − 237 = 78 kg.

19. d Average speed = $\dfrac{20 + 60}{\dfrac{20}{4} + \dfrac{60}{6}} = \dfrac{80}{15} = \dfrac{16}{3} = 5\dfrac{1}{3} \text{ miles / hr}$

20. b Let the incomes of Asha and Brinda be 3x and 2x, and their expenditures be 5y and 3y respectively.

Now, Savings = Incomes − Expenditures.

$\Rightarrow 1500 = 3x - 5y \qquad \ldots \text{(i)}$

and $1500 = 2x - 3y \qquad \ldots \text{(ii)}$

Multiplying (i) by 2 and (ii) by 3 and subtracting, we get

$3000 = 6x - 10y$

$4500 = 6x - 9y$

$-1500 = -y$

$\Rightarrow y = 1500$

$\therefore 1500 + 7500 = 3x$

$\Rightarrow \dfrac{9000}{3} = x \Rightarrow x = \text{Rs. } 3{,}000$

Thus, Brinda's income = Rs. 6,000.

21. b We have

$\left(2^{x+4}\right) - 2^{x+2} = 3$

$\Rightarrow 2^x \cdot 2^4 - 2^x \cdot 2^2 = 3$

$\Rightarrow 16 \cdot 2^2 - 4 \cdot 2^x = 3$

$\Rightarrow 12 \cdot 2^x = 3$

$\Rightarrow 2^x \cdot 3 \cdot 2^x = 3$

$\Rightarrow 3 \cdot 2^{x+2} = 3.2°$

Since the bases are same so comparing the exponents, we have $x + 2 = 0 \Rightarrow x = -2$.

22. d 18 pumps can raise 2,170 tonnes of water in $10 \times 7 = 70$ hr.

In 1 hr 18 pumps can raise $\dfrac{2170}{70} = 31$ tonnes

Let number of days taken by 16 pumps be x.

16 pumps can raise $\dfrac{1736}{9x}$ tonnes

According to the question,

18 days	31 tonnes
16 days	$\dfrac{1736}{9x}$

$x = \dfrac{18 \times 1736}{9 \times 16 \times 31} = 7$ days .

23. d LCM $(3, 4, 5, 6, 7) = 420$

$420 - 2 = 418$, is the number which when divided by 3, 4, 5, 6 and 7 leave the remainder 1, 2, 3, 4 and 5

Also, $418 \times 2 + 2 = 836 + 2 = 838$.

838 is the number which when divided by 3, 4, 5, 6 and 7, leave the remainder 1, 2, 3, 4 and 5.

Thus, there are 2 numbers.

24. c Suppose a train leaves Delhi at 9 p.m. on October 9 (you can take any date): The first train from Madhubani that it will cross will be the train that left Madhubani on October 9. The train from Delhi will reach Madhubani on October 11 at 9 a.m. Therefore, it will cross two more trains from Madhubani, i.e. the trains that left Madhubani on October 10 and 11.

25. c 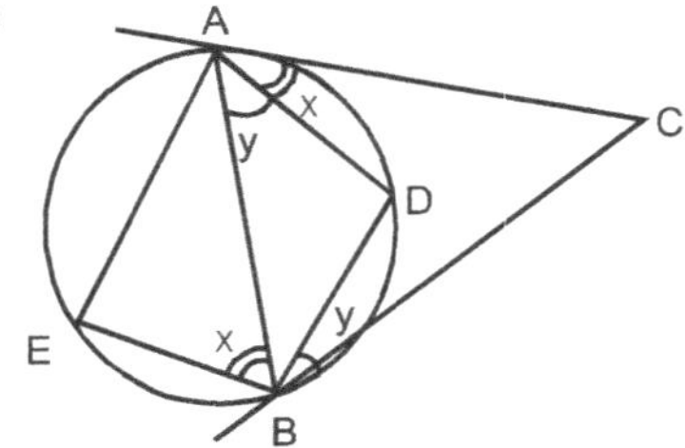

Let $\angle CAD$ be x° and $\angle CBD$ be y°.

$\angle CAD = \angle ABD$ (Angle in the alternate segment)

$\angle DBC = \angle BAD$ (Angle in the alternate segment)

$\therefore \angle CAB = \angle CBA = x + y$

$\therefore \angle ACB = 180° - 2(x + y)$

i.e. $40° = 180° - 2(x + y)$

$\therefore (x + y) = 70°$

$\angle ADB = 180° - \angle DAB - \angle DBA$

$= 180° - (x + y)$

$= 180° - 70° = 110°$.

26. d After 10 days, there is provision of food for 30 days

4000 men can consume the food in 30 days

1 men can consume the food in 30×4000

5000 men can consume the food in $\dfrac{30 \times 4000}{5000}$

$= 24$ days

27. d Cost of material $= \dfrac{3}{8}$ of the total cost

$\therefore 22.50 = \dfrac{3}{8}$ of total cost

$\therefore$ Total cost $= 22.5 \times \dfrac{8}{3} = $ Rs. 60

28. a $\dfrac{2 + \dfrac{1}{19}}{2 + \dfrac{5}{3 + \dfrac{4}{5}}} = \dfrac{2 + \dfrac{5}{19}}{2 + \dfrac{5}{19}} = 1$

29. b $N = 5Q + 1$

$N = 6P + 5$ for $P = 1$ the required N is 11

Which also satifies the requirement of first expression.

30. a In the given figure $= AC = BD = 4$ cm

So, area of shaded part = Area of ABCD – Area of circle of radius 2 cm

$= 4 \times 4 - \pi \times (2)^2$

$= 16 - \pi \times 4 = 16 - 4 \times 3.14$

$= 16 - 12.56 = 3.44$ cm^2

Number of questions: 25 **Time Allowed: 25 mins.**

1. If the sales turnover of a company increases from Rs. 100 crore to Rs. 300 crore in 3 years, what is the compounded annual growth rate of sales (approximately) for the company?
   (a) 42%
   (b) 44%
   (c) 48%
   (d) None of these

2. If the slope of the line joining $(-8, 11)$ and $(2, y)$ is $-\dfrac{4}{3}$, then what is the value of y?
   (a) $\dfrac{3}{4}$
   (b) $-\dfrac{3}{8}$
   (c) $-\dfrac{4}{7}$
   (d) $-\dfrac{7}{3}$

3. A T-shirt marked at Rs. 80 is sold for Rs. 68. The rate of discount is:
   (a) 15%
   (b) 12%
   (c) $17\dfrac{11}{17}\%$
   (d) 20%

4. The 15th term of an arithmetic progression is 5. If the total number of terms of the progression is 29, find the sum of all the terms of the progression.
   (a) 135
   (b) 195
   (c) 155
   (d) 145

5. Twenty litres of a milk solution contains milk and water in $3 : 1$ ratio. How much milk must be added to this solution to change the milk and water ratio to $4 : 1$?
   (a) 3 liters
   (b) 5 liters
   (c) 7 liters
   (d) 2 liters

6. Three years ago, the average age of Amin and Beena was 18 years. With Chetan joining them, the average age is 22 years now. How old is Chetan now?
   (a) 30 years
   (b) 25 years
   (c) 20 years
   (d) None of these

7. A can do a piece of work in 80 days. He works at it for 10 days and then B alone finishes the work in 42 days. How many days would A and B together take to complete the work?
   (a) $45\dfrac{1}{3}$ days
   (b) 48 days
   (c) $32\dfrac{2}{3}$ days
   (d) 30 days

8. A house-owner was having his house painted. He was advised that he would require 25 kg of paint. Allowing for 15% wastage and assuming that the paint is available in 2 kg cane, what will be the cost of paint purchased, if one cane cost Rs. 16?
   (a) Rs. 240
   (b) Rs. 180
   (c) Rs. 160
   (d) Rs. 360

9. If $\sin\theta$ and $\cos\theta$ are the roots of the equation $ax^2 + x + 1 = 0$ and $\sin\theta = p$, $\cos\theta = q$, then
   (a) $1 + 2pq = p^2 q^2$
   (b) $p + q = p^2 q^2$
   (c) $(p + q)^2 = p^2 + q^2$
   (d) None of these

10. The value of a diamond is directly proportional to the square of its weight. If a diamond weighing 4 kg breaks into two pieces, its total value decreases by 37.5%. Find the weights of the two pieces.
   (a) 2 kg, 2 kg
   (b) $2\dfrac{1}{2}$ kg, $1\dfrac{1}{2}$ kg
   (c) 3 kg, 1 kg
   (d) None of these

11. 'A' distributes Rs. 180 equally amongst a certain number of people. 'B' distributes the same sum but gives to each person Rs. 6 more than 'A' does, and gives to 40 persons less than 'A' does. How much does 'A' give to each person?
   (a) Rs. 2
   (b) Rs. 3
   (c) Rs. 4
   (d) Rs. 5

12. P, Q and R are three partners in a venture. Twice the investment of P is equal to thrice the capital of Q and the capital of Q is four times the capital of R. What is the share of R out of a total profit of Rs. 5,940?
   (a) Rs. 690
   (b) Rs. 720
   (c) Rs. 540
   (d) Rs. 940

13. A person has a total of Rs. 210 in Re. 1, 50 paise and 25 paise coins. They were in the ratio $2.5 : 3 : 4$. How many Re. 1 coins were there?
   (a) 89
   (b) 103
   (c) 92
   (d) 105

14. If you throw 5 fair coins, what is the probability of getting at least 3 heads?
   (a) $\dfrac{5}{16}$
   (b) $\dfrac{1}{2}$
   (c) $\dfrac{1}{3}$
   (d) $\dfrac{11}{16}$

15. If 'N' is a natural number, how many values of 'N' are possible such that $\dfrac{\left(17N^2 + 6N + 9\right)}{N}$ is also a natural number?

    (a) 3
    (b) Infinite
    (c) 2
    (d) 1

16. There would be 10% loss if a toy is sold at Rs.10.80 per piece. At what price should it be sold in order to earn a profit of 20%?

    (a) Rs. 12
    (b) Rs. 12.96
    (c) Rs. 14.40
    (d) None of these

17. Some quantity of tea worth Rs. 30.20 per kg is to be mixed with some quantity of tea worth Rs. 20.50 per kg so that the mixture may be worth Rs. 25.40 per kg. The ratio of the quantity of tea of the first kind to that of the second kind in the mixture should be

    (a) 48 : 49
    (b) 49 : 18
    (c) 49 : 24
    (d) 49 : 48

18. If the selling price of 8 items is equal to cost price of 7 items, then what is the profit or loss percentage? (You have to assume that CP or SP of all the items are same)

    (a) 12.5% profit
    (b) 14.2% loss
    (c) 12.5% loss
    (d) None of these

19. There are 3 numbers in the ratio 3 : 4 : 5 and the sum of their squares is 1250. Find the biggest of 3 numbers.

    (a) 20
    (b) 25
    (c) 30
    (d) 40

20. One root of $x^2 + kx - 8 = 0$ is square of the other. Find the value of 'k'.

    (a) – 4
    (b) – 2
    (c) 2
    (d) 4

21. Five distinct pairs of shoes are displayed. In how many different ways can 3 shoes be selected containing a matched pair?

    (a) 20
    (b) 60
    (c) 30
    (d) 40

22. The sum of the squares of two numbers is 68 and the square of their difference is 36. Find the product of the two numbers.

    (a) 32
    (b) 58
    (c) 104
    (d) 16

23. 1250 mangoes were distributed among a group of boys. Each boy got twice as many mangoes as the number of boys in the group. The number of boys in the group was:

    (a) 25
    (b) 45
    (c) 50
    (d) 625

24. If a, b, c be in A.P., then $\dfrac{1}{c}, \dfrac{b}{ac}, \dfrac{1}{a}$ are in

    (a) A.P
    (b) G.P
    (c) H.P
    (d) None of these

25. A certain distance is covered at a certain speed. If half of this distance is covered in double the time, the ratio of the two speeds is:

    (a) 4 : 1
    (b) 1 : 4
    (c) 2 : 1
    (d) 1 : 2

Answer Key

1. (b)	2. (d)	3. (a)	4. (d)	5. (b)	6. (d)	7. (d)	8. (a)	9. (a)	10. (c)
11. (b)	12. (c)	13. (d)	14. (b)	15. (a)	16. (c)	17. (d)	18. (c)	19. (b)	20. (b)
21. (d)	22. (d)	23. (a)	24. (a)	25. (a)					

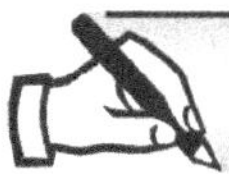

Explanations

1. b Suppose the initial turnover is x and the compounded annual growth rate is r, then we have

$$3x = x\left(1+\frac{r}{100}\right)^3 \text{ or } \left(1+\frac{r}{100}\right) = \sqrt[3]{3} = 1.4422$$

or r = 44.22%.

2. d $m = \dfrac{y_2 - y_1}{x_2 - x_1}$

where m : slope

$$\therefore \quad -\frac{4}{3} = \frac{y - 11}{2 + 8}$$

$$\Rightarrow -40 = 3y - 33$$

$$\Rightarrow 3y = -40 + 33$$

$$\Rightarrow y = -\frac{7}{3}.$$

3. a By applying the formula of M.P.

$$\therefore \text{ M.P.} = \frac{\text{Selling price} \times 100}{(100 - d\%)}$$

$$80 = \frac{68 \times 100}{(100 - d\%)}$$

$$8000 - 80d = 6800$$

$$1200 = 80d \%$$

$$\frac{1200}{80} = d\%$$

$$d = 15\%$$

4. d Let a denote the first term and d denote the common difference.

$$\therefore a + 14d = 5.$$

Lety S_n be the sum of n terms, then

$$S_n = \frac{n}{2}\left[2a + \overline{n-1}d\right]$$

$$= \frac{29}{2}[2a + 28d]$$

$$= \frac{29}{2} \times 2[a + 14d] = 29 \times 5 = 145$$

5. b Quantity of milk in the the given mixture = $\left(\dfrac{20 \times 3}{4}\right)$

= 15 litres.

Quantity of water in this mixture = (20 – 15) = 5 litres

Let X litres of milk be added to given mixture to have the requisite ratio of milk and water.

Then, $\left(\dfrac{15 + X}{5}\right) = \dfrac{4}{1}$ or 15 + X = 20 or X = 5

∴ Milk to be added = 5 litres.

6. d Let A denotes Amin, B denotes Beena and C denotes Chetn, then according to the question

$$\frac{A + B}{2} = 18 + 3 = 21 \Rightarrow A + B = 42 \qquad \text{... (i)}$$

$$\frac{A + B + C}{3} = 22 \Rightarrow A + B + C = 66 \qquad \text{... (ii)}$$

Using (i) in (ii), we get

42 + C = 66

⇒ C = 66 – 42 = 24 years.

7. d A's 10 day's work = $\dfrac{10}{80} = \dfrac{1}{8}$.

Remaining work = $\left(1 - \dfrac{1}{8}\right)$ is done by B in 42 days.

Therefore, B alone can finish the work in $\left(\dfrac{42 \times 8}{7}\right)$

= 48 days.

∴ B's 1 day's work = $\dfrac{1}{48}$

(A + B)'s 1 day's work = $\left(\dfrac{1}{80} + \dfrac{1}{48}\right) = \dfrac{1}{30}$.

∴ A and B together can finish the work in 30 days.

8. a Let the quantity of paint purchased be x kg

then (x – 15% of x) = 25 kg

x = 29.41 or 30 kg

So, he must purchase 15 cans

Total cost = 16 × 15 = Rs. 240

9. a $\sin\theta + \cos\theta = \dfrac{-1}{a}$

$\sin\theta \cos\theta = \dfrac{1}{a}$

$\therefore \sin\theta + \cos\theta = -\sin\theta \cos\theta$

or $(\sin\theta + \cos\theta)^2 = (-\sin\theta\cos\theta)^2$

or $\sin^2\theta + \cos^2\theta + 2\sin\theta \cos\theta = \sin^2\theta \cos^2\theta$

or $1 + 2pq = p^2q^2$

10. c Here, initial value $v_1 = k \cdot 4^2 = 16k$

Where k is a proportionality constant.

Suppose the diamond breaks into two pieces of weights x kg and 4 – x kg and their values are v_2 and v_3 respectively.

$v_2 = kx^2$ and $v_3 = k(4 - x)^2$

Total value = $v_2 + v_3 = k\{x^2 + (4 - x)^2\}$

= $k\{2x^2 - 8x + 16\}$

Given that $k(2x^2 - 8x + 16) = 62.5\%$ of $16k$

or $2k(x^2 - 4x + 8) = \dfrac{5}{8} \times 16k$

or $x^2 - 4x + 3 = 0$

or $x = 1$ or 3

$\therefore$ Weights of the parts are 1 kg and 3 kg.

11. b Let A distributes Rs. 180 among n persons.

Then, each person will have Rs. $\dfrac{180}{n}$.

B distributes Rs. 180 among $n - 40$ persons.

He gives Rs. 6 more than what A gives to every person

$\therefore \left(\dfrac{180}{n} + 6\right)(n - 40) = 180$

$\Rightarrow \dfrac{180}{n} + 6 = \dfrac{180}{n - 40}$

$\Rightarrow \dfrac{180}{n - 40} - \dfrac{180}{n} = 6$

$\Rightarrow 7200 = 6n(n - 40)$

$\Rightarrow n^2 - 40n - 1200 = 0$

$\Rightarrow n = 60, -20$ but $n = -20$ is not possible.

Clearly, A distributes Rs. $\dfrac{180}{n} = \dfrac{180}{60} = \text{Rs. } 3$ to every person.

12. c Let p, q and r denote the investments made by P, Q and R respectively. Then,

$2p = 3q$ and $q = 4r$

$\Rightarrow 2p = 3q = 12r$

Dividing the above equation by 12, we get

$\dfrac{p}{6} = \dfrac{q}{4} = \dfrac{r}{1}$ $\therefore$ p : q : r = 6 : 4 : 1

Total profit = Rs. 5,940

R's share $\dfrac{1}{6 + 4 + 1} \times 5940 = \dfrac{1}{11} \times 5940$ = Rs. 540

13. d Assume Re. 1 coins = 2.5x

Assume 50-paisa coins = 3x

Assume 25-paisa coins = 4x

Total amount = 210 = $1 \times 2.5x + \dfrac{1}{2} \times 3x + \dfrac{1}{4} \times 4x$

or x = 42 or Re. 1 coins = 105

14. b The total number of ways in which 5 coins can appear

$= 2^5 = 32$

Number of ways in which you can get 3 heads = $^5C_3 = 10$

Number of ways in which you can get 4 heads = $^5C_4 = 5$

Number of ways in which you can get all 5 heads $= {}^5C_5 = 1$

$\therefore$ The required probability $= \dfrac{10 + 5 + 1}{32} = \dfrac{1}{2}$

15. a Given expression is $\dfrac{17N^2 + 6N + 9}{N}$,

which can be written as $17N + 6 + \dfrac{9}{N}$.

An expression $17N + 6 + \dfrac{9}{N}$ is a natural number when N = 9 or N = 3 or N = 1

Thus only three values of N make an expression a natural number.

16. c Cost price $= \dfrac{10.80}{0.9} = \text{Rs.} 12$

Selling price $= 12 \times \dfrac{120}{100} = \text{Rs.} 14.40$

17. d Working conventionally, you would try the alligation method, but if you take a look at the problem, you find that both the additive mixtures are more or less equally separated from the resultant mixture, i.e. (30.20 – 25.40) is almost equal to (25.40 – 20.50). But the resultant is marginally closer to the costlier additive (the difference is smaller), which implies that there is more quantity of that additive. Hence, the answer is (d).

18. c Suppose the cost price of 1 item be Re. 1

Now SP of 8 items = CP of 7 items = Rs. 7

CP of 8 items = Rs. 8

$\therefore$ There is a loss of Re. 1 on Rs. 8

$\therefore$ 12.5% loss

19. b Let the numbers be 3x, 4x and 5x respectively.

$9x^2 + 16x^2 + 25x^2 = 1250$

$\Rightarrow 50x^2 = 1250$ or $x = 5$

The numbers are 15, 20 and 25.

$\therefore$ The biggest number is 25.

20. b Let α and β be the roots of the equation

$x^2 + kx - 8 = 0$

Given that $\alpha = \beta^2$

Now sum of the roots

$\alpha + \beta = \beta^2 + \beta = -k$

and product of the roots $= \alpha\beta = \beta^3 = -8$

$\Rightarrow \beta = -2$

$\therefore (-2)^2 + (-2) = -k$

$4 - 2 = -k$ $\therefore 2 = -k$

$\Rightarrow k = -2$

21. d One pair can be selected out of five pairs in five ways. Now we have 4 pairs of shoes, i.e. 8 distinct shoes, out of which one can be selected in

    $^8C_1 = 8$ ways.

    $\therefore$ Total number of ways = $5 \times 8 = 40$

22. d Let the two numbers be x and y

    Then $x^2 + y^2 = 68$ ... (i)

    and $(x - y)^2 = 36$

    $\Rightarrow x^2 + y^2 - 2 \times y = 36$

    $\Rightarrow 68 - 2xy = 36$ [Using (i)]

    $\Rightarrow 2xy = 68 - 36 = 32$

    $\Rightarrow xy = \dfrac{32}{2} = 16$

23. a Let the number of boys be x

    Number of mangoes each child gets = 2x

    $2 x \times x = 1250 \Rightarrow x^2 = 625 \Rightarrow x = 25$

24. a a, b, c are in A.P

    $\dfrac{a}{ac}, \dfrac{b}{ac}, \dfrac{c}{ac}$ are in A.P

    $\Rightarrow \dfrac{1}{c}, \dfrac{b}{ac}, \dfrac{1}{a}$ are in A.P

25. a Clearly, the speed is inversely proportional to time taken.

    Hence, ratio of speed is 4 : 1.

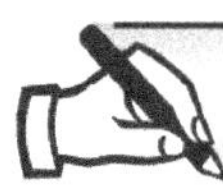

Practice Test-8

Number of questions: 25　　　　　　　　　　　　　　　　　　**Time Allowed: 30 mins.**

1. Ajay writes hundred whole numbers from 100 to 199. How many 1's does he write exactly two times?
   (a) 12　　　　　　　　(b) 11
   (c) 19　　　　　　　　(d) 10

2. If the difference between the CI and the SI at the end of 2 years is Rs. 100, what is the principal? Rate is 5% per annum in both the cases. (Assume same principal for both the cases.)
   (a) Rs. 50,000　　　　(b) Rs. 40,000
   (c) Rs. 10,000　　　　(d) None of these

3. The par value of the shares of company x and y is Rs. 10. The market price of the shares are Rs. 40 and Rs. 50 respectively. Find the ratio of the return on investment for an investor if the dividends are 20% and 40% respectively. Investment in both the cases is the same.
   (a) 5 : 8　　　　　　　(b) 8 : 5
   (c) 8 : 13　　　　　　(d) None of these

4. How many kilograms of rice costing Rs. 9 per kilogram must be mixed with 27 kg of rice costing Rs. 7 per kilogram so that 10% gain may be obtained by selling the mixture at Rs. 9.24 per kilogram?
   (a) 54 kg　　　　　　(b) 69 kg
   (c) 36 kg　　　　　　(d) 63 kg

5. A can build a wall in 15 days, which B alone can build in 20 days. If they build it together and get a total payment of Rs. 189, how much is B's share?
   (a) Rs. 108　　　　　(b) Rs. 81
   (c) Rs. 27　　　　　　(d) Rs. 96

6. A square and an equilateral triangle are inscribed in a circle of radius r. Then there sides are in the ratio
   (a) 1 : 3　　　　　　　(b) $\sqrt{2} : \sqrt{3}$
   (c) 1 : $\sqrt{3}$　　　　　(d) 2 : 3

7. The spring balance of a trader showed 1 kg for 900 gm. Find the profit/loss percentage if the trader marks up the price 10% above the cost price.
   (a) 20% profit　　　　(b) 22.22% loss
   (c) 22.22% profit　　(d) None of these

8. Find the value of $[10 \times 36$ of $\dfrac{1}{3} - (110 \div 11) \times 3 + 52]$.
   (a) 115　　　　　　　(b) 65
   (c) −430　　　　　　(d) None of these

9. If 15 men working 9 hr a day can reap a field in 16 days, in how many days will 18 men reap the same field, working 8 hr a day?
   (a) 15 days　　　　　(b) 17 days
   (c) 21 days　　　　　(d) 14 days

10. What is the remainder when 9875347 × 7435789 × 5789743 is divided by 4?
    (a) 1　　　　　　　　(b) 2
    (c) 3　　　　　　　　(d) None of these

11. If you pick up two numbers out of first 29 multiples of 11, what is the probability that the product of these two numbers is divisible by 3267?
    (a) $\dfrac{12}{^{29}C_2}$　　　　　(b) $\dfrac{13}{^{29}C_2}$
    (c) $\dfrac{41}{^{29}C_2}$　　　　　(d) $\dfrac{40}{^{29}C_2}$

12. In the adjacent figure, AE ⊥ ED, ED = 13 cm, CD ⊥ ED, CD = 3 cm, DC ⊥ CB, CB = 2 cm, AE = 11 cm. Find the length of AB.

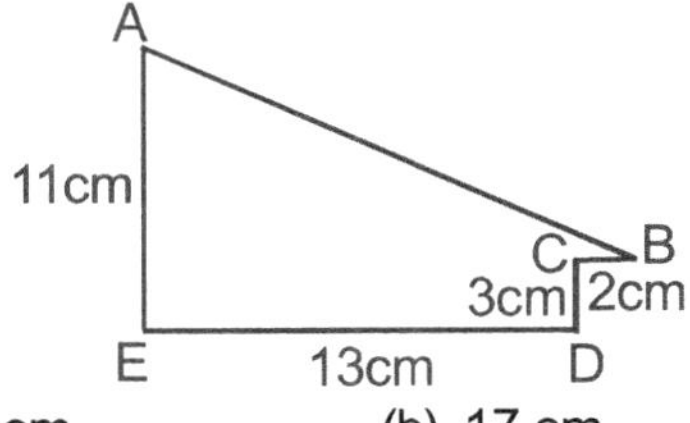

    (a) 8 cm　　　　　　(b) 17 cm
    (c) 12 cm　　　　　　(d) 14 cm

13. In how many ways can three integers be selected from the set {1, 2, 3, ⋯ 37} such that the sum of the three integers is an odd number?
    (a) 3876　　　　　　(b) 7638
    (c) 6378　　　　　　(d) 1938

14. S.I. on a sum at 4% p.a. for 2 years is Rs. 80. Find the C.I. on the same sum for the same period at the same rate of interest.
    (a) Rs. 81.60　　　　(b) Rs. 72.60
    (c) Rs. 181.60　　　(d) Rs. 66

15. A sum of money doubles itself in 7 years. In how many years will it become four-fold; if interest rate is simple?
    (a) 21 years
    (b) 21 years 3 months
    (c) 21 years 6 months
    (d) 22 years

16. A train crosses a platform, which is 250 m long. The speed of the train is 36 km/hr. The total time taken to cross the platform is 35 sec. Find the length of the train.
    (a) 120 m
    (b) 100 m
    (c) 120 km
    (d) 100 km

17. How many four-digit numbers can be made with the digits 0, 1, 2 and 7 so that at least one of the digits is repeated in every number?
    (a) 192
    (b) 96
    (c) 174
    (d) None of these

18. Two coins are such that the first has a tail and a head and the second has both heads. One of these coins is tossed and the result is a head. What is the probability that it is the coin with 2 heads?
    (a) $\dfrac{1}{2}$
    (b) $\dfrac{1}{3}$
    (c) $\dfrac{2}{3}$
    (d) $\dfrac{2}{7}$

19. A shopkeeper buys a table for Rs. 4,650 and marks its price 20% above its cost price. If he allows a discount of 15% on it, find the selling price.
    (a) Rs. 5,301
    (b) Rs. 4,743
    (c) Rs. 4,822
    (d) Cannot be determined

20. A man can row 12 km/hr in still water. If it takes him twice as long as to row up as to row down the river, find the speed of the stream.
    (a) 8 km/hr
    (b) 2 km/hr
    (c) 4 km/hr
    (d) 16 km/hr

21. If $2x + 5y = 54$ and $\dfrac{x}{y} = \dfrac{1}{5}$, find the value of $(x + y)$.
    (a) 10
    (b) 2
    (c) 8
    (d) 12

22. A garrison of 600 men had provisions for 28 days. After 4 days, a reinforcement of 200 men arrived. The food will now last for how many days?
    (a) 32 days
    (b) 21 days
    (c) 24 days
    (d) 18 days

23. Find the total length of fencing a rectangular area of dimensions 64 m × 36 m.
    (a) $2 \times 34 \times 36$ m
    (b) $\sqrt{64 \times 36}$ m
    (c) $\dfrac{64 \times 36}{3}$ m
    (d) 200 m

24. The cost of oil is Rs. 100 per L. After adulteration with another oil that costs Rs. 50 per L, Ram sells the mixture at Rs. 96 per kilogram, making a profit of 20%. In what ratio does he mixes the two?
    (a) 1 : 2
    (b) 3 : 2
    (c) 3 : 1
    (d) 3 : 4

25. A train travelling at the rate of 90 km/hr, crosses a pole in 10 sec. Its length is
    (a) 250m
    (b) 150m
    (c) 900m
    (d) 100m

Answer Key

1. (d)	2. (d)	3. (d)	4. (d)	5. (b)	6. (b)	7. (d)	8. (c)	9. (c)	10. (d)
11. (b)	12. (c)	13. (d)	14. (d)	15. (c)	16. (b)	17. (c)	18. (a)	19. (d)	20. (b)
21. (b)	22. (c)	23. (c)	24. (c)	25. (a)					

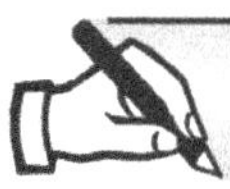

Explanations

1. c Hundred whole numbers from 100 to 199 are as follows.

101 102 ...110

111 112 ... 119 120

121...

131...

141...

151...

161...

171...

181...

191...

Thus number of 1's appearing exactly two times is

$2 + 9 + 8 = 19$ times

2. b Suppose the principal is P, $r = 5\%$ (given)

$$CI - SI \text{ (for 2 years)} = P\left(\frac{r}{100}\right)^2$$

or $100 = P\left(\frac{5}{100}\right)^2$

or P = Rs. 40,000.

3. a Par value for x as well as y = Rs. 10

Since dividends are 20% and 40% means Rs. 2 and Rs. 4 respectively.

So, return on investment for x = $\dfrac{2}{40}$

Return on investment for y = $\dfrac{4}{50}$

Ratio = $\dfrac{2}{40} : \dfrac{4}{50}$

$100 : 160 = 5 : 8$.

4. d Let x kg of rice costing Rs. 9 per kilogram is mixed.

Now according to the question

$$\frac{[(27 + x)\,9.24 - (9x + 27 \times 7)] \times 100}{9x + 27 \times 7} = 10$$

$\Rightarrow [27(9.24 - 7) + 0.24x] \times 10 = 9x + 27 \times 7$

$\Rightarrow 27(22.4 - 7) = 9x - 2.4x$

$\Rightarrow \dfrac{27(\times 5.4)}{6.6} = x \Rightarrow x = 63$ kg

5. b In one day A can build $\dfrac{1}{15}$ wall.

In one day B can build $\dfrac{1}{20}$ wall.

Working together for x days they can earn Rs. 189,

i.e. A + B = Rs. 189.

$\Rightarrow \dfrac{x}{15} + \dfrac{x}{20} = \text{Rs. } 189$

$\Rightarrow \dfrac{4x + 3x}{60} = \text{Rs. } 189 \Rightarrow x = \dfrac{189 \times 60}{7} = 27 \times 60$

So, B's share = $\dfrac{27 \times 60}{20} = 27 \times 3 = \text{Rs. } 81$

6. b

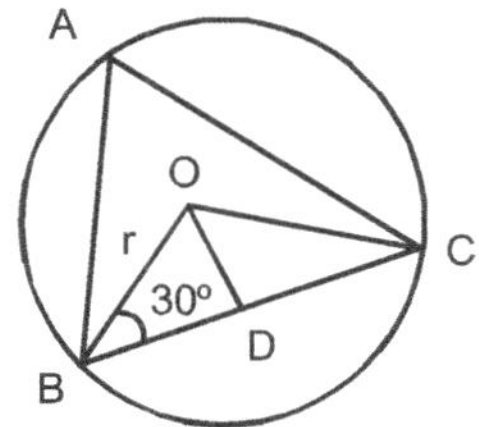

ABC is an equilateral triangle inscribed in a circle of radius r and centre O.

$\therefore BC = 2BD = 2 \cdot r \cdot \cos 30°$

$= 2 \cdot r \dfrac{\sqrt{3}}{2} = r\sqrt{3}$

$x\sqrt{2} = 2r$, where x is the side of the square

$\therefore x = \sqrt{2}\,r$ $\therefore$ Required ratio = $\sqrt{2} : \sqrt{3}$

7. c Suppose the CP be Rs. x per kg.

$\therefore$ Marked price = 1.1x per kg.

CP of 900 g = 0.9x

SP of 900 g = Marked price of 1 kg = 1.1x

$\therefore$ Profit percentage = $\dfrac{1.1x - 0.9x}{0.9x} \times 100 = 22.22\%$

8. d The given expression is

$$\left[10 \times 36 \text{ of } \frac{1}{3} - (110 \div 11) \times 3 + 52\right]$$

(Using BODMAS)

$10 \times 36 \times \dfrac{1}{3} - 10 \times 3 + 52$

$= 120 - 30 + 52 = 172 - 30 = 142$

9. a

	Men	hours	days
	15	9	16
	18	8	x

Also

Men	hours	
15	9 × 16	
18	8x	

Again in 1 hr   work done

Men	work
15	$\dfrac{1}{9 \times 16}$
18	$\dfrac{1}{8x}$

$$15 \times \frac{1}{8x} = 18 \times \frac{1}{9 \times 16} \Rightarrow \frac{15 \times 9 \times 16}{18 \times 8} = x$$

$\Rightarrow$ x = 15 days.

10. a $9875347 \times 7435789 \times 5789743$

= (9875344 + 3) (7435788 + 1) (5789740 + 3)

= $(4k_1 + 3)(4k_2 + 1)(4k_3 + 3)$.

When this is divided by 4, the remainder will be 1.

11. c   Two numbers can be picked up out of 29 numbers in $^{29}C_2$ ways. Product of two multiples of 11 is always divisible by 121, so in order to check whether the product is divisible by 3267 or not we just need to check whether the product is a multiple of $\dfrac{3267}{121} = 27$ or not. In first 29 natural numbers, we have,

Number of numbers divisible by 27 is 1.

Number of numbers divisible by 9 but not by 27 is 2.

Number of numbers divisible by 3 but not by 9 is 6.

Therefore, number of the pairs whose product is a multiple of 27 is 1 × 28 + 2 × 6 + 1 = 41

$\therefore$ The required probability = $\dfrac{41}{^{29}C_2}$

12. b   In right-angled triangle AFB

$(8)^2 + (13 + 2)^2 = AB^2$

$\Rightarrow 64 + 225 = AB^2$

$\Rightarrow 289 = AB^2 \Rightarrow AB = 17$ cm.

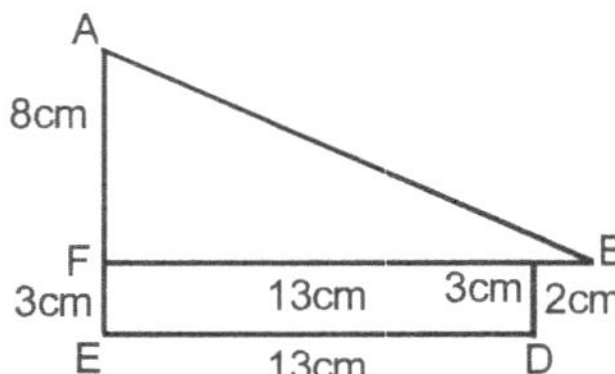

13. a   There are 18 even and 19 odd numbers in the given set. For odd sum either all the three numbers should be odd or two of them even and one odd.

This is possible in $^{19}C_3 + \left(^{18}C_2 \times \, ^{19}C_1\right) = 3876$.

14. a   Let the required amount be Rs. P.

$$80 = P \times 4 \times \frac{2}{100}$$

P = Rs. 1,000

$A = P\{1 + r/100\}^n$

$$A = 1,000 \times \left(\frac{26}{25}\right)^2$$

A = Rs. 1081.60

CI = A – P = Rs. 1081.60 – Rs. 1,000 = Rs. 81.60

15. a   Interest earned = Principal = x.

$$x = x \times \frac{R}{100} \times 7$$

$$\Rightarrow \frac{R}{100} = \frac{1}{7} \Rightarrow R = \frac{100}{7} = \frac{100}{7}$$

In order to become four-fold, interest = 3x

$$3x = x \times \frac{1}{100} \times \frac{100}{7} \times t \Rightarrow t = 21 \text{ years}$$

16. b   Let the length of the train be x m.

Also 36 km/hr = $\dfrac{36 \times 1000}{3600}$ = 10 m/sec

Now $\dfrac{250 + x}{10} = 35$

$\Rightarrow$ x = 100 m.

17. c   Total number of numbers that can be made is $3 \times 4^3 = 192$

Out of these 192 numbers, in $4! - 3! = 18$ numbers there will be no repetition.

$\therefore$ In remaining 192 – 18 = 174 numbers there will be at least one repetition.

18. c   Total number of heads on both the coins = 3

Number of heads on the second coin = 2

$\therefore$ The required probability = $\dfrac{2}{3}$.

19. b   C.P = Rs. 4,650

$$M.P = C.P + \frac{20}{100} \times C.P$$

$$= 4650 + \frac{20}{100} \times 4650 = 4650 + 930 = \text{Rs. } 5580$$

Discount allowed = 15%

S.P = M.P – Discount

$$= 5580 - \frac{15}{100} \times 5580$$

= 5580 – 837 = Rs. 4,743

20. c   Let the speed of the stream be x km/hr and distance travelled = d km.

Time taken by a man to row up = $\dfrac{d}{12 - x}$

Time taken by a man to row down = $\dfrac{d}{12 + x}$

Now, according to the question

$$\frac{2d}{12+x} = \frac{d}{12-x}$$

$\Rightarrow 24 - 2x = 12 + x$

$\Rightarrow x = 4$ km/hr.

21. d Given that $\dfrac{x}{y} = \dfrac{1}{5} \Rightarrow x = \dfrac{y}{5}$ … (i)

Also $2x + 5y = 54$ … (ii)

Using (i) in (ii), we get

$$2 \times \frac{y}{5} + 5y = 54$$

$\Rightarrow 2y + 25y = 270$

$\Rightarrow 27y = 270$

$\Rightarrow y = 10$ and $x = 2$, now $x + y = 12$

22. d

Men	Days	Consumption	
600	28	1	
600	1	$\dfrac{1}{28}$	… (i)
600	4	$\dfrac{1}{7}$	
800	x	$\dfrac{6}{7}$	
800	1	$\dfrac{6}{7x}$	… (ii)

Comparing (i) and (ii), we get

$$600 \times \frac{6}{7x} = 800 \times \frac{1}{28}$$

$\Rightarrow x = 18$ days.

23. d Length of fencing = Perimeter of rectangular field

= $2(64 + 36) = 2 \times 100 = 200$ m

24. b Cost price of mixture = $\dfrac{96 \times 100}{120} = $ Rs. 80

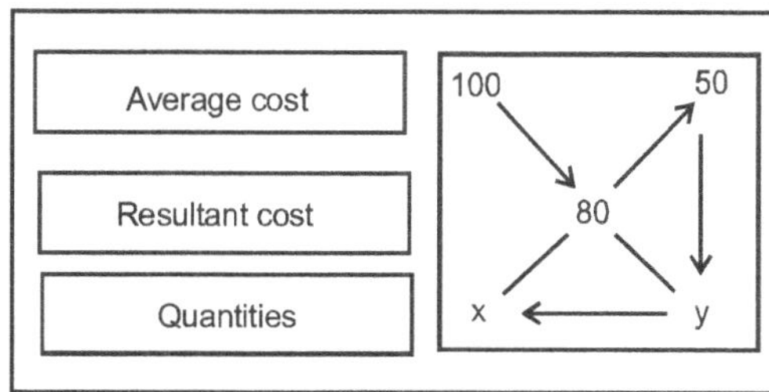

$$\frac{100-80}{80-50} = \frac{y}{x} \Rightarrow \frac{30}{20} = \frac{x}{y}$$

Hence, the ratio = 3 : 2.

25. a Speed of the train = 25 m/s

Length of the train = $25 \times 10 = 250$ m

Number of questions: 25 **Time Allowed: 25 mins.**

1. ABCD is a face of cube which has area 36 m². Nine equal cylinders are cut through its length as shown in the figure. Find the volume of the remaining portion.

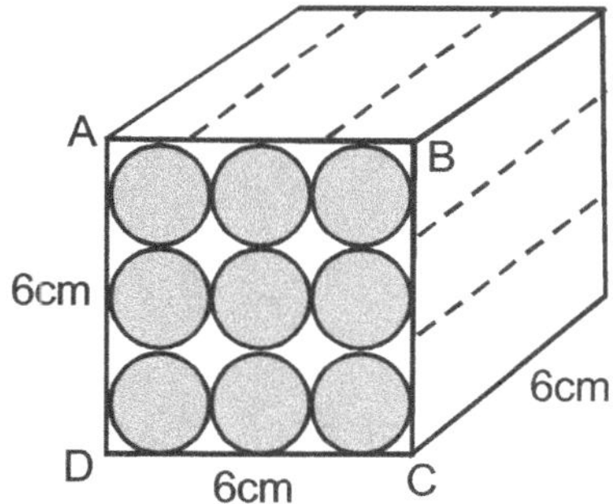

   (a) $90(4 - \pi)\, m^3$ (b) $45(4 - \pi)\, m^3$

   (c) $22.5(2 - \pi)\, m^3$ (d) None of these

2. 5% income of P is equal to 15% income of Q and 10% income of Q is equal to 20% income of R. If the income of R is Rs.4,000, then the total income of P, Q and R is

   (a) Rs. 12,000 (b) Rs. 18,000

   (c) Rs. 24,000 (d) Rs. 36,000

3. O is the centre of a circle of radius r. AOB is a diameter and circles are drawn on OA and OB as diameters. If a circle is drawn to touch these three circles, its radius is

   (a) $\dfrac{2r}{3}$ (b) $\dfrac{r}{2}$

   (c) $\dfrac{r}{4}$ (d) $\dfrac{r}{3}$

4. A man can travel a certain distance at a speed of 25 km/hr by motorcycle. He travels back the same distance at a speed of 10 km/hr. What is his average speed for the entire trip?

   (a) $10\dfrac{1}{7}$ km/hr (b) $12\dfrac{2}{5}$ km/hr

   (c) 13 km/hr (d) $14\dfrac{2}{7}$ km/hr

5. A milkman mixed 1 : 4 solution of milk and water with another 1 : 2 solution of milk and water in the volume ratio 3 : 2. If the profit earned by selling the first solution was 20% and the mixture was sold at the same price. What is the profit/loss percentage? You have to assume that water comes free of cost.

   (a) 5.26% profit (b) 5.26% loss

   (c) 6.25% loss (d) None of these

6. A production unit produces 10 articles of which 4 are defective. A quality inspector allows release of the products if he finds none out of the 3 articles he chooses at random to be defective. In how many ways can he select 3 articles such that he clears the release?

   (a) 10 (b) 20

   (c) 6! (d) 120

7. A boat covers 12 km upstream and 24 km downstream in 6 hr while it covers 24 km upstream and 12 km downstream in 9 hr. Find the speed of the current.

   (a) 7.5 km/hr (b) 12 km/hr

   (c) 9 km/hr (d) 4.5 km/hr

8. Two numbers x and y are such that when divided by 6, they leave remainders 4 and 5 respectively. Find the remainder when $x^3 + y^3$ is divided by 6.

   (a) 5 (b) 4

   (c) 3 (d) None of these

9. In the given figure, ABCD is a square with RC = 4 cm, AP = 2 cm and the area of the shaded portion is 88 cm². The side of the square ABCD is

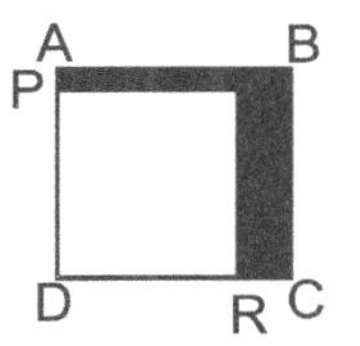

   (a) 14 cm (b) 12 cm

   (c) 16 cm (d) 18 cm

10. The wheel of an engine 25 decimetres in circumference makes 10 rotations in 4 sec. Find the speed of the wheel.

   (a) 16 km/hr (b) 24.5 km/hr

   (c) 32.8 km/hr (d) 22.5 km/hr

11. Machines A and B produce 8,000 clips in 4 hr and 6 hr respectively. They work alternately for 1 hr. A starts first, then 8,000 clips will be produced in

   (a) 4.33 hr

   (b) 4.66 hr

   (c) 5.33 hr

   (d) 5.66 hr

12. A cross section of the bottom platform of a flag staff is given in this figure. The width of each step is 30 cm and the height is 15 cm. The area of the cross section is

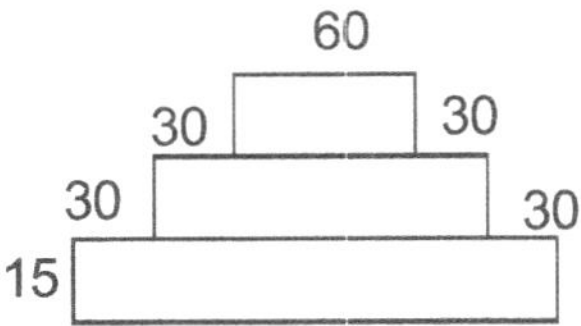

(a) 4,800 cm²   (b) 6,000 cm²
(c) 5,400 cm²   (d) None of these

13. In an urn there are 6 red, 4 black and 3 white balls. Three balls are drawn out of it simultaneously. What is the probability that all the three are of the same colour?

(a) $\dfrac{20}{286}$ (b) $\dfrac{9}{44}$

(c) $\dfrac{7}{220}$ (d) $\dfrac{25}{286}$

14. The table below shows the percentage change in the bottom line of five companies.

Company	1992-93	1993-94
A	10	−10
B	−20	9
C	5	12
D	−7	−15
E	17	−

Which company has the maximum percentage decrease in sales from 1992 to 1994?

(a) A   (b) B
(c) C   (d) D

15. A can complete a piece of work in 10 days which B alone can do in 12 days. In how many days can both complete it working together?

(a) 11 days   (b) 15 days

(c) $\dfrac{60}{11}$ days   (d) 8 days

16. A sum of money placed at compound interest doubles itself in 5 years. In how many years it will amount to eight times itself?

(a) 10 yr 8 months   (b) 15 yr
(c) 12 yr   (d) Cannot be determined

17. Due to an increase of 30% in the price of eggs, 3 eggs less than the previous amount are available for Rs.7.80. Find the present rate of eggs per dozen.

(a) Rs. 9.16   (b) Rs. 6.72
(c) Rs. 9.36   (d) Rs. 9.62

18. A sum of money is sufficient to pay A's wages for 21 days and B's wages for 20 days. It is then sufficient to pay the wages of both for

(a) 10.24 days   (b) 14 days
(c) 12.25 days   (d) 24.5 days

19. $\left\{\dfrac{\left(2x^2+4\right)}{3}\right\} + \dfrac{2}{6} \div \dfrac{1}{3} = \dfrac{23}{3}$, what is the value of x?

(a) −1   (b) 4
(c) −2   (d) None of these

20. The distance between the centres of two circles with radii 9 cm and 4 cm is 13 cm. The length of a direct common tangent between them is

(a) 10 cm   (b) 12 cm
(c) 11 cm   (d) 10.5 cm

21. A and B are moving on a circular track of length 200 m in the same direction. Find the time after which they would be together again. Speed of A is 23 m/s and that of B is 30 m/s. Assume that they start racing simultaneously from the starting point.

(a) $28\dfrac{5}{7}$ sec   (b) $28\dfrac{4}{7}$ sec

(c) $27\dfrac{4}{7}$ sec   (d) $26\dfrac{4}{7}$ sec

22. Two trains are running on parallel tracks and they travel at the rates of 25 miles/hr and 30 miles/hr. If the first train leaves an hour earlier than the second train, how long will it take for the second train to catch up with the first train?

(a) 3 hr   (b) 11 hr
(c) 6 hr   (d) 4.75 hr

23. A man 50 years old has 8 sons born at equal intervals. The sum of the age of the father and sons is 186 years. What is the age of the eldest son if the youngest is 3 year old?

(a) 33 years   (b) 28 years
(c) 31 years   (d) 29 years

24. A.M. between the roots of a quadraic equation is 8 and G.M. is 5, then the equation is

(a) $x^2 + 16x - 25 = 0$ (b) $x^2 - 8x + 5 = 0$
(c) $x^2 - 16x + 25 = 0$ (d) $x^2 - 16x - 25 = 0$

25. Vimla and Surjeet jointly started a business by investing Rs.9,000 and Rs.10,500, respectively. After 4 months, Jaya joined their business by investing Rs.12,500 but Surjeet withdraws Rs.2,000. At the end of the year there was a profit of Rs.4,770. Find the share of Jaya.

(a) Rs. 1500   (b) Rs.1375
(c) Rs. 1620   (d) Rs.1650

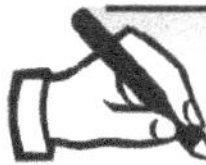

Answer Key

1. (d)	2. (d)	3. (d)	4. (d)	5. (b)	6. (b)	7. (d)	8. (c)	9. (c)	10. (d)
11. (b)	12. (c)	13. (d)	14. (d)	15. (c)	16. (b)	17. (c)	18. (a)	19. (d)	20. (b)
21. (b)	22. (c)	23. (c)	24. (c)	25. (a)					

Explanations

1. d The given figure out of which cylinders have been cut is a cube.

∴ The remaining volume

= Volume of cube − 9 × (Volume of cylinder)

$= 6^3 - 9 \times \pi \times 1 \times 1 \times 6 = 216 - 54 \times \pi$

$= 9(24 - 6\pi)$.

2. d According to the question

$$\frac{5}{100}P = \frac{15}{100}Q \qquad \ldots (i)$$

and $\dfrac{10Q}{100} = \dfrac{20}{100}R \qquad \ldots (ii)$

Given that income of R = Rs. 4,000

From (ii), we have

Q = 2 × 4000 = Rs. 8,000

∴ Income of P = 3Q

= 3 × 8000 = Rs. 24,000

Their total income

= P + Q + R = 4000 + 8000 + 24000 = Rs. 36,000

3. d

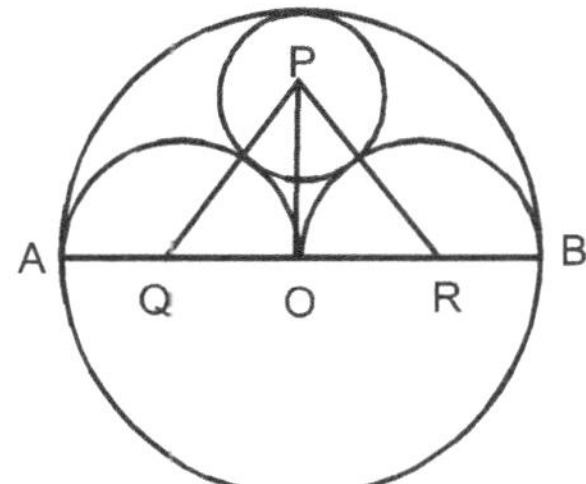

Let x be the radius of the circle which touches these three circles.

The radius of the circle on OB as diameter is $\dfrac{r}{2}$.

PO is perpendicular to OB.

Let R be the centre of the circle on OB as diameter.

$PR^2 = OP^2 + OR^2$

$$\left(\frac{r}{2}+x\right)^2 = (r-x)^2 + \left(\frac{r}{2}\right)^2 \Rightarrow \frac{r^2}{4} = \left(\frac{r}{2}+x\right)^2 - (r-x)^2$$

$\Rightarrow -r^2 + 3rx = 0 \Rightarrow -r + 3x = 0 \Rightarrow x = \dfrac{r}{3}$.

4. d Average speed = $\dfrac{\text{Total distance travelled}}{\text{Total time taken}}$

Let d km be the certain distance travelled by a man.

∴ Average speed = $\dfrac{2d}{\dfrac{d}{25} + \dfrac{d}{10}} = \dfrac{2d}{\dfrac{2d + 5d}{50}} = \dfrac{2d \times 50}{7d}$

$= \dfrac{100}{7} = 14\dfrac{2}{7}$ km/hr.

5. b Suppose the milkman takes 45 L of first and 30 L of second solutions.

Volume of milk in first solution = 9 L

Volume of milk in second solution = 10 L

Suppose cost price of milk is Re. 1 per litre.

∴ Total cost of first solution = Rs. 9

SP of first solution = 9 × 1.2 = Rs. 10.8

SP of 1 litre of first solution = $\dfrac{10.8}{45}$ = Rs. 0.24

SP of all 75 L of solution = 75 × 0.24 = Rs. 18

CP of all 75 L of solution = Rs. 19

(Since there was only 19 L of milk in all.)

∴ Loss percentage = $\dfrac{19-18}{19} \times 100 = 5.26\%$

6. b Since out of 10 articles 4 are defective, i.e. 6 articles are not defective.

Thus to clear the release an inspector will select an article in $^6C_3$ ways = 20.

7. d Let the speed of boat = x km/hr

and speed of current = y km/hr

Now according to the question

$$\frac{12}{x-y} + \frac{24}{x+y} = 6 \qquad \ldots \text{(A)}$$

$$\left[\text{Using Time} = \frac{\text{Distance}}{\text{Speed}} \right]$$

and $$\frac{24}{x-y} + \frac{12}{x+y} = 9 \qquad \ldots \text{(B)}$$

Put $\dfrac{1}{x-y} = u$ and $\dfrac{1}{x+y} = v$

Then (A) and (B) becomes

$$12u + 24v = 6 \qquad \ldots \text{(i)}$$
$$24u + 12v = 9 \qquad \ldots \text{(ii)}$$

Solving (i) and (ii), we get

$$u = \frac{1}{3}, v = \frac{1}{12}$$

Now $\dfrac{1}{x-y} = \dfrac{1}{3}$ or $x - y = 3$ … (iii)

and $\dfrac{1}{x+y} = \dfrac{1}{12}$ or $x + y = 12$ … (iv)

Solving (iii) and (iv), we get

Speed of boat = 7.5 km/hr

and speed of current = 4.5 km/hr.

8. c Suppose $x = 6k_1 + 4$ and $y = 6k_2 + 5$

$$x^3 + y^3 = (6k_1 + 4)^3 + (6k_2 + 5)^3$$
$$= 216\,k_1^3 + 432\,k_1^2 + 288\,k_1 + 64 + 216\,k_2^3$$
$$+ 540\,k_2^2 + 450\,k_2 + 125$$

All terms involving k_1 and k_2 and their higher powers are divisible by 6. The constant term being 189 which when divided by 6 leaves the remainder 3.

9. c

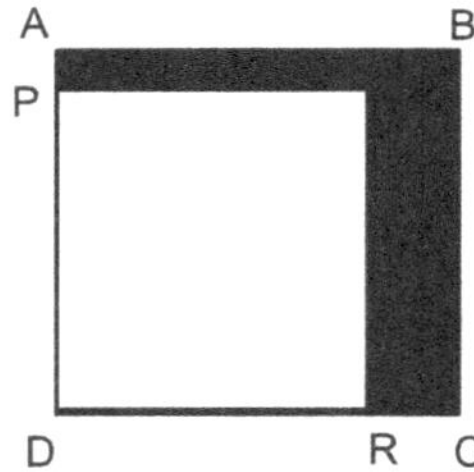

Let the side of the square be x cm.

Then PD = $x - 2$ and DR = $x - 4$

$\therefore x^2 - (x - 2)(x - 4) = 88$, i.e. $x^2 - (x^2 - 6x + 8)$

= 88 i.e. $6x = 96$, i.e. $x = 16$ cm

10. d 25 decimetres = 250 cm. In 10 revolutions, the wheel travels $250 \times 10 = 2,500$ cm

$\therefore$ In 4 s the wheel travels 2,500 cm

$\therefore$ In 1 s, the wheel travels $\dfrac{2500}{4}$ cm

$\therefore$ In 3,600 s (or 1 hr) it travels

$$\frac{2,500}{4} \times 3,600 = 22,50,000 \text{ cm/hr}$$

or the speed is 22.5 km/hr

11. b In 1 hr machine A produces $\dfrac{8000}{4} = 2000$ clips

In 1 hr machine B produces $\dfrac{8000}{6}$ clips

$$2000 + \frac{8000}{6} + 2000 + \frac{8000}{6} + \left(\frac{8000}{6} \times \frac{1}{2000} \right) = 8000$$

$$= 1 + 1 + 1 + 1 + \frac{4}{6} = 4.66 \text{ hr.}$$

12. c It consists of three rectangles.

The top most rectangle = 60×15 cm^2

The rectangle below it = 120×15 cm^2

The bottom most rectangle = 180×15 cm^2

$\therefore$ The total area of cross section

= $(60 + 120 + 180)15$ cm^2 = $5,400$ cm^2

13. d Ways of getting 3 balls out of 13 balls = $^{13}C_3$.

Probability of getting 3 balls of red colour = $\dfrac{^6C_3}{^{13}C_3}$

Probability of getting 3 balls of black colour = $\dfrac{^4C_3}{^{13}C_3}$

Probability of getting 3 balls of white colour = $\dfrac{^3C_3}{^{13}C_3}$

$\therefore$ Probability of getting all the three balls of same

colour = $\dfrac{^6C_3 + {}^4C_3 + {}^3C_3}{^{13}C_3} = \dfrac{25}{286}$.

14. d Obviously D, since in both the years, negative growth is recorded.

15. c A's 1 day work = $\dfrac{1}{10}$

B's 1 day work = $\dfrac{1}{12}$

(A + B)'s 1 day work = $\left(\dfrac{1}{10} + \dfrac{1}{12} \right) = \dfrac{11}{60}$ of entire job.

Both will finish the work in $\dfrac{60}{11}$ or $5\dfrac{5}{11}$ days.

16. b Let the prinicipal amount be Rs. p and rate of interest be r%.

A = Rs. 2p, n = 5 years and R = r%

$$A = P\left\{1 + \frac{r}{100}\right\}^n ; \quad 2p = p\left\{1 + \frac{r}{100}\right\}^5$$

$$2 = \left\{1 + \frac{r}{100}\right\}^5$$

Cubing the above equation we get

$$(2)^3 = \left\{\left(1+\frac{r}{100}\right)^5\right\}^3 \; ; \; 8 = \left\{1+\frac{r}{100}\right\}^{15}$$

For amount to become 8 times of itself, it would require 15 years.

17. c Let the original rate be X paise per egg.

Number of eggs bought for Rs.7.80 = $\frac{1}{2}$ paise

New rate = (130% of X) paise per egg

= $\frac{13X}{10}$ paise per egg.

Number of eggs bought for Rs.7.80

= $\frac{780 \times 10}{13X} = \frac{600}{X}$

$\therefore \frac{780}{X} - \frac{600}{X}$ = 3 or 3X = 180 or X = 60.

So, present rate = $\left(\frac{13 \times 60}{10}\right)$ paise per egg.

= 78 paise per egg

= Rs.9.36 per dozen

18. a Let total amount be Rs. x

A's wage per day is $\frac{x}{21}$.

B's wage per day is $\frac{x}{20}$.

When working together wage paid per day to them is $\frac{x}{20} + \frac{x}{21} = \frac{x \times 41}{420} \Rightarrow \frac{420}{41} = 10.24$ days

19. d Given expression is

$$\left[\frac{\left(2x^2 + 4\right)}{3}\right] + \frac{2}{6} \div \frac{1}{3} = \frac{23}{3}$$

$$\Rightarrow \frac{2x^2 + 4}{3} + \frac{2}{6} \times 3 = \frac{23}{3}$$

$$= \frac{2x^2 + 4 + 3}{3} = \frac{23}{3}$$

$$\Rightarrow 2x^2 = 23 - 7 = 16 \Rightarrow x^2 = 8 \Rightarrow x = \pm 2\sqrt{2}.$$

20. b

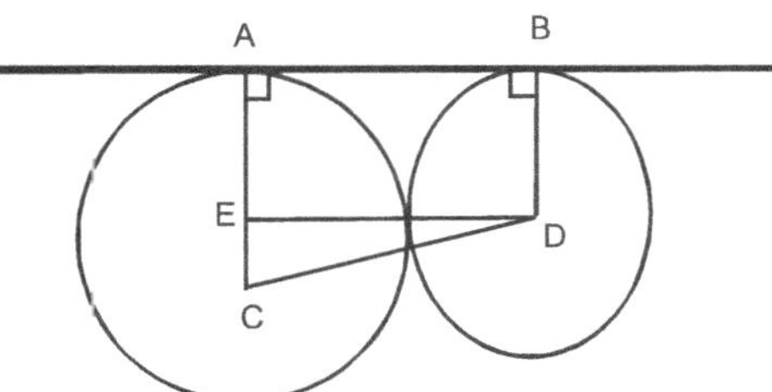

Let C and D be the centres of the two circles and let the direct common tangent be AB.

CA and DB are perpendicular to AB.

Draw DE perpendicular to CA.

$\therefore$ DEAB is a rectangle and CE = (9 − 4) cm = 5 cm,

CD = 13 cm

$\therefore$ DE^2 = CD^2 − CE^2 = 13^2 − 5^2 = 144 cm^2

DE = 12 cm

Hence, AB = 12 cm.

21. b A and B will be together once if B takes a lead of exactly one round over A, i.e. B takes a lead of 200 m over A. Relative speed of B with respect to A = 30 − 23 = 7 m/s

$\therefore$ Required time = $\frac{200}{7} = 28\frac{4}{7}$ sec

22. c Let the time taken by first train be t hr.

Then the time taken by second train to catch up with the first train be (t − 1)hr.

$\therefore$ 30 (t − 1) = 25t

$\Rightarrow$ 30t − 30 = 25t $\Rightarrow$ 5t = 30

$\Rightarrow$ t = 6 hr.

23. c Let the interval be x years

= 50 + 3 + (x + 3) + (2x + 3) + (3x + 3) + (4x + 3) + (5x + 3) + (6x + 3) + (7x + 3) = 186

= 50 + 28x + 24 = 186

$\Rightarrow$ 28x = 112 $\Rightarrow$ x = 4

Age of oldest son = 7x + 3 = 31 years.

24. c Let a and b be the roots of a quadratic equation

then, $\frac{a+b}{2} = 8$ or a + b = 16 $\Rightarrow$ S = 16

$\sqrt{ab} = 5$ or a.b = 25 $\Rightarrow$ P = 25

$\therefore$ Required equation is x^2 − Sx + P = 0

$\Rightarrow$ x^2 − 16x + 25 = 0

25. a Vimla invested Rs.9000 for 12 months.

Surjeet invested Rs.10500 for 4 months and Rs.8500 for 8 months.

Jaya invested Rs.12500 for 8 months.

$\therefore$ Ratio of capitals of Vimla, Surjeet and Jaya

= (9000 × 12) : (10500 × 4 + 8500 × 8) : (12500 × 8)

= 108000 : 110000 : 100000

= 108 : 110 : 100 = 54 : 55 : 50.

Sum of the ratios = (54 + 55 + 50) = 159

$\therefore$ Vimla's share = Rs. $\left(4770 \times \frac{54}{159}\right)$ = Rs.1620,

Surjeet's share = Rs. $\left(4770 \times \frac{55}{159}\right)$ = Rs.1650,

Jaya's share = Rs.[4770 − (1620 + 1650)] = Rs.1500.

Number of questions: 25   **Time Allowed: 25 mins.**

1. P is a prime number greater than 5. What is the remainder when P is divided by 6?
   - (a) 5
   - (b) 1
   - (c) 1 or 5
   - (d) None of these

2. A, B and C are moving on a circular track. A, who is the only one moving in the anticlockwise direction and moves at a speed twice that of B, and thrice that of C, takes 10 sec to cover the entire track. If all the three start simultaneously, when would they meet for the second time after the start?
   - (a) 120 sec
   - (b) 240 sec
   - (c) 360 sec
   - (d) None of these

3. How many 15-letter sets can be made using letters from {A, B, C, D} and requiring that there be at least 2 A's, at least 3 B's and at least 2 C's?
   - (a) 165
   - (b) 154
   - (c) 495
   - (d) 176

4. If X's income is 25% more than Y's and Y's income is 20% more than Z's, by what percentage is X's income more than Z's?
   - (a) 25%
   - (b) 33.33%
   - (c) 50%
   - (d) None of these

5. How many kg of sugar costing Rs. 6.10 per kg must be mixed with 125 kg of sugar costing Rs. 2.85 per kg so that 20% may be gained by selling the mixture of Rs. 4.80 per kg?
   - (a) 96 kg
   - (b) 189 kg
   - (c) 198 kg
   - (d) 69 kg

6. LCM of two distinct natural numbers is 211. What is their HCF?
   - (a) 37
   - (b) 211
   - (c) 1
   - (d) Data insufficient

7. If one root of $x^2 + px + 12 = 0$ is 4, while the equation $x^2 + px + q = 0$ has equal roots, then the value of 'q' is
   - (a) $-\dfrac{7}{2}$
   - (b) -7
   - (c) $\dfrac{49}{4}$
   - (d) $-\dfrac{49}{4}$

8. The average weight of a class dropped from 65 kg to 62 kg when a student weighing 77 kg was out of the class. How many students are there in the class now?
   - (a) 5
   - (b) 4
   - (c) 6
   - (d) None of these

9. A thief breaks away from a prison at 3.00 a.m. The police official at duty realizes it at 6.00 a.m and starts chasing the thief. The speed of the thief is 45 km/hr, while that of the police is 60 km/hr. At what time police official caught the thief?
   - (a) 6.00 p.m.
   - (b) 3.00 p.m.
   - (c) 5.00 p.m.
   - (d) 5.30 p.m.

10. A and B can complete a job in 12 days. B and C can do it in 16 days. After A's 5 days work, and B's 7 days work, C can finish the rest in 13 days. In how many days can C complete the work alone?
    - (a) 16 days
    - (b) 24 days
    - (c) 36 days
    - (d) 48 days

11. A mixture of 140 L of wine and water contains 20% water. How much water must be added to make water 84% of the resulting mixture?
    - (a) 560 L
    - (b) 700 L
    - (c) 440 L
    - (d) 588 L

12. In a class the average age of the students increases by one year when a student of 30 years joined them. If this new student was 20-years-old, the average age would have gone down by 1 year. Find the number of students originally in the class.
    - (a) 5
    - (b) 4
    - (c) 3
    - (d) 6

13. If $3 < \dfrac{3x - 4}{8} < 5$ and $x + y = 4$, then find the solution set for y.
    - (a) $\dfrac{-32}{3} < y < \dfrac{-16}{3}$
    - (b) $\dfrac{16}{3} < y < \dfrac{32}{3}$
    - (c) $\dfrac{8}{3} < y < \dfrac{32}{3}$
    - (d) $\dfrac{-32}{3} < y < \dfrac{-8}{3}$

14. There is a rectangle of dimensions 20 cm × 30 cm. A circle of radius 5 cm is drawn inside this rectangle. What is the probability that a point in the rectangle can never lie inside this circle?

    (a) $\dfrac{\pi}{24}$

    (b) $1 - \dfrac{\pi}{24}$

    (c) $\dfrac{1}{6} - \dfrac{\pi}{24}$

    (d) None of these

15. In a 200 m race, Ram beats Shyam by 35 m or 7 sec. What is Ram's time over the course?

    (a) 11 sec
    (b) 22 sec
    (c) 33 sec
    (d) None of these

16. The median AD of the $\triangle$ABC meets BC at D. The internal bisectors of $\angle$ADB and $\angle$ADC meet AB and AC at E and F respectively. Then EF

    (a) is perpendicular to AD
    (b) is parallel to BC
    (c) divides AD in the ratio AB : AC
    (d) None of these

17. The diagonal of a rectangle whose length is twice the breadth and is inscribed in a circle, is d. The area of the rectangle is

    (a) $\dfrac{4d^2}{3}$

    (b) $\dfrac{2d^2}{3}$

    (c) $\dfrac{3d^2}{5}$

    (d) $\dfrac{2d^2}{5}$

18. The 15th term of an arithmetic progression is 5. If the smallest term has a value anywhere between −30 and −20, what is the range of values between which the 21st term lies?

    (a) $15\dfrac{5}{7}, 20$

    (b) $21, 44\dfrac{3}{4}$

    (c) 36, 44
    (d) None of these

19. Ten cars are parked in a row. What is the probability that there are exactly 5 cars between two particular cars?

    (a) $\dfrac{8 \times 5!}{10!}$

    (b) $\dfrac{4 \times 5! \times 3! \times 2!}{10!}$

    (c) $\dfrac{8 \times 8!}{10!}$

    (d) $\dfrac{16 \times 8!}{10!}$

20. The sides of a cuboid increases by 20%. By what percentage does its volume increase?

    (a) 44%
    (b) 60%
    (c) 72.8%
    (d) None of these

21. Six bells commence tolling together at an interval of 2, 3, 6, 9, 12, and 15 sec respectively. In 6 hrs, how many times do they toll together?

    (a) 3
    (b) 180
    (c) 120
    (d) None of these

22. Two cards are drawn from a pack of well shuffled cards. Find the probability that one is a club and the other is an Ace.

    (a) $\dfrac{1}{13}$

    (b) $\dfrac{4}{13}$

    (c) $\dfrac{1}{52}$

    (d) $\dfrac{1}{26}$

23. The angles of depression of two ships from the top of a lighthouse are 45° and 30°. If the ships are 120 m apart, find the height of the lighthouse.

    (a) 44 m
    (b) 40 m
    (c) 47 m
    (d) 495 m

24. Vineet deposited Rs. 15,600 in a fixed deposit at SI at the rate of 10%. After every second year he converts his interests earnings into deposits. His interest in the fourth year is?

    (a) Rs. 3,744
    (b) Rs. 1,560
    (c) Rs. 3,432
    (d) Rs. 1,872

25. A conical flask which is 13 cm high with base radius 6 cm and upper radius 2 cm. Then the volume of the flask is

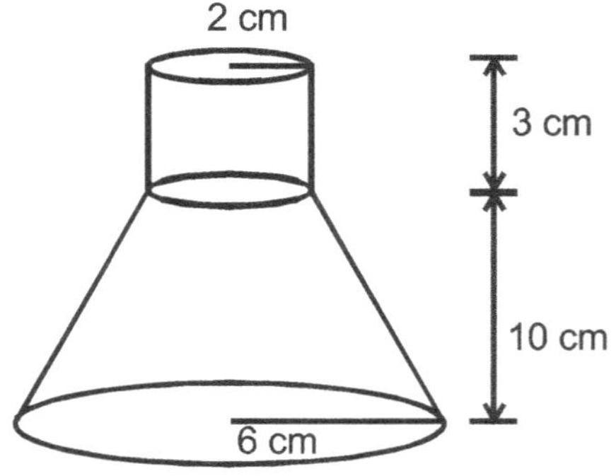

    (a) $\dfrac{520\pi}{3} \text{ cm}^3$

    (b) $\dfrac{556\pi}{3} \text{ cm}^3$

    (c) $\dfrac{484\pi}{3} \text{ cm}^3$

    (d) None of these

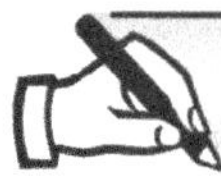

Answer Key

1. (c)	**2.** (a)	**3.** (a)	**4.** (c)	**5.** (d)	**6.** (c)	**7.** (c)	**8.** (b)	**9.** (b)	**10.** (b)
11. (a)	**12.** (b)	**13.** (a)	**14.** (b)	**15.** (c)	**16.** (b)	**17.** (d)	**18.** (a)	**19.** (c)	**20.** (c)
21. (c)	**22.** (d)	**23.** (a)	**24.** (a)	**25.** (b)					

Explanations

1. c Any prime number greater than 3 is of the form $6k \pm 1$. So, when it is divided by 6 the remainder will obviously be 1 or 5.

2. a Time taken by B and C to cover the entire track will be 20 sec and 30 sec respectively.

   They will meet for the first time after LCM (10, 20, 30), i.e. 60 sec

   $\Rightarrow$ They will meet for the second time after 120 sec.

3. a Out of 15 positions 7 positions are to be taken by 2 A's, 3 B's and 2 C's. Now we have to select letters for remaining 8 positions from 4 letters {A, B, C, D}, that can be done in

   $^{8+4-1}C_{4-1} = {}^{11}C_3 = 165$ ways.

4. c According to the question,

   $X = Y + \dfrac{1}{4}Y = \dfrac{5Y}{4}$ and $Y = Z + \dfrac{1Z}{5} = \dfrac{6}{5}Z$

   Also $X = \dfrac{5}{4} \times \dfrac{6}{5}Z = \dfrac{3}{2}Z = Z + \dfrac{Z}{2}$

   $\therefore$ X's income is 50% more than Z.

5. d Let x kg sugar costing Rs. 6.10 per kg be mixed with 125 kg sugar.

   Now according to the question,

   $\left(1 + \dfrac{1}{5}\right)[6.10x + 125 \times 2.85] = (x + 125)4.80$

   $\Rightarrow 6.10x + 125 \times 2.85 = (x + 125)\,4.80 \times \dfrac{5}{6}$

   $\Rightarrow 6.10x - 4x = 125(4 - 2.85)$

   $\Rightarrow 2.10x = 125(1.15) \Rightarrow x = \dfrac{125 \times 115}{210} \approx 69$ kg .

6. c 211 is a prime number. So, there is only one pair of distinct natural numbers possible whose LCM is 211, 1 and 211. HCF of 1 and 211 is 1.

7. c Let the other root of the equation $x^2 + px + 12 = 0$ be β.

   The sum of the root $4 + \beta = -p$

   $$4\beta = 12 \Rightarrow \beta = 3$$

   $\therefore p = -7$

   Now the equation $x^2 + px + q = 0$ has equal roots.

   $\therefore$ Discriminant $= b^2 - 4ac = 0$

   $\Rightarrow (-7)^2 - 4q = 0 \Rightarrow 49 - 4q = 0$

   $\Rightarrow q = \dfrac{49}{4}$.

8. b Suppose initially there were n students.

   So we have

   $\dfrac{65n - 77}{n - 1} = 62 \Rightarrow n = 5$

   $\therefore$ Now there are $5 - 1 = 4$ students.

9. b Let t hr be the time taken by the thief to run a distance whereas the police official will reach in time $(t - 3)$ hr.

   Therefore, $(t - 3)60 = 45t$

   $\Rightarrow t - 3 = \dfrac{3}{4}t \Rightarrow t = 12$ hr.

   $\therefore$ Police official caught the thief after 12 hr, i.e. 3.00 p.m.

10. b Let A do 'A' amount of work per day.

    B do 'B' amount of work per day.

    C do 'C' amount of work per day.

    $\Rightarrow A + B = \dfrac{1}{12}, \; B + C = \dfrac{1}{16}$

    $5A + 7B + 13\,C = 1$

    Solving these three equations, we get

    $C = \dfrac{1}{24}$

    $\therefore$ C will finish the work in 24 days.

11. a Content of water in 140 ℓ mixture = 28 ℓ

$\therefore$ Content of wine in 140 ℓ mixture = 112 ℓ

Now 16% of wine in new solution is 112.

Let x be the mixture containing 84% of water

$\therefore \dfrac{x \times 16}{100} = 112$

$\Rightarrow x = \dfrac{112 \times 100}{16} = 700\ \ell$

$\therefore$ Water added = 700 – 140 = 560 ℓ.

12. b Suppose initially there were n students and their average age was x, so we have

$\dfrac{nx + 30}{n+1} = x + 1$ and $\dfrac{nx + 20}{n+1} = x - 1$

Solving them, we get n = 4.

13. a $\dfrac{3x - 4}{8} > 3 \Rightarrow 3x - 4 > 24 \Rightarrow x > \dfrac{28}{3}$;

$\dfrac{3x - 4}{8} < 5 \Rightarrow 3x < 44 \Rightarrow x < \dfrac{44}{3}$;

$x + y = 4$

Hence, the value of y = 4 – x, i.e $y > 4 - \dfrac{44}{3}$ and

$y < 4 - \dfrac{28}{3}$

$\therefore \dfrac{-32}{3} < y < \dfrac{-16}{3}$.

14. b

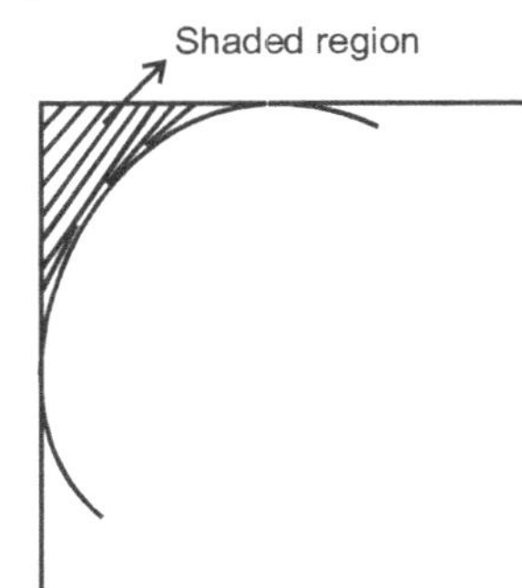

If a point does not lie in the circle, then the point must lie in the shaded region. At each of the four vertex such a shaded region is formed. The sum of the areas of all such shaded regions = $600 - 25\pi$

Hence, the required probability = $\dfrac{600 - 25\pi}{20 \times 30} = 1 - \dfrac{\pi}{24}$.

15. c Let Ram's time over the course be t second.

Ram travelled = 200 m

Shyam travelled = 165 m (in t seconds)

$\therefore$ Speed of Ram = $\dfrac{200}{t}$ m/sec

And speed of Shyam = $\dfrac{165}{t}$ m/sec.

Also, Ram beats Shyam by 7 sec.

$\therefore$ Shyam will take (t + 7) sec to complete the race.

So, $200 = \dfrac{200}{t} \times t = \dfrac{165}{t}(t + 7)$

$\Rightarrow 200t = 165(t + 7) \Rightarrow 35t = 165 \times 7 \Rightarrow t = 33$ sec

16. b

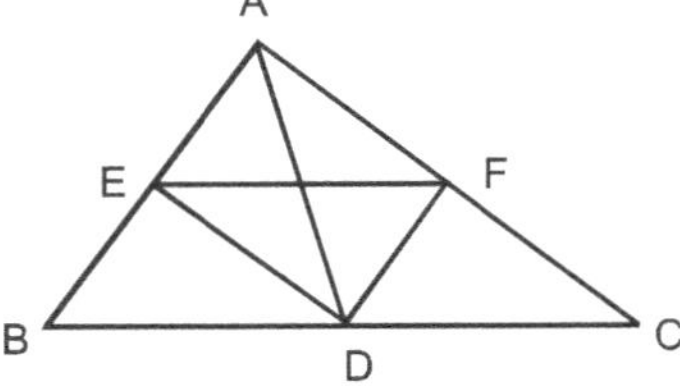

DE is the bisector of $\angle$ADB

$\therefore \dfrac{AE}{EB} = \dfrac{AD}{BD}$

DF is the bisector of $\angle$ADC.

$\therefore \dfrac{AF}{FC} = \dfrac{AD}{DC}$

Hence, $\dfrac{AE}{EB} = \dfrac{AF}{FC}$　　　　　$(\because$ BD = DC)

$\therefore$ EF is parallel to BC.

EF divides AD in the ratio AE : EB which is not AB : AC.

17. d

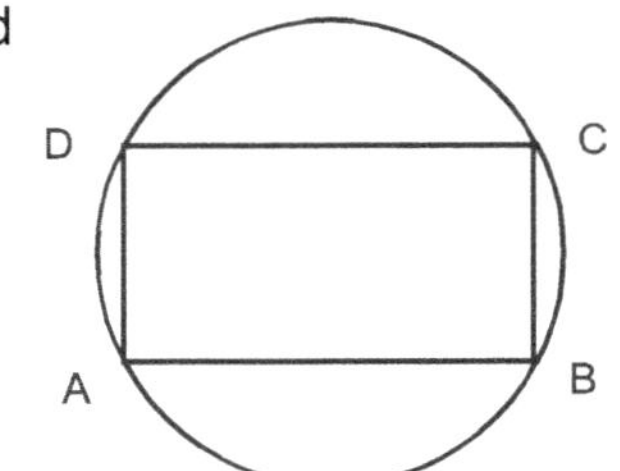

Let the breadth be x. Then its length is 2x.

$AD^2 + AB^2 = BD^2$, i.e. $x^2 + (2x)^2 = d^2$,

i.e. $5x^2 = d^2$

The area of the rectangle = $2x^2 = \dfrac{2d^2}{5}$.

18. a $a + 14d = 5$

When a = –20

$d = \dfrac{25}{14}$

When a = –30, $d = \dfrac{35}{14} = \dfrac{5}{2}$

$\therefore$ 21st term will be between

$\left\{-20 + 20 \times \dfrac{25}{14}\right\}$ and $\left\{-30 + 20 \times \dfrac{5}{2}\right\}$

i.e. $15\dfrac{5}{7}$ and 20

19. c Suppose there are 10 positions for cars namely 1, 2, 3, …, 10. To have exactly five cars in between, those two cars should be on positions 1 and 7 or 2 and 8 or 3 and 9 or 4 and 10. Now in any of these positions these two cars can interchange their positions.

So, we have 4 × 2 = 8 arrangements for these two particular cars. Remaining 8 cars can be arranged in 8! ways. Therefore, total number of favourable arrangements = 8 × 8!

$\Rightarrow$ The required probability = $\dfrac{8 \times 8!}{10!}$.

20. c Let the sides of the cuboid be x cm, y cm and z cm.

Then the volume of the cuboid = xyz cm^3.

Now if the sides are increased by 20%,

then the dimensions will be

$x + \dfrac{1}{5}x,\, y + \dfrac{1}{5}y,\, z + \dfrac{1}{5}z$, i.e. $\dfrac{6x}{5},\dfrac{6y}{5},\dfrac{6z}{5}$

$\therefore$ Volume = $\dfrac{6 \times 6 \times 6}{5 \times 5 \times 5}$(xyz) s = $\dfrac{216}{125}$(xyz)

So, increase in volume = $\dfrac{216 - 125}{125} \times 100 = 72.8\%$

21. c Interval when they toll together

= LCM of (2, 3, 6, 9, 12 and 15) sec = 180 sec

Bells toll together after 180 sec

No. of times they toll together in 6 hrs

= $\dfrac{6 \times 60 \times 60}{180}$ = 120 times

22. d Let A be the event that one is a club, which is not an Ace, the other is Ace of club

Let B be the event that one is any club card and the other is a non club Ace.

$\therefore$ Required probability = P (A) + P(B)

= $\dfrac{^{12}C_1 \times\, ^1C_1}{^{52}C_2} + \dfrac{^{13}C_1 \times\, ^3C_1}{^{52}C_2}$

= $\dfrac{2(12 \times 1)}{52 \times 51} + \dfrac{2(13 \times 3)}{52 \times 51} = \dfrac{24 + 78}{52 \times 51} = \dfrac{1}{26}$

23. a Let AB, the height of the light house = x m

$\therefore \angle$MAP = $\angle$APB = 30° and $\angle$NAQ = $\angle$AQB = 45°

Let the length between P and B be y m

So, the length between B and Q is (120 – y)m.

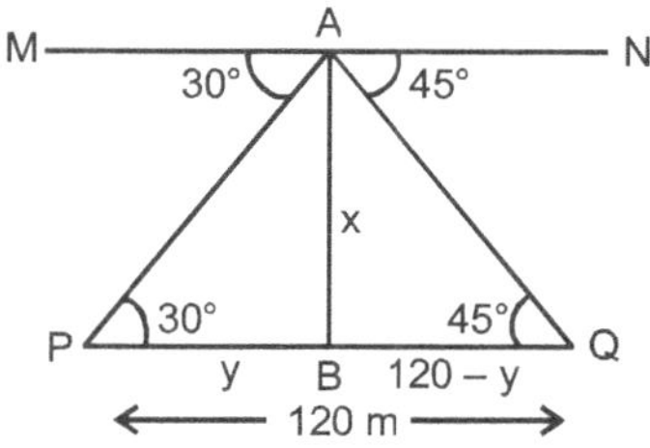

In $\triangle$ ABP,

$\tan 30° = \dfrac{AB}{BP} \Rightarrow \dfrac{1}{\sqrt{3}} = \dfrac{x}{y} \Rightarrow y = x\sqrt{3}$ … (i)

Again in $\triangle$ ABQ

$\tan 45° = \dfrac{AB}{BQ}, \Rightarrow 1 = \dfrac{x}{120 - y} \Rightarrow x = 120 - y$ … (ii)

From (i) and (ii)

x = 120 – x$\sqrt{3}$ or x$\left(1 + \sqrt{3}\right)$ = 120

$\Rightarrow x = \dfrac{120}{1 + \sqrt{3}} \approx 44m$

24. a Amount deposited = Rs. 15,600

Rate of interest = 10%

$\Rightarrow$ Interest for 2 year = $\dfrac{15600 \times 10 \times 2}{100}$ = Rs. 3,120

As he is converting interest of two year into deposits the amount of deposit after two years becomes

Rs. 15,600 + Rs. 3,120 = Rs. 18,720

$\Rightarrow$ Hence, the interest for 4th year

= $\dfrac{18720 \times 10 \times 2}{100}$ = Rs. 3,744

25. b Volume = $\pi r_1^2 h_1 + \dfrac{\pi}{3} h_2 \left(r_1^2 + r_2^2 + r_1 r_2\right)$

= $\dfrac{\pi}{3}\left[3 \times 4 \times 3 + 10(4 + 36 + 12)\right]$

= $\dfrac{\pi}{3}(36 + 520) = \dfrac{556}{3}\pi$ cm^3

ENGLISH USAGE AND VOCABULARY

Practice Test-1

Number of questions: 30   **Time Allowed: 30 mins.**

Directions for questions 1 to 5 : Fill in the following blanks with the appropriate choices.

1. For almost seven years, Mrs Jacob _____ unable to move her head.

   (a) was   (b) looks

   (c) had been   (d) is

2. Biofeedback training is based on the _____ that we can gain control of our bodily functions.

   (a) understanding   (b) aspect

   (c) feeling   (d) premise

3. The sharp cracking of a twig along with a bird's _____ made a great impact on him.

   (a) cry   (b) shriek

   (c) squawk   (d) scream

4. It is possible to listen to _____ as well as to sound, just as it is possible to see both light and shadow.

   (a) music   (b) silence

   (c) instrument   (d) voice

5. He prefers swimming _____ any other sport.

   (a) than   (b) over

   (c) to   (d) against

Directions for questions 6 to 10: In each of the following sentences, a part of the sentence is underlined. Four different ways of phrasing the underlined part are indicated beneath each sentence. Choose the best alternative among the four given options.

6. He considers <u>me as a fool</u>.

   (a) I as a fool   (b) me for a fool

   (c) I for a fool   (d) me a fool

7. The accountant has <u>already given</u> the balance sheet.

   (a) already gave   (b) already give

   (c) already given   (d) allready given

8. Jack may be <u>a better player to me</u>.

   (a) a better player than me

   (b) a better player than I

   (c) the better player to me

   (d) the better player than I

9. <u>He not only was competent</u> but also intelligent.

   (a) Not only he was competent

   (b) He was not competent

   (c) Not only was he competent

   (d) He was competent not only

10. There <u>have been heavy rainfall</u> since yesterday.

    (a) have been strong rainfall

    (b) has been strong rainfall

    (c) has been heavy rainfall

    (d) was been heavy rainfall

Directions for questions 11 to 20: In each of the following questions, a word is followed by four alternatives. Choose the one which best expresses the meaning of the given word.

11. Ostensible

    (a) Absurd   (b) Obvious

    (c) Practical   (d) Apparent

12. Serendipitous

    (a) Accidental   (b) Selective

    (c) Discriminate   (d) Pure

13. Murky

    (a) Ugly   (b) Dangerous

    (c) Gloomy   (d) Lazy

14. Gregarious

    (a) Sociable   (b) Turbulent

    (c) Pugnacious   (d) Clumsy

15. Accost

    (a) Hesitate   (b) Speculate

    (c) Bargain   (d) Confront

16. Sagacity

    (a) Morality   (b) Wisdom

    (c) Sanity   (d) Uprightness

17. Angst

    (a) Anxiety   (b) Pride

    (c) Modesty   (d) Simplicity

18. Vulgar

    (a) Enthusiastic   (b) Wild

    (c) Coarse   (d) Noisy

19. Umbrage
    (a) Sensitive   (b) Shabbiness
    (c) Premature   (d) Resentment
20. Hiatus
    (a) Break   (b) Contempt
    (c) Tight   (d) Narrow

Directions for questions 21 to 25 : Identify the word which has the correct spelling.

21. (a) Perseverance   (b) Persevirance
    (c) Persiverance   (d) Persivirance
22. (a) Recieve   (b) Receive
    (c) Recive   (d) Riceive
23. (a) Opthalmolgy   (b) Opthalmolagy
    (c) Optometrist   (d) Opitician
24. (a) Comission   (b) Commision
    (c) Comision   (d) Commission
25. (a) Discipline   (b) Disciplene
    (c) Dicsipline   (d) Discepline

Directions for questions 26 to 30: Identify the part of the sentence that contains a grammatical or spelling error. Mark that part as your answer.

26. Ram <u>asked me</u> <u>whether I had a car</u>
        (a)   (b)
    <u>and would I</u> <u>pick him up</u>.
        (c)   (d)
27. Everybody <u>among the guests were</u> <u>enjoying</u>
                        (a)
    <u>his drink</u> <u>when the theft</u> <u>took place</u>.
        (b)   (c)   (d)
28. Although <u>these buildings</u> are <u>in need of</u> repair
                    (a)   (b)
    <u>there have been</u> much improvement <u>in their</u>
            (c)
    <u>appearance</u>.
        (d)
29. <u>I am disappointed</u>   <u>in not having saw</u>
            (a)   (b)
    <u>a single stage play while</u> <u>I was in Baroda</u>.
            (c)   (d)
30. <u>Americans are</u> <u>accustomed</u> <u>drinking coffee</u>
        (a)   (b)   (c)
    <u>with their meals</u>.
        (d)

Answer Key

1. (a)	**2.** (d)	**3.** (c)	**4.** (b)	**5.** (c)	**6.** (d)	**7.** (c)	**8.** (b)	**9.** (c)	**10.** (c)
11. (d)	**12.** (a)	**13.** (c)	**14.** (a)	**15.** (d)	**16.** (b)	**17.** (a)	**18.** (c)	**19.** (d)	**20.** (a)
21. (a)	**22.** (b)	**23.** (c)	**24.** (d)	**25.** (a)	**26.** (c)	**27.** (a)	**28.** (c)	**29.** (b)	**30.** (b)

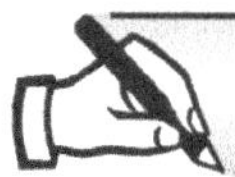 # Explanations

1. a Since the action is in the past tense, the verb will be 'was'.

2. d The answer is 'premise' because a premise is a basis for any logical deduction.

3. c The sound made by a bird is 'squawk'.

4. b The blank word has to be the opposite of sound as 'light' and 'shadow' are opposites. 'silence' is the correct option.

5. c We normally say 'prefer ....to....'

6. d There is no need to use *as*.

7. c (c) has the right tense structure.

8. b The complete sentence should read ... *better player than I (am)*.

9. c 'Not only was he competent' has the right idiomatic structure.

10. c 'Has been heavy rainfall' is the correct option.

11. d 'Ostensible' means apparent or seeming to be true.

12. a 'Serendipitous' means to come upon or find by accident.

13. c 'Murky' means gloomy, cloudy or dark.

14. a A 'Gregarious' person is sociable.

15. d To 'Accost' is to confront someone and talk to him/her in an unfriendly way.

16. b 'Sagacity' is to be as wise as a sage.

17. a 'Angst' is to be anxious and worried.

18. c A 'vulgar' joke is coarse and not refined.

19. d 'Umbrage' is a feeling of resentment caused by being offended.

20. a A 'Hiatus' is a break in something, or interruption in continuity.

26. c It should be 'whether I would' instead of 'would I'.

27. a 'Everybody' is a universal pronoun, which should be followed by a verb in the singular case, i.e. 'was' and not 'were'.

28. c 'Improvement' is singular case pronoun, so the verb should be 'has' and not 'have'.

29. b 'Not having saw' is grammatically wrong, say 'not having seen'.

30. b The statement should read 'accustomed to'.

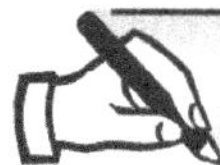

Practice Test-2

Number of questions: 30   **Time Allowed: 30 mins.**

Directions for questions 1 to 5: Fill in the following blanks with the most appropriate choice.

1. The student _____ the conversation without waiting for the speaker to stop talking.
   (a) interpreted   (b) intuned
   (c) interrupted   (d) interfered

2. I could not finish the work in time because I was very _____.
   (a) energetic   (b) fatigue
   (c) lazy   (d) tired

3. I am _____ to having a hearty breakfast in the morning.
   (a) fond   (b) liking
   (c) desirous   (d) used

4. Primitive men probably _____ eclipses of the sun and the moon a source of awe and terror.
   (a) discovered   (b) created
   (c) regarded   (d) believed

5. Martha's appeal for mercy was met with a _____ response from her kidnapper.
   (a) callous   (b) hard
   (c) curious   (d) fantabulous

Directions for questions 6 to 10: Identify the word which has the correct spelling.

6. (a) Glycerene   (b) Glycirine
   (c) Glycerine   (d) Glycirene

7. (a) Conspicous   (b) Conspicuous
   (c) Conspicuos   (d) Conspicus

8. (a) Infloresence   (b) Inflorecence
   (c) Infloresense   (d) Inflorescence

9. (a) Unconcious   (b) Unconsious
   (c) Unconscius   (d) Unconscious

10. (a) Vicissitude   (b) Viccissitude
    (c) Viccisitude   (d) Vicisitude

Directions for questions 11 to 15: The following passage contains blanks that are to be filled in with an appropriate word from the four given options. Choose the best word from the given alternatives.

I make lists to keep my ...**11**... level down. If I write down 15 things to be done, I ...**12**... that vague, nagging sense that there are an overwhelming ...**13**... of things to be done, all of which are on the ...**14**... of being forgotten. Ed, on the other hand, controls his ...**15**... precisely by forgetting them.

11. (a) anxiety   (b) blood
    (c) tension   (d) shopping

12. (a) win   (b) lose
    (c) gain   (d) get

13. (a) sense   (b) number
    (c) list   (d) time

14. (a) edge   (b) brim
    (c) verge   (d) curve

15. (a) accuracy   (b) stress
    (c) money   (d) statement

Directions for questions 16 to 20: Read each of the following sentences to find out whether there is any grammatical error in it. The error, if any, will be in one part of the sentence. Mark the number of that part as the answer.

16. The music teacher (a)/ let (b)/ Radhika and I (c)/ play the piano (d).

17. Falling on the (a)/ roof, the rain (b)/ attached (c)/ my attention (d).

18. The dog (a)/ barks loud (b)/ whenever it sees (c)/ a stranger (d).

19. She is (a)/ more older (b)/ to (c)/ her sister (d).

20. Your stomach (a)/ can hold (b)/ about a (c)/litre of foods (d).

Directions for questions 21 to 25: The following passage contains blanks that are to be filled in with an appropriate word from the four given options. Choose the best word from the given alternatives.

After a cancer scare, I was warned ...**21**... pursuing my dream of having a baby. Still my brush with ...**22**... inspired me to try to find a child who was in ...**23**..., to save a ...**24**..., if I could not create one. So my husband and I decided to ...**25**... a child.

21. (a) for   (b) against
    (c) by   (d) to

22. (a) mortals   (b) creation
    (c) mortality   (d) fever

23. (a) danger   (b) risk
    (c) fertility   (d) awe
24. (a) death   (b) conscious
    (c) life   (d) purpose
25. (a) adopt   (b) adapt
    (c) give   (d) adept

Directions for questions 26 to 30: Fill in the following blanks with the appropriate choices.

26. Because of his excellent _____ skills, he could mesmerize the crowd with the power of his speech.
    (a) loquacious   (b) convincing
    (c) presentation   (d) oratory
27. The patriot was given a tumultuous welcome _____ his countrymen.
    (a) with   (b) from
    (c) among   (d) by

28. There is no time like the _____ to start thinking about owning a house.
    (a) current   (b) past
    (c) present   (d) future
29. Practice will _____ pay its dividends.
    (a) finally   (b) eventually
    (c) sooner   (d) later
30. When certain kinds of monkeys are _____, they act just like human beings.
    (a) domesticated
    (b) pet
    (c) beaten
    (d) flattered

✍ Answer Key

1. (c)	2. (d)	3. (d)	4. (c)	5. (a)	6. (c)	7. (b)	8. (d)	9. (d)	10. (a)
11. (a)	12. (b)	13. (b)	14. (c)	15. (b)	16. (c)	17. (c)	18. (b)	19. (b)	20. (d)
21. (b)	22. (c)	23. (a)	24. (c)	25. (a)	26. (d)	27. (d)	28. (c)	29. (b)	30. (a)

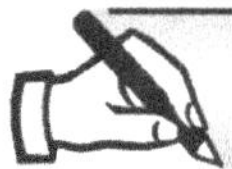 # Explanations

1. c 'Interrupted' is the most logical answer.

2. d 'tired' is the most logical answer.

3. d 'used to ....' is the right usage. The other choices have different prepositions. For example, 'fond of...' have a liking towards...', desirous of...' .

4. c The answer is 'regarded' because it implies the 'treatment' the primitive men gave to the sun and the moon.

5. a 'Hard response' does not make sense. Also, one cannot figure out what is a 'curious response'. 'Callous' means 'cold hearted or indifferent' which is the most suitable choice.

11. a *Anxiety* is the best word to describe *vague, nagging sense.*

12. b *'Lose'* makes sense because the list helps matters.

13. b *'Number'* is the best choice because *15* is already mentioned once.

14. c *'Verge of being forgotten'* which means *almost forgotten* is the most appropriate phrase.

15. b 'Anxiety' is a recurring theme in this paragraph. Hence, the correct word to be used is 'stress'.

16. c 'Me' as an object pronoun will replace 'I'.

17. c 'caught my attention' is the correct idiomatic usage.

18. b 'Loudly' as an adverb should be used to modify the verb 'barks'.

19. b Usage of 'elder' instead of 'more older' is correct as elder is used for individuals of the same family. The correct sentence is: 'she is elder to her sister'.

20. d use. . . 'a litre of food'.

21. b The usage of the word 'warned' before the blank gives us the hint that the word used in the blank has to be a negative one and hence 'against' is most appropriate.

22. c The correct word to be used here is 'mortality' because the author just survived a cancer scare, hence had a brush with *mortality*.

23. a The blank requires a negative word because the writer gives a hint before this blank that he is in search of a child who needs help. Hence, the correct answer is 'danger'.

24. c 'Life' is the correct word to be used as the writer gives a hint about saving a child if she is not able to create one.

25. a Keeping in mind the meaning of the entire paragraph, the word that would fit in the last blank is 'adopt' because the couple are planning to save the life of a child who needs help.

26. d A 'loquacious' person is a talkative person and need not be a good public speaker. So, choice (a) is incorrect. It is hard to understand the relation of 'convincing' skills and power of speech. Choice (c) is wrong as presentation skills need not necessarily make a good orator. Thus, choice (d) is the correct answer.

27. d The answer should be 'by' as you are given something 'by' somebody. The other choices don't make sense grammatically.

28. c *'present'* is the best word that can fit in this commonly advocated sentence.

29. b 'eventually' is the correct word because the results of any practice come after some time.

30. a The correct word to be used here is 'domesticated', which means to train an animal to live in a human environment.

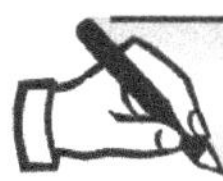

Practice Test-3

Number of questions: 30 | **Time Allowed: 30 mins.**

Directions for questions 1 to 5: The following passage contains blanks that are to be filled in with an appropriate word from the four corresponding options. Choose the best word from the given alternatives.

The ...1... of education has also been a potent instrument in emphasizing and shaping the underlying unity of mankind. The best ...2... perhaps in which we can describe the present decade is to call it a 'decade of promise'. The marvel of science, the immense ...3... of harnessing nuclear energy for peaceful purposes and the urge to ...4... resources to their optimum level have all significantly contributed in tackling problems on a ...5... scale rather than attempting to solve these baffling issues of ignorance, poverty and disease separately individual and national scales.

1. (a) need   (b) mode
   (c) spread   (d) development
2. (a) way   (b) method
   (c) format   (d) manner
3. (a) effects   (b) labour
   (c) possibilities   (d) capability
4. (a) materialise   (b) utilise
   (c) synthesise   (d) pressurise
5. (a) global   (b) globe
   (c) world   (d) universal

Directions for questions 6 to 10: Fill in the following blanks with the appropriate choices.

6. He is looking for a job, _____ times are tough.
   (a) and   (b) but
   (c) so   (d) in
7. The corporation is working towards _____ its existing training institutes.
   (a) vitalizing   (b) vitiating
   (c) vapourizing   (d) revitalizing
8. Insurance itself has become a _____ subject in the curriculum of business administration.
   (a) half-baked   (b) fledgling
   (c) hybrid   (d) full-fledged
9. They have held _____ a demonstration outside the consulate.
   (a) most   (b) lot
   (c) to   (d) many
10. Many areas have _____ or no capability to respond to terrorist attacks.
   (a) lots   (b) many
   (c) little   (d) full

Directions for questions 11 to 20: The following passage contains blanks that are to be filled in with an appropriate word from the four corresponding options. Choose the best word from the given alternatives.

Over the entire field of ...11... making, the problems facing the government are ...12... scientific and technological in ...13... . Our decisions in defence and foreign ...14... are increasingly governed by the developments in military and civil technology, ...15... in such matters as armament and disarmament, the ...16... of a new law for the seas or an international regime for space. The ...17... field of industry and agriculture, education, health and welfare confronts us with a wide range of technological choices, and even decisions in such ...18... nonscientific areas as taxation and procurement ...19... affect the pace and ...20... of the nation's technological progress.

11. (a) peace   (b) talks
   (c) policy   (d) strategy
12. (a) increasingly   (b) contentiously
   (c) especially   (d) decreasingly
13. (a) intent   (b) content
   (c) essence   (d) pith
14. (a) events   (b) happenings
   (c) affairs   (d) conditions
15. (a) in particular   (b) especially
   (c) virtually   (d) seemingly
16. (a) detail   (b) elaboration
   (c) spreading   (d) dimension
17. (a) complete   (b) entire
   (c) all   (d) whole

18. (a) obviously   (b) clearly
    (c) seemingly   (d) thin
19. (a) willingly   (b) profoundly
    (c) superficially   (d) intensely
20. (a) quality   (b) caliber
    (c) talent   (d) intensity

Directions for questions 21 to 25: Correct the underlined portion in a given sentence by replacing it with the correct choice from among the four given alternatives.

21. When <u>harassed or threatened a puffer fish literally puffs up by gulping water stored in an offshoot of their</u> stomach.
    (a) harassed or threatened, a puffer fish literally puffs up by gulping water stored in an offshoot of their
    (b) harassed or threatened, a puffer fish literally puffs up by gulping in water stored in an offshoot of their
    (c) harassed or threatened, a puffer fish literally puffs up by gulping water stored in an offshoot of its
    (d) it feels harassed or threatened, a puffer fish literally puffs up by gulping water stored in an offshoot of their

22. Bats are over a million years <u>older in age to mammals.</u>
    (a) older in age to mammals.
    (b) older in age than other mammals.
    (c) old in age like mammals.
    (d) older in age than mammals.

23. It is possible to hold a certain <u>image in your mind for long periods, and this can have a salutary impact on your</u> own behaviour and character.
    (a) image in your mind for long periods, and this can have a salutary impact on your
    (b) image in your mind for long periods, and this can have a salutary impact on one's
    (c) image in your mind for long periods, and this has a salutary impact on your
    (d) image in your mind for a long period, and this can have a salutary impact on your

24. John Maynard Keynes, <u>the greatest economist of the 20th century, once wrote an essay on fellow Cambridge genius, the scientist and mathematician</u> Isaac Newton.
    (a) the greatest economist of the 20th century, once wrote an essay on fellow Cambridge genius, scientist and mathematician
    (b) the great economist of the 20th century, once wrote an essay on fellow Cambridge genius, scientist and mathematician
    (c) the greatest economist of the 20th century, once wrote an essay about fellow Cambridge genius, scientist and mathematician
    (d) the greatest economist of the 20th century, once wrote an essay on fellow Cambridge genius, who was a scientist and the mathematician

25. After his journey to India, Alexander the Great <u>took with him 200 peafowls, which were as appreciated in Europe as any other place.</u>
    (a) took with him 200 peafowls, which were as appreciated in Europe as any other place.
    (b) took back with him 200 peafowls, which were as appreciated in Europe as in any other place.
    (c) took back with him 200 peafowls, which were as appreciated in Europe as any other place.
    (d) took with him 200 peafowls, which were appreciated in Europe as well as in all other places.

Directions for questions 26 to 30: Each of the following questions contains a sentence that is broken up into parts. Rearrange the parts so as to make a meaningful sentence.

26. A. that would be a
    B. good enough reason
    C. by itself
    D. to switch to
    E. this system
    (a) ABCDE   (b) BACDE
    (c) ABDCE   (d) EABCD

27. A. varying indirect tax rates
    B. the present labyrinth of
    C. in different states
    D. constitutes a formidable barrier to
    E. interstate trade
    (a) ABCDE   (b) BACDE
    (c) ABDCE   (d) EABCD

28. A. he cannot
    B. be
    C. for this
    D. solely blamed
    E. fresh delay
    (a) ABCDE   (b) BACDE
    (c) ABDCE   (d) EABCD

29. A. finest filmmakers
    B. had few
    C. or no problems
    D. with the CBFC
    E. some of our
    (a) ABCDE   (b) BACDE
    (c) ABDCE   (d) EABCD

30. A. even fashion shows on satellite television
    B. have had to don a
    C. fig leaf of propriety before they
    D. privacy of homes
    E. can be telecast into the
    (a) ABCDE   (b) BACDE
    (c) ABDCE   (d) ABCED

Answer Key

1. (d)	**2.** (d)	**3.** (c)	**4.** (b)	**5.** (a)	**6.** (b)	**7.** (d)	**8.** (d)	**9.** (d)	**10.** (c)
11. (c)	**12.** (a)	**13.** (b)	**14.** (c)	**15.** (b)	**16.** (b)	**17.** (b)	**18.** (c)	**19.** (b)	**20.** (a)
21. (c)	**22.** (b)	**23.** (d)	**24.** (a)	**25.** (b)	**26.** (a)	**27.** (b)	**28.** (c)	**29.** (d)	**30.** (d)

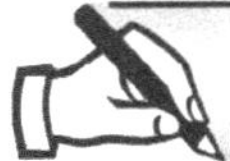

Explanations

1. d If you read further, you will see that the context of the passage is talking about education and human development. Hence (d) is the best choice.

2. d 'Manner of description' is the right diction.

3. c 'To harness nuclear energy', we need the word 'possibilities'.

4. b Resources are meant to be 'utilised'.

5. a Clearly, the correct choice is (a).

6. b 'but' brings out the regretful tone.

7. d 'revitalizing' means that the 'existing' is being improved.

8. d 'full-fledged' fits in correctly as it emphasizes on the fact that insurance has gained itself an a place in business administration curriculum.

9. d 'many a' is the right usage. It means 'lots'.

10. c 'little' means almost none at all, and goes with 'no capability'.

11. c The paragraph deals with policy making by the government in different areas.

12. a If you read the passage further you will find that the government's problems are primarily scientific and technological in nature and need immediate attention. Hence, 'increasingly' is the correct word.

13. b Since the government's problems are primarily scientific and technological in nature, the word that fits in here is 'content'.

14. c 'foreign affairs' is the popularly used term, also most generically applicable.

15. b The only word to fit the blank is choice (b). The rest appear weak.

16. b Contextually, choice (b) is the most appropriate as we are discussing policy-making guidelines.

17. b 'entire' is the most appropriate word in this situation, as a big list is mentioned here.

18. c 'seemingly' fits the context of the passage as it brings out the contrast.

19. b None of the other choices is good enough to fit the blank, 'profoundly' brings out the depth.

20. a The word 'quality' goes with the positive tone of 'pace'.

21. c Choice (c) is the most concise and has singular agreement between the verb and the pronoun.

22. b The right term is 'older in age than other mammals' and not 'older in age to mammals'. Also, (d) is incorrect because bat itself comes under the mammals category.

23. d Choice (b) is wrong as it uses your mind in the beginning but one's later. Choice (c) replaces 'this can' by 'this has'. 'This' introduces an element of certainty, which is absent in the original sentence. Choice (a) is wrong as it uses the phrase 'for long periods'. Hence, choice (d) is most appropriate.

24. a Choice (b) changes the superlative 'greatest' to 'great'. Choice (c) is wrong as it uses 'essay about' instead of 'essay on'. Choice (d) is wrong because when read in continuation with rest of the sentence, it would imply that the essay was on two different people, which is not correct. Hence, choice (a) is the correct answer.

25. b Choices (a) and (c) are wrong as in the second part of the sentences, we should say 'as in any other place'. Choices (a) and (d) also fail to specify where the peafowls were taken.

26. a 'AB' forms a mandatory pair as B describes the subject 'that' (mentioned in A) as a 'good enough reason. C follows B as the reflexive pronoun 'itself' (stated in C) refers to 'that' (subject). The correct sentence is - 'That would be a good enough reason by itself to switch to this system'.

27. b 'BA' is the opening mandatory pair as it gives us the subject of the sentence i.e. labyrinth of varying indirect taxes. This pair is present only in option (b), hence this is the correct option.

28. c B follows A in order to complete the verb form 'cannot be' (infinitive). 'CE' is a mandatory pair as the demonstrative pronoun 'this' (used in C) modifies the noun 'fresh delay' (mentioned in E). Hence, 'ABDCE' is the correct sequence.

29. d 'EA' is the obvious opener as it gives us the subject of the sentence i.e. some of our finest filmmakers. Hence, option (d) is the correct answer.

30. d 'ABC' is a mandatory sequence as C describes what the fashion shows have to don (fig leaf of propriety). 'ED' follows as it gives a reason behind this.

Number of questions: 30 **Time Allowed: 30 mins.**

Directions for questions 1 to 5: Identify the part of the sentence that contains a grammatical or spelling error. Mark that part as your answer.

1. Nothing but fraud and double-dealing
   (a) (b)
   are discernible in his actions.
   (c) (d)

2. You look much handsome now.
   (a) (b) (c) (d)

3. They discovered a large number of hoarded
   (a) (b) (c)
   sugar in his shop.
   (d)

4. The social reformer worked for the benefit
   (a) (b) (c)
   of disabled.
   (d)

5. I think it is quite allright if you stay.
   (a) (b) (c) (d)

Directions for questions 6 to 10: The following passage contains blanks that are to be filled in with an appropriate word from the four given options. Choose the best word from the given alternatives.

It is difficult to ...6... the future course of events. We cannot be ...7... . I see some danger ...8... . We cannot afford to ...9... . We have to be prepared for every sacrifice. We ...10... do without some necessities of life.

6. (a) depict   (b) predict
   (c) judge   (d) edict

7. (a) satisfied   (b) deficient
   (c) complacent   (d) implemented

8. (a) in front   (b) before
   (c) lead   (d) ahead

9. (a) lax   (b) relax
   (c) hoax   (d) try

10. (a) was to   (b) may have to
    (c) might had to (d) will have to

Directions for questions 11 to 15: Each of the following questions contains a sentence that is broken up into parts. Rearrange the parts so as to make a meaningful sentence.

11. A. the world's best-selling
    B. doll seems to have been
    C. overtaken by a
    D. mid-life
    E. crisis
    (a) ABCDE   (b) BACDE
    (c) ABDCE   (d) EABCD

12. A. is plummeting fast
    B. demand
    C. and even resale values
    D. are at an
    E. all-time low
    (a) ABCDE   (b) BACDE
    (c) ABDCE   (d) EABCD

13. A. their products are
    B. a clever amalgamation
    C. sociology
    D. of psychology
    E. and technology
    (a) ABCDE   (b) BACDE
    (c) ABDCE   (d) EABCD

14. A. toys is not
    B. restricted to children
    C. alone but
    D. also to adults
    E. the appeal of
    (a) ABCDE   (b) BACDE
    (c) ABDCE   (d) EABCD

15. A. the human
    B. crisis is
    C. all about
    D. questions
    E. existential
    (a) ABCDE   (b) BACDE
    (c) ABDCE   (d) ABCED

Directions for questions 16 to 20: Complete the following sentences with the appropriate choice from among the given alternatives.

16. Stalkers hit the headlines _______ stalking celebrities.
    (a) and   (b) by
    (c) so   (d) on

17. He rammed his car _______ her stationary vehicle.
    (a) on   (b) by
    (c) through   (d) into

18. He should not waste his _______ furies off the sets.
    (a) create   (b) creation
    (c) criole   (d) creative

19. There maybe a _______ of black buck in California.
    (a) most   (b) a lot
    (c) tonnnage   (d) shortage

20. It does not mean that their films have been _______ of social and political content.
    (a) looted   (b) devoid
    (c) devoured   (d) tool

Directions for questions 21 to 25: Identify the part of the sentence that contains a grammatical or spelling error. Mark that part as your answer.

21. I cannot hardly read the letter.
    (a) (b)   (c)   (d)

22. Less men are present today.
    (a)   (b)   (c)   (d)

23. The streets were flooded when the pipe
      (a)   (b)   (c)
    bursted.
      (d)

24. None of the two guests participated
         (a)   (b)
    in the games or danced.
        (c)   (d)

25. The government plan to put an electronic
         (a)   (b)   (c)
    system in place.
      (d)

Directions for questions 26 to 30: Complete the following sentences with the appropriate choice from among the given alternatives.

26. He has no apologies _______ offer.
    (a) to   (b) but
    (c) so   (d) and

27. I don't _______ create controversies.
    (a) purpose   (b) purposely
    (c) purposeful   (d) purposly

28. You _______ like him too much, did you?
    (a) did   (b) did do
    (c) didn't   (d) do

29. She shouldn't have gone to the _______ in the first place.
    (a) pressed   (b) pressure
    (c) pressing   (d) press

30. She was a very beautiful woman _______.
    (a) as   (b) well
    (c) and well   (d) as well

✎ Answer Key

1. (c)	**2.** (c)	**3.** (c)	**4.** (d)	**5.** (c)	**6.** (b)	**7.** (c)	**8.** (d)	**9.** (b)	**10.** (b)
11. (a)	**12.** (b)	**13.** (c)	**14.** (d)	**15.** (d)	**16.** (b)	**17.** (d)	**18.** (d)	**19.** (d)	**20.** (b)
21. (b)	**22.** (a)	**23.** (d)	**24.** (a)	**25.** (b)	**26.** (a)	**27.** (b)	**28.** (c)	**29.** (d)	**30.** (d)

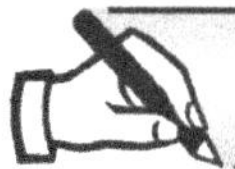 # Explanations

1. c The subject of the sentence is 'nothing' singular and not 'fraud and double-dealing'. Hence, 'is', not 'are'.

2. c The adverb 'much' cannot be used here. It should be 'you look very handsome now'.

3. c Amount refers to bulk or mass, number to individuals or units. (e.g. a large number of cars) and large amount of sugar. Hence, 'numbers' should be replaced by 'amount'.

4. d 'Of the disabled' is the right usage as we refer to a class, hence the article 'the' is required.

5. c 'alright' is the correct spelling.

6. b Since we are talking about the 'future course of events', the right word is 'predict'.

7. c If you read the following lines that follow, you will know that the right word is 'complacent' to fit into the context.

8. d 'ahead' is grammatically correct.

9. b 'relax' is the right verb here. The rest don't fit sensibly into the sentence.

10. b Choices (c) and (d) are incorrect because (c) is grammatically incorrect while (d) implies that the future course of events is predetermined. Choice (a) implies a command which does not fit here. Choice (b) is the correct option as it includes an element of uncertainty.

11. a The mandatory pair 'AB' opens the sentence by introducing the subject of the sentence 'world's best-selling doll'. 'DE' is a mandatory pair as it gives us the complete word 'mid-life crisis'. Hence, option (a) is the correct answer.

12. b A follows B as it describes the 'demand' i.e. *it is plummeting fast*. Hence, 'BA' is a mandatory pair. However, this can be found only in option (b). Hence, it is the correct option.

13. c 'AB' is a mandatory pair as B describes the subject i.e. 'their products'. D follows B as the preposition *of* is required here. Hence, 'ABDCE' is the correct sequence.

14. d 'EA' is the obvious opener as it gives us the subject of the sentence i.e. 'the appeal of toys'. Hence, option (d) is the correct answer.

15. d 'AB' is the opening mandatory pair as it introduces the subject i.e. 'the human crisis'. 'ED' is also a mandatory pair, as the adjective *existential* will precede the noun *questions.* Hence, 'ABCED' is the correct sequence.

16. b 'by' is the correct preposition to be used.

17. d You ram something 'into' something else.

18. d 'creative' is the right adjective form to be used to modify 'furies'.

19. d 'shortage' indicates scarcity.

20. b 'devoid' indicates 'lack of something'.

21. b Since 'hardly' conveys a negative meaning, 'can' should be used.

22. a Use 'fewer' to indicate individuals, 'less' is used to refer to bulk or mass.

23. d Use 'burst', there is no such word as 'bursted'.

24. a Use 'neither' as we are referring to two persons only.

25. b Use the singular verb 'plans' to refer to the government (singular noun).

26. a 'to offer something' is the right usage.

27. b 'purposely' is the right usage in the context.

28. c 'didn't' goes as a negative with the positive 'did'.

29. d 'press' refers to the journalists here.

30. d 'as well' adds on to the positive qualities that must have come prior to this sentence.

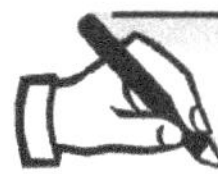

Practice Test-5

Number of questions: 20　　　　　　　　　　　　　　　　**Time Allowed: 20 mins.**

Directions for questions 1 to 5: Each of the following questions contains a sentence that is broken up into parts. Rearrange the parts so as to make a meaningful sentence.

1. A. she wanted
   B. to get
   C. to the
   D. top and
   E. stay there
   (a) ABCDE　　　　(b) BACDE
   (c) ABDCE　　　　(d) EABCD

2. A. technology decisions
   B. making good
   C. crucial as
   D. is as
   E. ever
   (a) ABCDE　　　　(b) BADCE
   (c) ABDCE　　　　(d) EABCD

3. A. and that's before
   B. the cost of training
   C. employees to
   D. use the
   E. stuff
   (a) ABCDE　　　　(b) BACDE
   (c) ABDCE　　　　(d) EABCD

4. A. major IT
   B. projects require
   C. in an
   D. radical changes
   E. organization
   (a) ABCDE　　　　(b) BACDE
   (c) ABDCE　　　　(d) EABCD

5. A. CEOs need to
   B. stay current
   C. to make sure
   D. stay competitive
   E. their companies
   (a) ABCDE　　　　(b) BACDE
   (c) ABDCE　　　　(d) ABCED

Directions for questions 6 to 10: Fill in the following blanks with the most appropriate choice.

6. Women have always dressed to _____ figure flaws.
   (a) disfigure　　　　(b) show
   (c) camouflage　　　(d) delineate

7. Being watched by the enemy is not nearly as _____ as being bombed by them.
   (a) comfortable　　　(b) unsettling
   (c) crazy　　　　　　(d) universal

8. Rain was pouring from the night sky at a rate that would have _____ Noah.
   (a) alarmed　　　　(b) praised
   (c) vindicated　　　(d) enraged

9. It's amazing how happy one can be, with _____ expectations of one's ownself.
   (a) high　　　　　(b) over
   (c) unrealistic　　(d) low

10. If, indeed, we have stopped going hammer and tongs at each other, let us ensure we replace it with something _____ and _____.
    (a) substantive … constructive
    (b) destructive … quarrelsome
    (c) superb … delicious
    (d) metallic … shiny

Directions for questions 11 to 15: Correct the underlined portion in a given sentence by replacing it with the correct choice from among the four alternatives given.

11. There they stood on the top shelf, all 20 volumes, <u>their red binding and gold lettering undoubtedly making them the most attractive between all the books on</u> the bookshelf.
    (a) their red binding and gold lettering undoubtedly making them the most attractive between all the books on
    (b) their red binding and gold lettering undoubtedly making them the most attractive among all the books in
    (c) their red binding and gold lettering having undoubtedly made them the most attractive among the books in
    (d) their red binding and gold lettering undoubtedly making them the most attractive among all the books on

12. Anyone who has worked with children <u>will confirm that children respond instinctively to nature and are capable of assimilating</u> even very complicated concepts.

    (a) will confirm that children respond instinctively to nature and are capable of assimilating

    (b) will confirm that they respond instinctively to nature and are capable to assimilate

    (c) will confirm that they respond instinctively to nature and are capable of assimilating

    (d) will confirm that children who respond instinctively to nature are capable to assimilating

13. Everything in the world <u>decays, it comes to an end and also dies inevitably.</u>

    (a) decays, it comes to an end and also dies inevitably.

    (b) decays, comes to an end and dies inevitably.

    (c) decays and as it comes to an end it dies inevitably.

    (d) decay, they come to an end and then they die inevitably.

14. Minkowski, who was Einstein's teacher, used to say that <u>a human being is a metaphor of both, the body and the soul, something that according to him symbolized</u> the ultimate creation of God.

    (a) a human being is a metaphor of both, the body and the soul, something that according to him symbolized

    (b) a human being is a metaphor of both, the body and the soul and symbolized

    (c) a human being which is a metaphor of both, the body and the soul, was something which to him symbolized

    (d) a human being is a metaphor of both, the body and the soul, which symbolized to him

15. According to experts in Britain, use of fitted carpets, that encourage dust mite to grow, <u>has contributed to a significant increase in the number of cases of asthma which in turn reduces their</u> immunity to other allergies.

    (a) has contributed to a significant increase in the number of cases of asthma which in turn reduces their

    (b) have contributed to a significant increase in the number of cases of asthma among the British, which in turn reduces their

    (c) has contributed to a significant increase in the number of cases of asthma among the British, which in turn reduces their

    (d) has contributed by significantly causing an increase in the number of cases of asthma among the British which in turn reduces their

Directions for questions 16 to 20: Identify the part of the sentence that contains a grammatical or spelling error. Mark that part as your answer.

16. <u>This secret and</u> <u>complex web of terror</u>
      (a)   (b)
<u>are now</u> <u>being exposed</u>.
  (c)   (d)

17. <u>Suvakar and Ammar</u> <u>does not</u> <u>play</u> <u>cricket</u>.
    (a)   (b)   (c) (d)

18. <u>Both PPL and JL</u> <u>have been</u> <u>suffering from</u>
   (a)   (b)   (c)
<u>huge loss</u>.
 (d)

19. <u>He presented</u> <u>a picture of how</u>
   (a)   (b)
<u>different revive schemes have</u>
      (c)
<u>failed to do any good</u>.
    (d)

20. <u>We do not want to</u> <u>throw good money</u>
   (a)   (b)
<u>behind bad money</u> <u>at this stage</u>.
  (c)   (d)

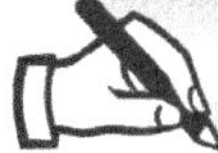

Answer Key

1. (a)	**2.** (b)	**3.** (a)	**4.** (c)	**5.** (d)	**6.** (c)	**7.** (b)	**8.** (a)	**9.** (d)	**10.** (a)
11. (d)	**12.** (c)	**13.** (b)	**14.** (b)	**15.** (c)	**16.** (c)	**17.** (b)	**18.** (d)	**19.** (c)	**20.** (b)

Explanations

1. a 'ABCD' is a mandatory sequence as it states what 'she' wanted and where did she want to reach (the top). Hence, option (a) is the correct answer.

2. b 'BA' is the obvious opener as it gives us the subject of the sentence i.e. *making good technology decisions.* However, this can be found only in option (b). Hence, it is the correct option.

3. a 'CDE' is a mandatory sequence that follows B as it states what the training is provided for. Hence, option (a) is the correct answer.

4. c 'AB' provides the topic of the discussion i.e. *major IT projects* and 'DCE' states what they require. Hence, 'ABDCE' is the correct sequence.

5. d B follows A as it states what CEOs need to do – *stay current.* 'CED' states the reason behind this – *to make sure their companies remain competitive.* Hence, option (d) is the correct answer.

6. c Option (c) is the answer because women make an attempt to conceal flaws through stylishly cut garments.

7. b 'unsettling', which means weakening or shaking is a result of bombing. Hence, option (b) is the correct answer.

8. a Option (a) is the answer because it rained so much that even Noah (of Noah's Ark) was scared.

9. d The sentence wants to convey the fact that one can be happy if one keeps low expectation from himself. Hence, option (d) i.e. *low* is the correct answer.

10. a Options (c) and (d) are illogical. We are looking for an answer that would be the opposite of 'hammer and tongs' which is (a).

11. d Choice (a) is wrong in usage because of the phrase 'the most attractive between'. *Between* is used when two things are compared. In case of comparison of many things, among should be used. Choice (b) is wrong in using 'books in'. It should be 'books on' the bookshelf. Choice (c) uses a past continuous perfect tense 'having undoubtedly made' and hence the sentence seems awkward and incomplete. Thus, choice (d) is the correct answer.

12. c Choice (a) is awkward as children should be replaced by a pronoun. Choice (b) is wrong in using 'to assimilate'. The correct usage is 'of assimilating'. Choice (d) wrongly uses the phrase 'capable to assimilating'.

13. b The sentence has parallel construction. Hence, there is no need to repeat the subject.

14. b Choice (a) is wrong as it uses a redundant phrase 'that according to him'. Choice (c) has a double use of 'which' that makes it very awkward and confusing. Choice (d) also uses a 'which clause' that is unnecessary.

15. c Choice (a) is wrong as 'their' has no noun to refer to. Choice (b) is wrong as it uses a plural verb 'have' for a singular noun 'use of carpets'. Choice (d) by saying 'has contributed by' implies a positive contribution which is not the case.

16. c The noun 'web' is singular, so the verb is 'is'.

17. b 'Do not play cricket' should be used as the two subjects together are plural.

18. d It should be 'losses' for two companies.

19. c It should be 'revival' and not revive.

20. b The correct usage is 'good money after bad money'.

Number of questions: 30 **Time Allowed: 30 mins.**

Directions for questions 1 to 10: The following passage contains blanks that are to be filled in with an appropriate word from the four given options. Choose the best word from the given alternatives.

Even in a world where high seas are common, the news that a group of Kiwi **...1...** is planning to hold the world's highest **...2...** party on the peak of Argentina's 7,000 metres high Mount Aconcagua could **...3...** an eyebrow or two. In the context of the recent economic **...4...** in Argentina and the riots which swept out more than one head of state from power, there are those who might quip that the safest place to have a **...5...** three-course meal complete with tablecloth, cutlery, wine and freeze-dried food is at the highest point in the Andes since the 'agitating descamidos' (Evita Peron's phrase for the shirtless peasants) would find it a bit too cold to **...6...** . The Kiwi group is, of course, **...7...** not so much on the current socio-politico-economic developments in Argentina as on breaking the record set by their rivals from Down Under, the Australia Social Climbers having dined and wined on the peak of Peru's 6,768 metres high Mount Huascaran. One table and six chairs will be **...8...** the Kiwi climbers to the top of Mount Aconcagua. The five male mountaineers will be wearing tuxedoes under their **...9...** of woolly clothing while the **...10...** female will be decked in a size-20 dress big enough to fit over both her size-12 frame and the bulky mountaineering outfit. The dinner date is for early February and the team is all set to leave for South America.

1. (a) helpers (b) coolies
   (c) designers (d) climbers
2. (a) lime (b) refreshments
   (c) snack (d) dinner
3. (a) rose (b) praise
   (c) raise (d) lower
4. (a) crisis (b) ferry
   (c) lull (d) room
5. (a) formal (b) casual
   (c) orgy (d) bash
6. (a) buy (b) share
   (c) welcome (d) gatecrash
7. (a) focused (b) peered
   (c) lose (d) blurred

8. (a) lugged (b) carried
   (c) flown (d) accompanying
9. (a) rolls (b) designed
   (c) sweaters (d) swathes
10. (a) rich (b) solitary
    (c) lonely (d) pretty

Directions for questions 11 to 15: Complete the following sentences with the appropriate choice from among the given alternatives.

11. This one is a ______ hit.
    (a) universe (b) uno
    (c) numero (d) universal
12. ______, India was the first country to air the ad early this month.
    (a) Incidence (b) Incidentaly
    (c) Insidiously (d) Incidentally
13. Suddenly a collision of Sumo wrestlers ______ the team and challenges them to play a game of football.
    (a) approach (b) beats
    (c) tackle (d) approaches
14. It was a very ______ logistic exercise.
    (a) complete (b) opening
    (c) frontal (d) complex
15. That perhaps ______ the cost of producing this mega-budget commercial.
    (a) justify (b) just
    (c) match (d) justifies

Directions for questions 16 to 20: Identify the part of the sentence that contains a grammatical or spelling error. Mark that part as your answer.

16. He is in the amidst of intense negotiations.
     (a)   (b)   (c)   (d)
17. Hollywood's antipathy for big business
              (a)   (b)
    may seems strange.
      (c)   (d)
18. Good marketing consists of give people
              (a)   (b)
    what they want.
      (c)   (d)

19. <u>Public sentiment</u> <u>has a</u> <u>way of</u>
         (a)   (b)   (c)
<u>swinging dramatical</u>.
         (d)

20. <u>The American</u> <u>legal system</u> <u>reflect the</u>
         (a)   (b)
<u>nation's cultural</u> <u>mistrust of big business</u>.
         (c)   (d)

Directions for questions 21 to 25: Complete the following sentences with the appropriate choice from among the given alternatives.

21. Successful companies have been forced to break up because they were perceived as ______ to consumer interest.
    (a) good   (b) benevolent
    (c) detrimental   (d) rusty

22. Compelling sagas need a ______, positive character.
    (a) weak   (b) imperial
    (c) moron   (d) strong

23. Michael Douglas could probably ______ through the part and still churn out an award-winning performance.
    (a) act   (b) brave
    (c) essay   (d) sleep-walk

24. May they never have to wake up one day, as thousands of Enron employees did, to find that the lines that ______ art and life have vanished overnight.
    (a) draw   (b) sketch
    (c) cartoon   (d) demarcate

25. We cannot sleep well during the night, ______ someone may enter the house.
    (a) happy   (b) satisfied
    (c) free   (d) fearing

Directions for questions 26 to 30: Each of the following questions contains a sentence that is broken up into five parts. Rearrange the parts so as to make a meaningful sentence.

26. A. our delegation took off
    B. on January 26, 2002, on a
    C. visit to South Africa, Nigeria
    D. and our last stop was Senegal
    E. before returning home
    (a) ABCDE   (b) BADCE
    (c) ABDEC   (d) EABCD

27. A. though their long walk
    B. to freedom rid them of
    C. whose dreams have to be translated to reality
    D. apartheid, they were aware that
    E. there still remained a section
    (a) ABCDE   (b) BADCE
    (c) ABDEC   (d) EABCD

28. A. sense
    B. in some
    C. order
    D. the old
    E. continues
    (a) ABCDE   (b) BADCE
    (c) ABDEC   (d) EABCD

29. A. rate is
    B. the unemployment
    C. rising and
    D. the expectations
    E. so are
    (a) ABCDE   (b) BADCE
    (c) ABDEC   (d) BACED

30. A. the evening is
    B. a venture in itself
    C. undertaken hesitantly for
    D. fear of being robbed
    E. a walk in
    (a) ABCDE   (b) BADCE
    (c) ABDEC   (d) EABCD

✍ Answer Key

1. (c)	**2.** (d)	**3.** (c)	**4.** (b)	**5.** (a)	**6.** (b)	**7.** (d)	**8.** (d)	**9.** (d)	**10.** (c)
11. (c)	**12.** (a)	**13.** (b)	**14.** (c)	**15.** (b)	**16.** (b)	**17.** (b)	**18.** (c)	**19.** (b)	**20.** (a)
21. (c)	**22.** (d)	**23.** (a)	**24.** (a)	**25.** (b)	**26.** (a)	**27.** (b)	**28.** (c)	**29.** (d)	**30.** (d)

✍ Explanations

1. d The passage is about mountaineering. So, 'climbers' is the most appropriate word to be used.

2. d The passage, in the later lines, talks about dining at the mountain heights.

3. c The sentence is about disbelief shown by the gesture of raising an eyebrow.

4. a The 'economic crisis' led to the revolt/riots.

5. a It is a 'formal' three-course dinner with all courtesies observed.

6. d 'gatecrash', which means to arrive uninvited or to interrupt is the correct answer.

7. a The focus is on breaking the record and not on the revolution.

8. d The table set would go along with the climbers for the dinner. Hence, accompanying' is with the climbers the correct option.

9. d The mountaineers are wrapped and covered in layers of wooly clothing. Thus, we use the word 'swathes'.

10. b There is only one female, hence use 'solitary'.

11. d A 'universal' hit is a hit anywhere in the world.

12. d 'Incidentally' means as a matter of coincidence. Rest of the options are either misspelt or logically incorrect.

13. d 'approaches' and 'challenges' have the right parallel structure.

14. d 'complex' means that it was tough to handle.

15. d 'justifies', which means to prove right or just is the correct answer.

16. c 'midst' is the right use, meaning *in the middle of*.

17. c Use 'seem' (singular verb) with 'hollywood' (singular subject).

18. b The word 'giving' should be used here and not 'give'

19. d 'dramatically' is the right adverb to be used here.

20. c Use singular verb 'reflects' for the singular noun 'system'.

21. c 'detrimental' brings out the reason why the companies have been forced to break up.

22. d 'strong' goes with 'positive'.

23. d 'sleep-walk' indicates that Michael Douglas can put in a performance without trying too hard and still be the best.

24. d 'demarcate' means to draw a line that separates movies and real life.

25. d They cannot sleep because they are afraid. Hence, 'fearing' is used.

26. a A is the opening sentence which states that the delegates took off. This is followed by the pair 'BC', which states when and where they went. Hence, the correct sequence is 'ABCDE'.

27. c 'AB' is a mandatory pair as the pronouns 'their' and 'them' used in these sentences refer to the same persons. B states that *they* could get rid of something and D states what exactly they could get rid of (apartheid). Hence, 'ABD' is a mandatory sequence. Note that this sequence can be found only in option (c). Hence, this is the correct option.

28. b B definitely follows A in order to complete a logically correct phrase i.e. *in some sense*. The correct sentence is 'In some sense the old order continues'.

29. d C follows A in order to complete the verb form i.e. *is rising*. The correct sequence is 'BACED'.

30. d 'EA' is the opening mandatory pair as it gives us the subject of the sentence i.e. 'a walk in the evening'. This leaves us with only one possible option, which is option (d).

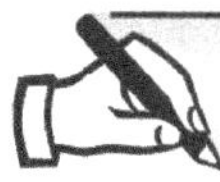

Practice Test-7

Number of questions: 30   **Time Allowed: 30 mins.**

Directions for questions 1 to 5: The following passage contains blanks that are to be filled in with an appropriate word from the four given options. Choose the best word from the given alternatives.

Four months after the city government enforced its People's Right to Information Act, the Delhi administration still operates in secrecy that verges on ...**1**... . Bureaucratic straitjackets continue as almost 75 per cent of the government departments are totally ...**2**... of the provisions of the Act. The government's failure to tutor its officials on the provisions of the Act, staff shortage and infrastructural facilities have made the much-touted law ...**3**... . Delhi Chief Secretary P. S. Bhatnagar ...**4**... that only 25 per cent of the administration has responded positively to the new law and made preliminary arrangements to enforce it. "The rest have not even taken the first step in enforcing the law," he said. The Delhi Vidyut Board which has ...**5**... a list of 25 officials who could act as competent authorities for dispensing information complained that it did not have the supporting staff to ensure enforcement.

1. (a) claustrophobia   (b) agoraphobia
   (c) paranoia   (d) dementia
2. (a) aware   (b) famous
   (c) popular   (d) ignorant
3. (a) bribed   (b) ineffectual
   (c) ignored   (d) work
4. (a) conceded   (b) succeeded
   (c) clapped   (d) refused
5. (a) retracted   (b) regressed
   (c) held   (d) forwarded

Directions for questions 6 to 10: Identify the part of the sentence that contains a grammatical or spelling error. Mark that part as your answer.

6. <u>Cleopatra</u> <u>as well as her retinue of slaves</u>
       (a)   (b)
<u>are sailing</u> <u>down the Nile.</u>
     (c)   (d)
7. <u>I</u> <u>do not know</u> <u>to read</u> <u>the scriptures.</u>
   (a)   (b)   (c)   (d)
8. <u>This</u> <u>is</u> <u>a best book</u> <u>on the subject.</u>
    (a) (b)   (c)   (d)
9. <u>He</u> <u>broke</u> <u>a antique and expensive</u> <u>vase.</u>
   (a)   (b)   (c)   (d)
10. <u>He</u> <u>made</u> <u>some derogatively remarks</u>
   (a) (b)   (c)
<u>about his uncle.</u>
     (d)

Directions for questions 11 to 15: From the options given in each question, choose the grammatically correct sentence.

11. (a) I have been travelling since last two months.
    (b) I have been travelling since the last two months.
    (c) I have been travelling for the last two months.
    (d) I have been travelling from the last two months.
12. (a) What is needed is not more politicians but more leaders.
    (b) What are needed is not more politicians, but rather more leaders.
    (c) What is needed are not more politicians, but more leaders.
    (d) What is are needed are not more politicians, but more leaders.
13. (a) I doubt that he will not succeed in this venture.
    (b) I doubt if he will not succeed in this venture.
    (c) I doubt whether he will succeed in this venture.
    (d) I doubt that he will succeed in this venture.
14. (a) He tried to blame it on to me.
    (b) He tried to blame it to me.
    (c) He tried to blame me.
    (d) He tried to put the blame on to me.
15. (a) I shall go tomorrow certainly.
    (b) I shall certainly go tomorrow.
    (c) I certainly shall go tomorrow.
    (d) I shall go certainly tomorrow.

Directions for questions 16 to 20: Choose the alternative that is closest in meaning to the underlined expression.

16. Sobhraj could easily be arrested because the police were <u>tipped off</u> in advance.
    (a) tricked   (b) bribed
    (c) given information   (d) threatened

17. Women should be paid the same as men when they do the same job, for surely, <u>what is sauce for the goose is sauce for the gander</u>.
    (a) what is thought to be acceptable for a man should also be so for a woman
    (b) goose and gander eat the same sauce
    (c) both goose and gander should equally be treated
    (d) the principle of equal treatment should be implemented

18. She wanted to get a bodytop as it was <u>the rage</u> on the fashion scene.
    (a) hated
    (b) subject of argument
    (c) very popular
    (d) leading to violence

19. The chest of drawers <u>was knocked down for a paltry sum</u>.
    (a) was broken down
    (b) was sold cheaply at an auction
    (c) was split into pieces
    (d) was dismantled

20. She stood by him through <u>thick and thin</u> in those difficult times.
    (a) she made him fat
    (b) she put fat in the fire
    (c) she was fat
    (d) under all circumstances

Directions for questions 21 to 25: The following questions consist of two words each that have a certain relationship with each other followed by alternatives. Select the alternative that has the same relationship as depicted in the original pair of words.

21. Wealth : Poverty
    (a) Part : Whole   (b) Good : Excellent
    (c) Prodigal : Miser   (d) Wicked : Sinful

22. Misfortune : Catastrophe
    (a) Miniature : Big
    (b) Limited : Infinite
    (c) Knowledge : Learning
    (d) Happiness : Elation

23. Molecule : Atoms
    (a) Family : Sisters   (b) Light : Bulb
    (c) Tissue : Cells   (d) Body : Limb

24. Limp : Walk
    (a) Flap : Fly   (b) Run : Race
    (c) Stutter : Talk   (d) Chew : Digest

25. Riddle : Solve
    (a) Mirage : Illusion   (b) Joke : Amuse
    (c) Mystery : Unravel   (d) Target : Sim

Directions for questions 26 to 30: Fill in the following blanks with the appropriate choices.

26. Could I rely _____ you to be discreet?
    (a) at   (b) on
    (c) in   (d) over

27. We _____ tennis in the garden when you telephoned.
    (a) had played   (b) playing
    (c) were playing   (d) are playing

28. It is _____ that he is unhappy with your performance today.
    (a) understandable   (b) only but natural
    (c) a natural   (d) by nature

29. If he had taken his doctor's advice, he _____ recovered soon.
    (a) would be   (b) would have
    (c) would have been   (d) should be

30. There are some birds in Siberia that _____ every year to the Ghana bird sanctuary.
    (a) migrated   (b) have migrated
    (c) are migrating   (d) migrate

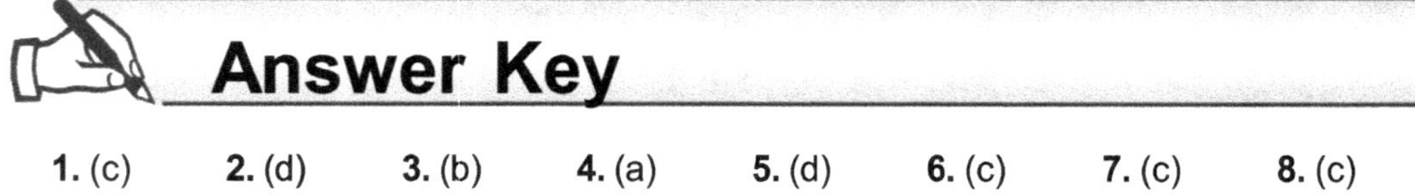

Answer Key

1. (c)	**2.** (d)	**3.** (b)	**4.** (a)	**5.** (d)	**6.** (c)	**7.** (c)	**8.** (c)	**9.** (c)	**10.** (c)
11. (c)	**12.** (a)	**13.** (c)	**14** (c)	**15.** (b)	**16.** (c)	**17.** (a)	**18.** (c)	**19.** (b)	**20.** (d)
21. (c)	**22.** (d)	**23.** (c)	**24.** (c)	**25.** (c)	**26.** (b)	**27.** (c)	**28.** (a)	**29.** (b)	**30.** (d)

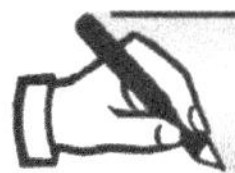

Explanations

1. c Paranoid people are very secretive. Hence, 'paranoia' is the correct word.

2. d The departments are unaware of the Act. Hence, 'ignorant' is the correct word.

3. b The law is not working, hence it is 'ineffectual'.

4. a The correct word to be used is 'conceded', which means to admit the truth.

5. d The list has been handed over — 'forwarded'.

6. c 'is sailing down the Nile' is the correct phrase because the subject of this sentence is 'Cleopatra'(singular), not 'slaves'.

7. c 'how to read' is the correct phrase as the verb 'to know' cannot be followed directly by an infinitive ('to read'), but takes a conjunction, e.g. how, which, what, when, whether, etc.

8. c The definite article 'the' should be used before a superlative (best).

9. c The article 'an' should be used in place of 'a' before a word beginning with a vowel or vowel sound (antique).

10. c The correct adjective to be used here is 'derogatory', which qualifies the noun 'remark' in the given sentence.

11. c 'Since' implies a specific point of time, while 'for' indicates a 'generic span of time'. Hence, in this case 'for' is a better word to indicate a generic span of time.

12. a Statement (a) is correct. 'Rather' is redundant as they both (but and rather) mean the same. Also 'what' requires the verb 'is' in this case.

13. c When there are two plausible outcomes, the word 'whether' is suitable. 'I doubt whether…'

14. c Option (c) is the answer that gives the direct effect.

15. b Option (b) is the answer as it has the adverb('certainly') rightly placed.

16. c 'to tip off' means to give advance information.

17. a The meaning of the phrase — what is sauce for the goose is sauce for the gander — implies that whatever is acceptable for the man should be acceptable for the woman.

18. c A 'rage' means a very popular fad.

19. b 'to knock down' means to sell off at an auction. A 'paltry sum' means a meagre amount.

20. d 'Through thick and thin' means that the two of them went through both good and bad times together.

21. c 'Prodigal' means extravagant while 'Miser' means stingy. These words are almost antonyms, just as the original pair.

22. d 'Catastrophe' is an advanced form of 'Misfortune'. 'Elation' is a higher form of 'happiness'.

23. c 'Molecule' is made up of 'Atoms'. 'Tissue' is made up of 'Cells'. Body is not made up of limb, but limbs.

24. c 'Limping' is an incorrect form of 'walking'. 'Stuttering' is an incorrect form of 'talking'.

25. c You 'solve a riddle', and 'unravel a mystery'.

26. b You can rely 'on' somebody, not 'over' or 'in' somebody.

27. c The action has to be a past continuous tense as the people were doing the action in the past. Hence, the phrase 'were playing' is used.

28. a 'understandable' is the correct option. The remaining options do not fit in logically.

29. b 'The conditional verb phrase 'would have' will be used here as the sentence puts a condition to 'his recovery', which is 'if he had taken the doctor's advice'.

30. d Simple present tense is mostly used to convey a habitual action. Hence, the verb 'migrate' is used.

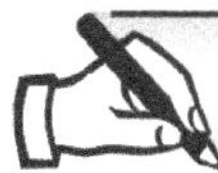

Practice Test-8

Number of questions: 20   **Time Allowed: 20 mins.**

Directions for questions 1 to 5 : Fill in the following blanks with the appropriate choices.

1. They lament and express their despair ______ the way Gandhi has been forgotten in his own land.
   (a) over   (b) of
   (c) in   (d) with

2. The council ______ on this issue.
   (a) is divided   (b) are divided
   (c) is being divided   (d) is getting divided

3. After having sought my help, ______.
   (a) my friend left me all alone
   (b) I was left all alone by my friend
   (c) I was alone
   (d) I asked her to leave me alone

4. I have known her ______ the end of the World War II.
   (a) from   (b) since
   (c) during   (d) towards

5. The landlady ______ since morning.
   (a) has gossiped   (b) has been gossiping
   (c) gossiped   (d) has gossiped

Directions for questions 6 to 15 : Identify the part of the sentence that contains a grammatical or spelling error. Mark that part as your answer.

6. She has arrived when we reached the station.
   (a)   (b)   (c)   (d)

7. This is the eldest manuscript in the library.
   (a) (b)   (c)   (d)

8. Moliere's plays are greater than
         (a)   (b)
   any other dramatist in France.
         (c)   (d)

9. This is the most unique insect.
   (a) (b)   (c)   (d)

10. He have no parallel in the
          (a)   (b)   (c)
    world of country music.
             (d)

11. The two brothers were quarreling
         (a)   (b)
    with one another.
         (c)   (d)

12. I had to do so because I felt
              (a)
    that the safety of my sister-nurses
              (b)
    and female attendants were in peril.
           (c)   (d)

13. I did not wait because
        (a)   (b)
    he had went before I reached his place.
            (c)   (d)

14. Judge in him prevailed and he
        (a)   (b)   (c)
    sentenced his son to imprisonment.
             (d)

15. There are no news today.
       (a) (b)   (c)   (d)

Directions for questions 16 to 20: In each of the following questions, a word is followed by four alternatives choose the one which is most opposite in meaning to the given word.

16. Audit
    (a) Check   (b) Bother
    (c) Study   (d) Overlook

17. Authentic
    (a) Real   (b) Genuine
    (c) Confirm   (d) Duplicate

18. Avid
    (a) Eager   (b) Passive
    (c) Interested   (d) Energetic

19. Baffle
    (a) Conjure   (b) Clarify
    (c) Confound   (d) Perplex

20. Baleful
    (a) Malevolent   (b) Destructive
    (c) Benign   (d) Destroy

✎ Answer Key

1. (a)	**2.** (b)	**3.** (a)	**4.** (b)	**5.** (b)	**6.** (b)	**7.** (c)	**8.** (c)	**9.** (c)	**10.** (a)
11. (d)	**12.** (d)	**13.** (c)	**14.** (a)	**15.** (b)	**16.** (d)	**17.** (d)	**18.** (b)	**19.** (b)	**20.** (c)

✎ Explanations

1. a 'To despair over something' is the right use of the preposition.

2. b Council takes plural verb 'are' because the sentence talks about members who have different views.

3. a After the modifier clause, the noun being modified 'my friend' should immediately succeed the modifier clause.

4. b 'Since' indicates a point of time when the action began and has continued till the present.

5. b 'has been gossiping' shows a continuous action that is still going on.

6. b 'had arrived' is the correct phrase. When the adverb clause of time is in the simple past tense (reached), the main clause must be in the past perfect tense.

7. c Use 'the oldest manuscript' as 'elder' and 'eldest' apply to persons only.

8. c The correct phrase is 'those of any other dramatist' as the comparison is between the plays of Moliere and those of other dramatists.

9. c 'A unique insect' should be used as unique expresses a superlative meaning. Hence, we cannot say most unique (two superlatives can't be together).

10. a 'He' as a singular subject will take the singular verb 'has'.

11. d Replace 'one another' by 'each other' because the reference is only to two persons.

12. d The subject of the clause is a singular one, i.e. 'safety'. Hence, the singular auxiliary verb 'was' will be used.

13. c 'had gone' is the past perfect tense and is the correct usage.

14. a The definite article 'the' should be used before judge.

15. b 'There is no news today'. News is a singular noun. It always takes a singular verb.

16. d An audit is a check to determine whether things are done properly. So, its opposite is 'overlook'.

17. d 'authentic' means genuine, its opposite is 'duplicate'.

18. b An avid person is active. Its opposite is passive.

19. b To baffle is to confuse someone. 'clarify' is its opposite.

20. c 'baleful' means being evil or destructive in influence. Hence, its opposite is 'benign', which means being gentle.

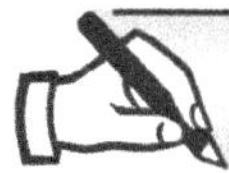

Practice Test-9

Number of questions: 20 **Time Allowed: 20 mins.**

Directions for questions 1 to 5: Select the odd word from the given set of four alternatives.

1. (a) Feasible   (b) Workable
   (c) Practicable   (d) Fantastic
2. (a) Lazy   (b) Idle
   (c) Go-getter   (d) Sluggard
3. (a) Mettlesome   (b) Spineless
   (c) Spirited   (d) Fiery
4. (a) Shouting   (b) Bleating
   (c) Roaring   (d) Whining
5. (a) Ploy   (b) Tactic
   (c) Driver   (d) Maneuver

Directions for questions 6 to 10: Choose the alternative that is closest in meaning to the underlined expression.

6. The car <u>seems to have disappeared which was following us.</u>
   (a) seems to have disappeared which was following us.
   (b) seems to be disappearing and which was following us.
   (c) seems to have disappeared which is following us.
   (d) which was following us seems to have disappeared.

7. The girl <u>John is going to marry is whom extremely beautiful.</u>
   (a) John is going to marry is whom extremely beautiful.
   (b) John will marry whom is extremely beautiful.
   (c) whom John is going to marry is extremely beautiful.
   (d) whom John wants to marry is extreme beautiful.

8. Amundsen <u>to reach was the first man the south pole.</u>
   (a) to reach was the first man the south pole.
   (b) to reach the first man was the south pole.
   (c) to reach the south pole was the first man.
   (d) was the first man to reach the south pole.

9. The police <u>to kidnap a prominent diplomat have been investigating a plot.</u>
   (a) to kidnap a prominent diplomat have been investigating a plot.
   (b) have been investigating to kidnap a plot of a prominent diplomat.
   (c) have to investigate a plot to kidnap a prominent diplomat.
   (d) have been investigating a plot to kidnap a prominent diplomat.

10. His wife <u>tried to conceal that he was seriously ill the fact.</u>
    (a) tried to conceal that he was seriously ill the fact.
    (b) tried concealing the fact that he was ill seriously.
    (c) tried and concealed the fact that he was ill seriously.
    (d) tried to conceal the fact that he was seriously ill.

Directions for questions 11 to 15: Identify the part of the sentence that contains a grammatical or spelling error. Mark that part as your answer.

11. <u>What needs</u> <u>to be</u> <u>done</u> <u>is poverty</u>
        (a)   (b)   (c)   (d)
    <u>should eradicate.</u>

12. <u>They wanted to</u> <u>know that</u> <u>why they</u>
         (a)   (b)   (c)
    <u>were wrong.</u>
        (d)

13. <u>Her health</u> <u>was too bad</u> <u>that she could not</u>
        (a)   (b)   (c)
    <u>recover soon.</u>
        (d)

14. <u>Once I</u> <u>return back</u> <u>from Mumbai,</u>
       (a)   (b)   (c)
    <u>I will meet you.</u>
          (d)

15. <u>The cake</u> <u>was cut to</u> <u>four equal parts.</u>
        (a)   (b)   (c)   (d)

Directions for questions 16 to 20: The following questions consist of two words each that have a certain relationship with each other followed by alternatives. Select the alternative that has the same relationship as depicted in the original pair of words.

16. TRAINING : HEREDITY
    (a) Unnatural : Usual
    (b) Ornithologist : Birds
    (c) Habits : Instinct
    (d) Astute : Ingenious

17. FRAGRANT : INCENSE
    (a) Frequent : Sound
    (b) Sneeze : Nostrils
    (c) Noxious : Garbage
    (d) Noisome : Pleasant

18. TRIANGLE : HEXAGON
    (a) Cone : Sphere
    (b) Rectangle : Octagon
    (c) Pentagon : Heptagon
    (d) Angle : Quadrilateral

19. ABRIDGE : LENGTHEN
    (a) Root : Trunk
    (b) Stop : End
    (c) Lend : Borrow
    (d) Prize : Reserve

20. Soup : Liquid
    (a) Water : Thirst
    (b) Book : Knowledge
    (c) Oxygen : Gas
    (d) Writer : Publisher

Answer Key

1. (d)	**2.** (c)	**3.** (b)	**4.** (a)	**5.** (c)	**6.** (d)	**7.** (c)	**8.** (d)	**9.** (d)	**10.** (d)
11. (d)	**12.** (b)	**13.** (b)	**14.** (b)	**15.** (b)	**16.** (a)	**17.** (c)	**18.** (b)	**19.** (c)	**20.** (c)

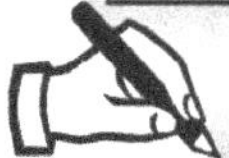

Explanations

1. d Fantastic bears no relation to the rest of the words that are synonyms.

2. c Go-getter is an antonym of the other three words.

3. b Spineless is an opposite of the other three words.

4. a Shouting is not the sound of an animal, the rest of the words are.

5. c A driver is a person, the rest of the words denote strategies or moves.

6. d The underlined part has an adjective clause 'which was following us' which describes the 'car' and the main clause 'seems to have disappeared'. The adjective clause should be placed immediately after the noun that it qualifies so that there is no scope for ambiguity.

7. c The word 'whom' modifies 'the girl', hence should be placed immediately after it. Also, the adverb 'extremely' should be used and not 'extreme'.

8. d All choices except (d) have an incorrect word order. The infinitive phrase 'to reach the south pole' has to be correctly placed next to the noun 'man' which it describes.

9. d The infinitive clause, 'to kidnap a prominent diplomat' has been misplaced in choices (a) and (b), hinting that the police might be doing the kidnapping. Choice (c) also suggests that the police have not started the investigation and is incorrect. Choice (d) is the answer as all these ambiguities are resolved in it.

10. d 'The fact' is 'that he was seriously ill' and hence the clause 'that he.......ill' has to be placed after 'the fact'. Choice (d) is the answer as it uses the right structure.

11. d 'poverty' cannot eradicate on its own, but has to be eradicated. Therefore, the correct phrase is 'poverty should be eradicated'.

12. b The word 'that' is not required. 'Wanted to know why' ..... is the right usage.

13. b 'too bad' is incorrect usage and should be replaced by 'so bad', where the word so indicates the extent to which her health was bad.

14. b 'Return back' is wrong because of repetition. It should be either 'come back' or plainly 'return'.

15. b Cakes are 'cut into pieces'.

16. a 'Training' is the opposite of 'Heredity'. Similarly, 'Unnatural' is the opposite of 'Usual'.

17. c Incense emits Fragrance just as Garbage emits a Noxious smell.

18. b The second word in the pair has double the sides of the first word. Triangle - 3 sides, Hexagon - 6 sides; Rectangle - 4 sides, Octagon - 8 sides.

19. c 'Abridge' (shorten) is the opposite of 'Lengthen' and 'Lend' is the opposite of 'Borrow'.

20. c Soup is a liquid. Similarly, oxygen is a gas.

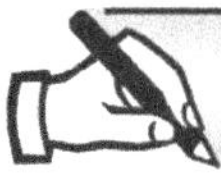

Practice Test-10

Number of questions: 30 **Time Allowed: 30 mins.**

Directions for questions 1 to 10: The following passage contains blanks that are to be filled in with an appropriate word from the four given options. Choose the best word from the given alternatives.

The British Cabinet Mission, which had come to India to work out the strategy for transfer of power, left without any success after a stay of more than three months. It had been a ...1... period of ...2... and sustained negotiations conducted in the ...3... heat of an Indian summer from which the Cabinet Mission could have derived no mental ...4... or physical relief. But they had not allowed their efforts to ...5... . They ...6... tirelessly to find a solution to a near ...7... problem, ...8... all kinds of odds and difficulties. There was Sir Stafford Cripps on the one hand, with his ...9... energy and flashes of intellectual genius, and Lord Pethick-Lawrence on the other, with his ...10... practical outlook and undoubted sympathy for Indian aspirations — a combination which might surely have been expected to produce the results for which everyone had hoped.

1. (a) dire (b) monumental
   (c) provocative (d) remarkable
2. (a) intractable (b) excited
   (c) political (d) arduous
3. (a) powerful (b) boiling
   (c) simmering (d) sweltering
4. (a) strain (b) consolation
   (c) recognition (d) achievement
5. (a) sustain (b) abandon
   (c) strengthened (d) flag
6. (a) extracted (b) endeavoured
   (c) projected (d) followed
7. (a) insurmountable (b) invincible
   (c) uncontrollable (d) irrevocable
8. (a) observing (b) maintaining
   (c) enduring (d) avoiding
9. (a) inscrutable (b) irresistible
   (c) unattainable (d) indefatigable
10. (a) essentially (b) unnaturally
    (c) superficially (d) adequately

Directions for questions 11 to 15: Combine the sentences given below into a single sentence and indicate which of A, B or C can be a starter for the complete sentence.

11. I had my lunch. I still had the snack.
    A. As I ...
    B. In spite of ...
    C. Being that I am ...
    (a) A only (b) B only
    (c) C only (d) A and B

12. We may run out of battery. Better take a spare one along.
    A. As we ...
    B. We better ...
    C. Being that I am ...
    (a) A only (b) B only
    (c) C only (d) A and B

13. You must go to Sir. Or you will feel worse.
    A. You as ...
    B. Despite ...
    C. You must ...
    (a) A only (b) B only
    (c) C only (d) A and B

14. We must study. Else, we will fail the examination.
    A. If I ...
    B. If we ...
    C. Being that we are ...
    (a) A only (b) B only
    (c) C only (d) A and B

15. I would have slapped her. But I am decent.
    A. Had it ...
    B. In spite of ...
    C. If only he ...
    (a) A only (b) B only
    (c) C only (d) None of these

Directions for questions 16 to 20: Identify the part of the sentence that contains a grammatical or spelling error. Mark that part as your answer.

16. The booty was cut between the two thieves.
        (a)   (b) (c)   (d)

17. The room can be shared between five
        (a)   (b)   (c)

    people easily.
        (d)

18. I will go to a postgraduate program
    (a)   (b)   (c)

    in America.
        (d)

19. It is the easiest to solve quantitative
        (a)   (b)   (c)

    problems than logical ones.
        (d)

20. The pollution in Mumbai is more than Delhi.
    (a)   (b)   (c)   (d)

Directions for questions 21 to 25: Complete the following sentences with the correct choice from the given alternatives.

21. The town looks different because _____ your marriage.
    (a) from   (b) of
    (c) at   (d) in

22. She was in the habit of interfering _____ his affairs.
    (a) on   (b) by
    (c) with   (d) in

23. When I was young, I always went to school _____ foot.
    (a) by   (b) with
    (c) on   (d) upon

24. Even educated people sometimes believe _____ superstitions.
    (a) in   (b) of
    (c) about   (d) for

25. Parents are usually blind _____ the faults of their children.
    (a) against   (b) about
    (c) to   (d) of

Directions for questions 26 to 30: Complete the following sentences with the correct choice from the given alternatives.

26. Neither of the men _____
    (a) have done satisfactory work.
    (b) has done satisfactory work.
    (c) have not done satisfactory work.
    (d) have done satisfactory work.

27. We expect everyone _____
    (a) to do his duty.   (b) to do their duty.
    (c) to do our duty.   (d) to do one's duty.

28. I have been trying to get in touch with her _____ morning.
    (a) from   (b) for
    (c) since   (d) within

29. They are trying to settle their dispute _____ third-party intervention.
    (a) in   (b) through
    (c) about   (d) for

30. They had been trying to contact us _____ two days.
    (a) from   (b) for
    (c) since   (d) within

Answer Key

1. (d)	**2.** (d)	**3.** (d)	**4.** (b)	**5.** (d)	**6.** (b)	**7.** (a)	**8.** (c)	**9.** (d)	**10.** (a)
11. (b)	**12.** (d)	**13.** (c)	**14.** (b)	**15.** (d)	**16.** (b)	**17.** (c)	**18.** (b)	**19.** (a)	**20.** (d)
21. (b)	**22.** (d)	**23.** (c)	**24.** (a)	**25.** (c)	**26.** (b)	**27.** (a)	**28.** (c)	**29.** (b)	**30.** (b)

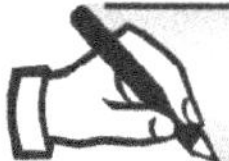

Explanations

For questions 1 and 2 :

First solve question 2. The word to fill the blank has to complement the word 'sustained'. 'Arduous', which means laborious or difficult is, therefore, right. Now for arduous and sustained negotiations, the period cannot be dire, monumental provocative. It has to be remarkable.

3. d 'sweltering' heat is the right usage. 'boiling heat' is a wrong expression.

4. b The blank has to be filled with a word that complements 'relief'. 'consolation' is the correct word.

5. d Here the meaning of 'flag' is to become limp or feeble. Contextually, this is the right answer.

6. b The answer is connected to the previous sentence. 'Not allow their efforts to flag' means to 'endeavour tirelessly'.

7. a A problem that cannot be solved is called an insurmountable problem.

8. c 'enduring' all odds and difficulties is the best answer choice available because one has to sustain or endure difficulties in order to find a solution.

9. d 'indefatigable' means 'never getting fatigued or tired'. Since it is implied that Sir Stafford Cripps is untiring, it has to be indefatigable energy.

10. a 'essentially' practical outlook is the best choice as it is expected to produce favourable results

11. b The correct sentence is - 'In spite of having my lunch, I still had the snack'.

12. d A — 'As we may run out of battery, we better take a spare one along'. B — 'We better take a spare battery along as we may run out of batteries'.

13. c 'You must go to Sir, otherwise you will feel worse' is the correct sentence.

14. b The correct sentence is - 'If we don't study for the examination, we will fail the examination'.

15. d None of A, B or C fits for a starter.

16. b 'Booty' is not cut, it is divided'.

17. c When there are more than two people, we use 'among'. We use 'between' for two people.

18. b 'I will do a post . . .' or 'I will go for a . . .' or 'I will pursue . . .' are the right phrases.

19. a For comparison of two things, we use the comparative degree 'easier'.

20. d The comparison is illogical as pollution is compared to Delhi. The better substitute is 'pollution of Mumbai is more than that in Delhi.'

21. b 'Because of' is the correct prepositional phrase. Hence, (b) is correct.

22. d 'Interfering in' other's affairs — is correct. It denotes 'intrusion' into a particular task.

23. c Though we commonly speak of 'going to' a place 'by foot', it is wrong English. The right usage is 'going on foot' to some place. However, when you use other modes of transportation like car or bus, you say, 'going by car/bus'.

24. a The answer is 'believe in' as you 'believe in' a concept. It is wrong to say 'believe about'.

25. c In English, we say that one is 'blind to' certain things, not 'blind against'.

26. b 'Neither' is a singular pronoun, therefore you use the singular verb 'has'.

27. a 'Everyone' is a singular pronoun; therefore, you use the complementary singular pronoun 'his'.

28. c 'Since' indicates a period of time that began in the past and still continues.

29. b One solves a problem 'through' some means.

30. b 'For' indicates a generic period of time while 'since' indicates a specific time period.

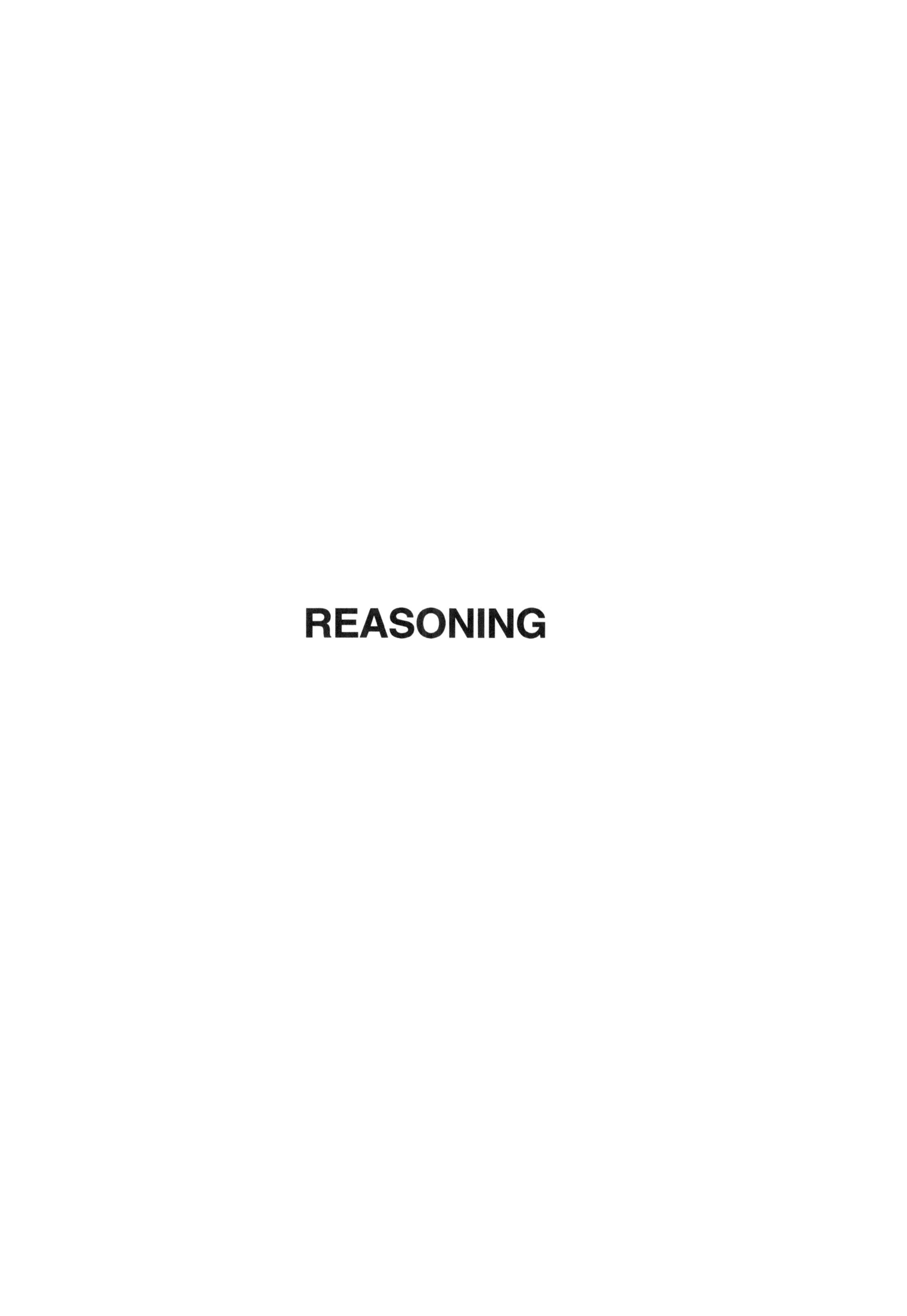

REASONING

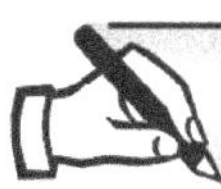

Practice Test-1

Number of questions: 30   **Time Allowed: 30 mins.**

Directions for questions 1 to 5: Answer the following questions based on the information given below.

XYZ Tourism arranges tours to six different cities, viz. A, B, C, D, E and F in the span of 7 days, i.e. from Monday to Sunday, as per following conditions:

I.   Tour to city A should not be organized on Friday.

II. Tour to city C should be organized immediately after tour to city F.

III. There should be a gap of two days between tour to city E and tour to city D.

IV. On one day, there won't be any tour.

V.   Tour to city B should be organized on Wednesday and should not be followed by tour to city D.

VI. On Saturday, tour has to be arranged to any one of the cities.

VII. Tour to city D must be followed by a holiday.

1. Which day is a holiday?
    (a) Tuesday   (b) Saturday
    (c) Monday   (d) Can't be determined

2. How many tours are to be organized between C and E?
    (a) None   (b) One
    (c) Two   (d) Can't be determined

3. On which day will the tour to city F be organized?
    (a) Friday   (b) Saturday
    (c) Sunday   (d) Monday

4. Which tour will be the last tour in this series?
    (a) A   (b) B
    (c) C   (d) Can't be determined

5. Which of the following information is not required in finding the complete sequence of tours?
    (a) I only   (b) II only
    (c) V only   (d) None of these

Directions for questions 6 and 7: In the following questions, a statement is followed by two explanatory statements numbered I and II. These explanatory statements have been given to answer the question asked in the main statement.

Choose your answer as:

(a) If the data in statement I alone is sufficient to answer the question.

(b) If the data in statement II alone is sufficient to answer the question.

(c) If the data in both the statements together is not sufficient to answer the question

(d) If the data in both the statements is needed to answer the question.

6. A test was conducted in a class of 50 students. The test was of 100 marks. Was 70 the average marks on a class test?
    I.   In the test, half of the class had marks below 70 and half of the class had marks above 70.
    II. The lowest marks in the test was 45 and the highest marks was 95.

7. Four books are kept on a rack. Yellow coloured book is to the right of blue coloured book. Black coloured book is to the right of red coloured book. Which colour book is to the extreme left?
    I.   Red coloured book is to the left of black coloured book.
    II. Black coloured book is to the left of blue coloured book.

Directions for questions 8 and 9: From the given options find the missing numbers to replace and complete the series.

8. 0.56, 1.12, 1.40, 1.54, ?
    (a) 3.99   (b) 1.61
    (c) 2.24   (d) 3.33

9. 5 8 13 9 13 17 13 18 21 17 23 ?
    (a) 25   (b) 27
    (c) 23   (d) 19

Directions for questions 10 and 11: Answer the questions independently.

10. If A + B means 'A is brother of B', A ÷ B means 'A is father of B' and A × B means 'A is sister of B', which of the following means 'M is uncle of P'?
    (a) M + N × P   (b) N × P ÷ M
    (c) M ÷ K × P   (d) M + N ÷ P

11. Pointing to an old man, Ramu said, "His son is my son's uncle." How is the old man related to Ramu?
    (a) Uncle   (b) Brother
    (c) Father   (d) Grandfather

Directions for questions 12 to 15: In the following questions, there are two statements followed by two conclusions numbered I and II. You have to take the given statements to be true even if they seem to be at variance with commonly known facts. Read the conclusions and then decide which of them logically follows.

Mark answer:

(a) If only conclusion I follows

(b) If only conclusion II follows

(c) If both conclusions I and II follow

(d) If neither conclusion I nor II follows

12. **Statements:**

    All girls are boys.

    Some boys are idiots.

    Conclusions:

    I.   All idiots are girls.

    II. All boys are girls.

13. **Statements:**

    All Chinese are dwarfs.

    Some dwarfs are Indians.

    Conclusions:

    I.   Some dwarfs are Chinese.

    II. Some dwarfs are not Indians.

14. **Statements:**

    All scientists are eccentric.

    Abhinav is eccentric.

    Conclusions:

    I.   Abhinav is a scientist.

    II. Some scientists are eccentric.

15. **Statements:**

    All cars are costly.

    No car is black.

    Conclusions:

    I.   Some cars are costly.

    II. Some cars are not black.

Directions for question 16 to 19: Answer the questions independently.

16. In a certain code language PROPER is coded as UWTUJW, what will be the code for EXTRACT in the same code language?

    (a) JYCWFHY   (b) JCYWHFY

    (c) JCYFWHY   (d) JCYWFHY

17. In a certain code language FATHER is coded as HCVJGT, what will be the code for HUMANITY in the same language?

    (a) JWODPKVA   (b) JWOCPKAV

    (c) JWOPCKVA   (d) JWOCPKVA

18. Sunil travelled 25 m straight towards the north. Then he took a left-turn and moved another 20 m. After that he took a left-turn and moved 50 m straight. Then he turned to his right and moved another 20 m. How far is he from the starting point?

    (a) 50 m   (b) 47.16 m

    (c) 65 m   (d) 68.42 m

19. A starts from his office and walks 3 km towards north. He then turns right and walks 2 km and then turns right and walks 5 km. He then turns right and walks 2 km, and then again turns right and walks 2 km. In which direction is he now from the starting point?

    (a) South

    (b) North-east

    (c) South-east

    (d) He is at the starting point

Directions for questions 20 to 24: Arrange the following sentences in a logical order and answer the questions that follow.

A. Well, they didn't really confiscate it.

B. The Security people had confiscated my cigar cutter.

C. And I was still annoyed.

D. I was fresh off a flight from Raleigh-Durham.

E. I heard the story at just the right time.

20. Which of the following should be the FIRST sentence?

    (a) B   (b) A

    (c) C   (d) E

21. Which of the following should be the SECOND sentence?

    (a) A   (b) E

    (c) B   (d) D

22. Which of the following should be the THIRD sentence?

    (a) E   (b) B

    (c) C   (d) A

23. Which of the following should be the FOURTH sentence?

    (a) A   (b) B

    (c) C   (d) D

24. Which of the following should be the FIFTH sentence?

    (a) A   (b) B

    (c) C   (d) D

Directions for questions 25 to 29: From the options given below, choose the one that best rearranges the letters given below to construct a meaningful word:

25. E O I S S R H P N C
    1 2 3 4 5 6 7 8 9 10

    (a) 10, 1, 9, 5, 2, 6, 4, 7, 3, 8

    (b) 6, 9, 5, 7, 10, 2, 1, 4, 8, 3

    (c) 4, 1, 10, 6, 9, 5, 8, 3, 7, 2

    (d) 3, 6, 2, 4, 7, 5, 1, 10, 8, 9

26. E A E R L B I R V O C
    1 2 3 4 5 6 7 8 9 10 11

    (a) 10, 4, 9, 11, 1, 5, 8, 3, 7, 2, 6

    (b) 1, 9, 11, 5, 8, 2, 10, 7, 3, 6, 4

    (c) 7, 10, 6, 8, 5, 2, 11, 9, 4, 1, 3

    (d) 7, 4, 8, 3, 9, 10, 11, 2, 6, 5, 1

27. O U S D R H
    1 2 3 4 5 6

    (a) 314652   (b) 154632

    (c) 365124   (d) 352641

28. T T I I W N
    1 2 3 4 5 6

    (a) 314652   (b) 154632

    (c) 643125   (d) 631542

29. I V O J L A
    1 2 3 4 5 6

    (a) 432156   (b) 432165

    (c) 231564   (d) 432561

30. There are five persons: Ram, Keshav, Lalit, Pawan and Prabhat. Lalit is older than Pawan but not younger than Keshav. Ram is older than Keshav but younger than Pawan. Who is the eldest?

    (a) Lalit

    (b) Prabhat

    (c) Ram

    (d) Can't be determined

Answer Key

1. (a)	**2.** (b)	**3.** (a)	**4.** (a)	**5.** (d)	**6.** (c)	**7.** (b)	**8.** (b)	**9.** (a)	**10.** (d)
11. (c)	**12.** (d)	**13.** (a)	**14.** (b)	**15.** (c)	**16.** (d)	**17.** (d)	**18.** (b)	**19.** (d)	**20.** (d)
21. (d)	**22.** (c)	**23.** (b)	**24.** (a)	**25.** (a)	**26.** (d)	**27.** (c)	**28.** (d)	**29.** (b)	**30.** (d)

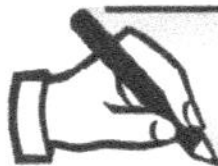

Explanations

For questions 1 to 5 :

The tours can be arranged in the following manner:

Monday	– D
Tuesday	– off
Wednesday	– B
Thursday	– E
Friday	– F
Saturday	– C
Sunday	– A

6. c Statement I cannot answer the problem.

   ∴ Suppose half of the class get 50 and half of the class get 72, then average of the class

   $= \dfrac{50+72}{2} = \dfrac{122}{2} = 61$ which is not 70.

   Statement II gives us the extreme values of the data. As extreme values doesn't help in determining the average value, so it doesn't give us the answer of the problem.

7. b With the given information, the only confusion is whether blue-coloured book or the red coloured book is at the extreme left. Statement I is just the reverse of the statement that black coloured book is to the right of red coloured book. Statement II says that black coloured book is to the left of blue coloured book. So blue book can't be the left most. So red book at the left most position.

8. b The series is moving as the difference between the consecutive terms is halved of the previous difference and is added to the next term of the series to continue the given series.

   1.12 – 0.56 = 0.56

   1.40 – 1.12 = 0.28

   1.54 – 1.40 = 0.14

   1.54 + 0.07 = 1.61

9. a There are three parallel series moving in the question such as (5, 9, 13, 17....), (8, 13, 18 , 23.....) and (13, 17, 21 , 25...).

10. d Among the given options only option (d) conveys that M is the uncle of P. As M is the brother of N and N is the father of P. Hence, we can conclude that M is the uncle of P.

11. c Ramu's son's uncle - Ramu's brother. So, the old man's son is Ramu's brother, i.e. the old man is Ramu's father.

For questions 12 to 15: Draw different types of Venn diagrams based on the statements and then draw common conclusions.

12. d 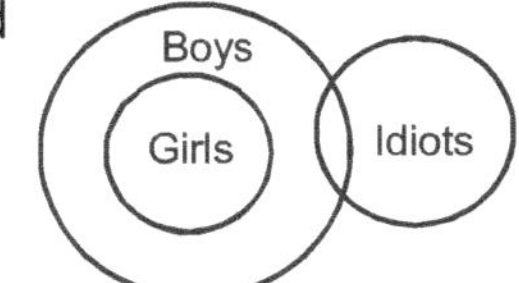

From the above venn diagram we can conclude that neither I nor II follows.

13. a 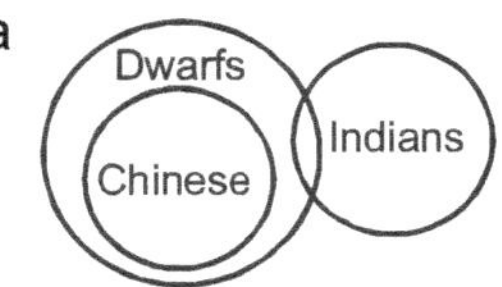

From the above venn diagram we can see that only I definitely follows. II does not follow because 'Some dwarfs are Indian' does not mean that 'Some dwarfs are not Indian'. This is an incorrect inference.

14. b 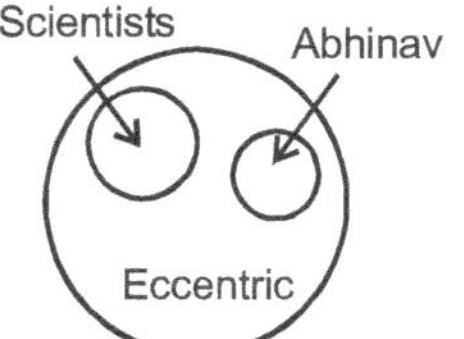

From the above venn diagram we can deduce that only II follows. Abhinav may or may not be a scientist.

15. c 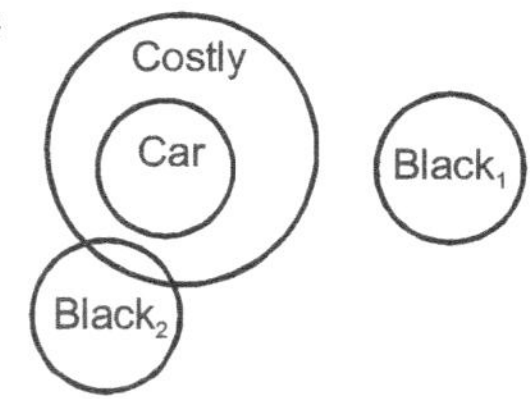

From the above venn diagram we can conclude that both I and II follow. 'Some' is included in 'All' - therefore 'some cars are costly' and 'some cars are not black'.

16. d The coding follows as

P(16) + 5 = U(21)	E(5) + 5 = J(10)
R(18) + 5 = W(23)	X(24) + 5 = C(3)
O(15) + 5 = T(20)	T(20) + 5 = Y(25)
P(16) + 5 = U(21)	R(18) + 5 = W(23)
E(5) + 5 = J(10)	A(1) + 5 = F(6)
R(18) + 5 = W(23)	C(3) + 5 = H(8)
	T(20) + 5 = Y(25)

17. d 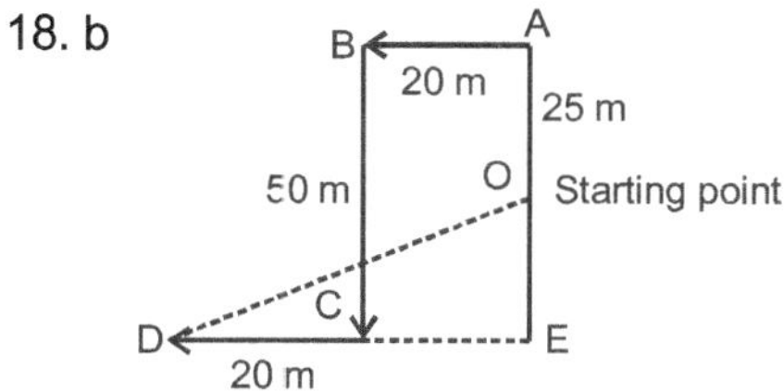

F(6) + 2	H(8)	H(8) + 2	J (10)
A(1) + 2	C(3)	U(21) + 2	W(23)
T(20) + 2	V(22)	M(13) + 2	O(15)
H(8) + 2	J(10)	A(1) + 2	C(3)
E(5) + 2	G(7)	N(14) + 2	P(16)
R(18) + 2	T(20)	I(9) + 2	K(11)
		T(20) + 2	V(22)
		Y(25) + 2	A(1)

18. b 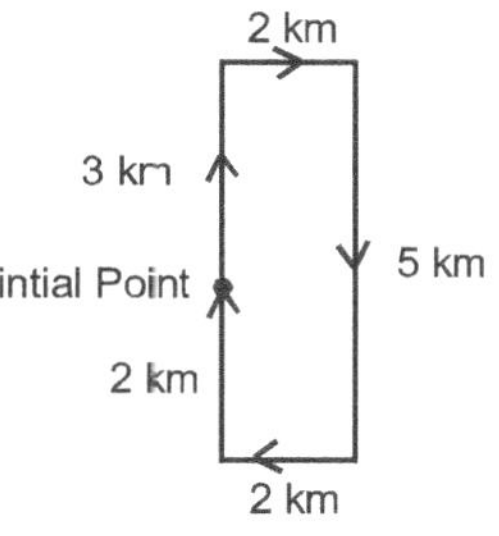

We have to find out

$$OD = \sqrt{OE^2 + ED^2} = \sqrt{(CB - OA)^2 + (EC + CD)^2}$$

$$= \sqrt{(25)^2 + (40)^2} = \sqrt{625 + 1600} = \sqrt{2225}$$

Therefore, OD = 47.16 m.

19. d The movement is:

For questions 20 to 24:

E is the opening sentence as it does not fit in anywhere else in the passage. The mandatory pair 'DC' follows E as it states where the story began (at the airport) and what were the author's feelings/ state of mind at that moment (annoyed). B follows as it states the reason for his annoyance and A follows it as the pronoun 'they' mentioned in A refers to 'the security people' mentioned in B. Hence, the correct sequence is 'EDCBA'.

For questions 25 to 29:

The sentence reads 'But the smiles suddenly turned into grins on the faces of cynics as the drug dragon surfaced over her head'.

25. a The word formed is CENSORSHIP. To solve this question unravel the first four letters only. It helps you to narrow down your choice to the right answer.

26. d To solve this question, first check 'a'. 10,4,9 sequence gives you 'ORV' this does not form any word. 1,9,11 of choice b gives you 'EVC', eject. Choice 'c' is also rejected for the same reason.

27. c SHROUD

28. d NITWIT

29. b JOVIAL

30. d Cannot be determined because there is no information about Prabhat.

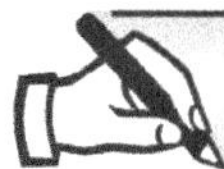

Practice Test-2

Directions for questions 1 to 5 : Arrange the following sentences in a logical order and answer the questions that follow.

A. Absence of other parental figures in the family has worsened the situation.

B. Drug abuse amongst youngsters seems to be on the increase.

C. The need for many mothers to work has put an additional claim on the time available for the children.

D. Breakdown of the extended family has put a lot of burden on the parent.

E. Psychologists attribute this to the growing alienation of the new generation from their parents.

1. Which sentence should be LAST in the paragraph?
   - (a) A
   - (b) B
   - (c) C
   - (d) D

2. Which sentence should come FIRST in the paragraph?
   - (a) A
   - (b) B
   - (c) E
   - (d) D

3. Which sentence should come FOURTH in the paragraph?
   - (a) A
   - (b) B
   - (c) C
   - (d) E

4. Which sentence should come SECOND in the paragraph?
   - (a) B
   - (b) C
   - (c) D
   - (d) E

5. Which sentence should come THIRD in the paragraph?
   - (a) A
   - (b) B
   - (c) C
   - (d) D

Directions for questions 6 to 10: Read the following information and answer the questions given under

There are five persons P, Q, R, S and T. One is a footballer, one is a cricketer, and one a table tennis player.

P & S are unmarried ladies and do not take part in any game. None of the ladies play football or cricket. There is a married couple in which T is a husband. Q is the brother of R and Q is neither a cricketer nor a table tennis player.

6. Who is the footballer ?
   - (a) Q
   - (b) R
   - (c) S
   - (d) T

7. Who is the table tennis player ?
   - (a) Q
   - (b) R
   - (c) S
   - (d) T

8. Who is the cricketer ?
   - (a) Q
   - (b) R
   - (c) S
   - (d) T

9. Who is the wife of T ?
   - (a) P
   - (b) S
   - (c) R
   - (d) Q

10. The three ladies in the group are.
    - (a) PQR
    - (b) PRS
    - (c) QRS
    - (d) PST

Directions for questions 11 and 12: In the following questions, a statement is followed by two explanatory statements numbered I and II. These explanatory statements have been given to answer the question asked in the main statement.

Choose your answer as:

(a) If the data in statement I alone is sufficient to answer the question.

(b) If the data in statement II alone is sufficient to answer the question.

(c) If the data in both the statements together is not sufficient to answer the question

(d) If the data in both the statements is needed to answer the question.

11. A and B are 2 sisters. P is A's friend. N is P's brother. X is M's best friend. Who is Y's friend?
    - I. Y is sister of X.
    - II. Z is very close to one of X or Y.

12. A child wants to buy 4 toys from a shop. His dad is not allowing him to buy the gun in the shop and has told him to buy anything else. The stock of dolls is no more with the shopkeeper. Which toy will the child surely buy?
    - I. The boy is fond of toy cars.
    - II. The toy car that the boy selected in the shop was most costly.

Directions for questions 13 and 14: Find the missing number in place of '?' from the options given in the questions.

13. 5, 9, 15, 23, 33, ?
    (a) 41   (b) 45
    (c) 48   (d) 49

14. 2, 4, 8, 14, 16, 22, ?
    (a) 24   (b) 25
    (c) 26   (d) 29

15. If Amar is the son of Mohan and Mohan is the son of Sohan, then how is Sohan related to Amar?
    (a) Father-in-law
    (b) Grandfather
    (c) Grandmother
    (d) Can't be determined

16. If 'A @ B' means 'A is sister of B'; 'A × B' means 'A is father of B'; and 'A – B' means 'A is brother of B'; then 'M is uncle of P' will be denoted by _____.
    (a) M @ K × P   (b) K – P @ M
    (c) M – K × P   (d) M × K – P

Directions for questions 17 to 20: In the following questions, there are two statements followed by two conclusions numbered I and II. You have to take the given statements to be true even if they seem to be at variance with commonly known facts. Read the conclusions and then decide which of them logically follows.

Mark answer:

(a) If only conclusion I follows

(b) If only conclusion II follows

(c) If both conclusions I and II follow

(d) If neither conclusion I nor II follows

17. **Statements:**
    All Indians are intellectuals.
    Some intellectuals are fools.
    Conclusions:
    I.   Some Indians are not intellectuals.
    II. All intellectuals are Indians.

18. **Statements:**
    Some students are hardworking.
    No hardworking is intelligent.
    Conclusions:
    I.   Students who are not hardworking are not intelligent.
    II. No intelligent is hardworking.

19. **Statements:**
    Some cats are rats.
    All bats are rats.
    Conclusions:
    I.   Some rats are bats.
    II. Cats which are not rats are bats.

20. **Statements:**
    All books are beautiful.
    No beautiful is good.
    Conclusions:
    I.   Some books are not beautiful.
    II. Some books are good.

21. In a certain code language ROMAN is coded as MZLNQ, what will be the code for ENGLISH in that code language?
    (a) GRHFKMD   (b) GRHKFND
    (c) GRHKFMD   (d) GRFHKMD

22. In a certain code language 'tin tun ton' stands for 'live the life', 'tun kun mun' stands for 'life and me', 'ton cot nus' stands for 'live your dreams', what will be the code for 'live' in that code language?
    (a) tun   (b) ton
    (c) tin   (d) mun

23. Ajay facing east, travelled 10 km straight, took a left turn and moved another 5 km and then took another left turn and moved further 10 km. How far is he from the starting point?
    (a) 15 km   (b) 5 km
    (c) 10 km   (d) 20 km

24. I am facing east. I turn 180° in the clockwise direction and then 135° in the anticlockwise direction. Which direction am I facing now?
    (a) East   (b) South-east
    (c) West   (d) South-west

25. In the English alphabet, which letter is exactly in between the 6th letter, from left, and 10th letter from right?
    (a) U   (b) V
    (c) H   (d) There is no such letter

Directions for questions 26 to 30: Answer the following questions based on the alphanumeric series given below.

O S 4 L 2 8 A J Q 3 C 7 E F 6 5 X 9 H G O V I M

26. Three of the following 4 characters are alike, with respect to their position in the above sequence, and form a group. Which is the one that does not belong to that group?

   (a) A   (b) E

   (c) J   (d) H

27. Which character is the 7th character to the right of the 13th character from the left-hand side, if the second half of the above series is reversed?

   (a) X

   (b) H

   (c) E

   (d) 3

28. If the first half of the above series is reversed and the second half is kept the same, how many such letters would you find which are immediately preceded by a letter and immediately followed by a number?

   (a) 1   (b) 4

   (c) 2   (d) None of these

29. Three of the following 4 characters (numbers) are alike, with respect to their positions in the above sequence, and form a group. Which is the one that does not belong to that group?

   (a) 4   (b) 3

   (c) 7   (d) 8

30. Which character is the 8th character to the left of the 12th character from the right-hand side, if the first half of the above series is reversed?

   (a) 6   (b) L

   (c) Q   (d) None of these

Answer Key

1. (d)	**2.** (b)	**3.** (a)	**4.** (d)	**5.** (c)	**6.** (a)	**7.** (b)	**8.** (d)	**9.** (c)	**10.** (b)
11. (c)	**12.** (b)	**13.** (b)	**14.** (c)	**15.** (d)	**16.** (c)	**17.** (d)	**18.** (b)	**19.** (a)	**20.** (d)
21. (c)	**22.** (b)	**23.** (b)	**24.** (b)	**25.** (d)	**26.** (c)	**27.** (a)	**28.** (c)	**29.** (d)	**30.** (d)

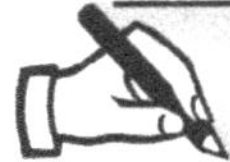

Explanations

For questions 1 to 5:

B is the opening sentence as it states the subject of the passage i.e. 'Drug abuse amongst youngsters'. E follows as the word 'this' mentioned in it refers to the 'drug abuse' mentioned in B. 'CA' forms a mandatory pair as C continues the point stated in E, that alienation from parents is responsible for increased drug abuse, by blaming the mother. A follows as it refers to 'other parental figures' apart from the mother. D is the last sentence as it continues the earlier statements in an extended mode. Hence, the correct sequence is 'BECAD'.

For questions 6 to 10:

The information can be collated in the form of a table as shown below.

Person	Gender	Game	Wife/Husband
P	Female	–	–
Q	Male	Footballer	–
R	Female	T.T.	Wife of T
S	Female	–	–
T	Male	Cricketer	Husband of R

6. a Q is the footballer.

7. b R is the Table Tennis player.

8. d T is the cricketer.

9. c R is the wife of T.

10. b P & S are ladies as given in the initial information. R is the wife of T. Hence the ladies in the group are PRS.

11. c Even both the statements together are unable to answer the problem as the problem involves friends.

12. b Statement II implies that the toy car that the boy liked was available in the shop. Also given that his father has allowed him to buy anything other than toy gun. So he must buy the toy car.

13. b The series is the $1^2 + 4$, $2^2 + 5$, $3^2 + 6$, $4^2 + 7$, $5^2 + 8$ and the next term would be $6^2 + 9$.

14. c Multiples of 2 excluding multiples of 3 or 5.

15. d Can't be determined because we don't know the sex of Sohan.

16. c Obviously (c) as M is brother of K who is father of P

For questions 17 to 20:

Draw the different types of Venn diagrams based on the given statements. The valid conclusion is the one which is common in all different Venn diagrams.

17. d 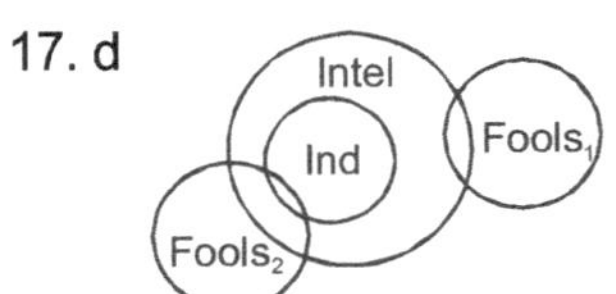

From the given venn diagram we can see that neither conclusion I nor II follows.

18. b 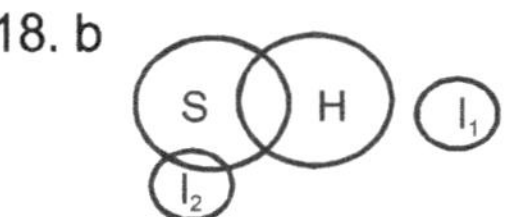

From the given venn diagram we can see that conclusion II definitely follows.

19. a 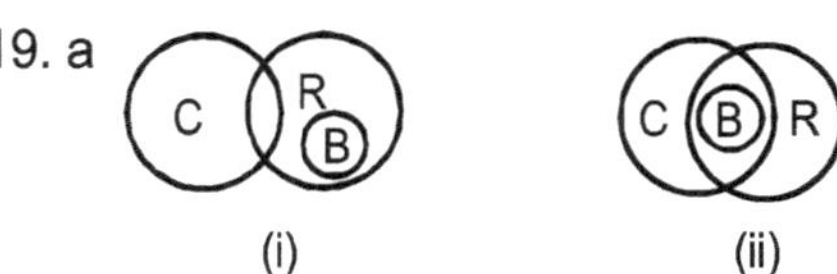

There are 2 possible venn diagrams for this. When we observe both of them, we see that only conclusion I definitely follows.

20. d 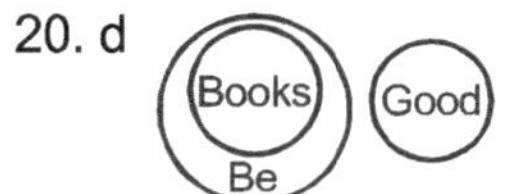

None of the given conclusions follows.

21. c The coding follows as

 R(1) – 1 = M(5) E(1) – 1 = G(7)
 O(2) – 1 = Z(4) N(2) – 1 = R(6)
 M(3) – 1 = L(3) G(3) – 1 = H(5)
 A(4) – 1 = N(2) L(4) – 1 = K(4)
 N(5) – 1 = Q(1) I(5) – 1 = F(3)
         S(6) – 1 = M(2)
         H(7) – 1 = D(1)

22. b From (I) and (III) we get 'ton' = 'live'.

23. b 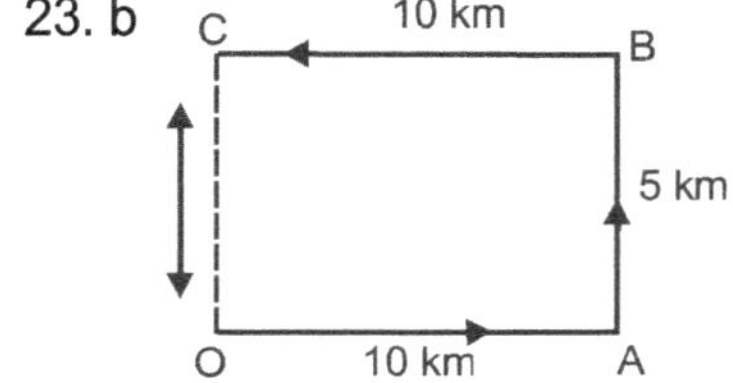

24. b 180° CW + 135° ACW = 180 − 135 = 45° CW

So he will be facing in south-east, which is equal to 45° clockwise turn.

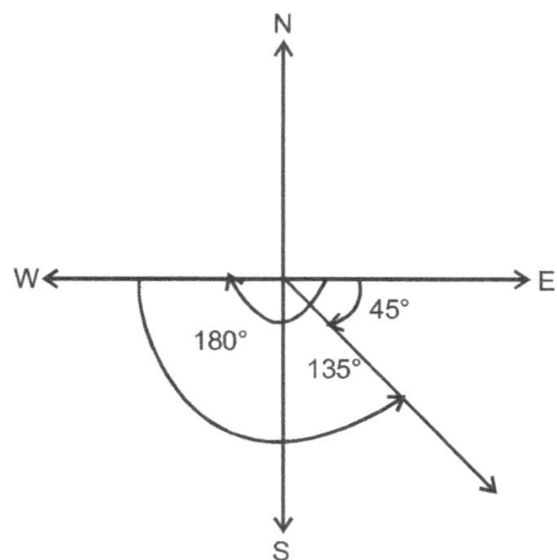

25. d Tenth letter from right end = 17th letter from left end, so midway letter in $\dfrac{6+17}{2} = \dfrac{23}{2}$ hence, there is no such letter.

26. c Except for J, all other options are in between a number or a letter.

27. a If the above half of the series is reversed then the given series would look like as

O S 4 L 2 8 A J Q 3 C 7 M I V O G H 9 X 5 6 F E

Hence, the 7th character to the right of the 13th character from the left hand side is X.

28. c If the first half of the series is reversed then the given series would look like as

7 C 3 Q J A 8 2 L 4 S O E F 6 5 X 9 H G O V I M

There are only two such letters.

29. d Except for the number 8, all the others are between two English letters.

30. d After the reversal of the first half

7C3QJA82L4SOEF65X9HGOVIM

The 12th character from the right is the letter 'O' and the 8th character to its left is the 'J'.

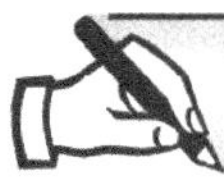# Practice Test-3

Directions for questions 1 to 4: In the following questions, there are two statements followed by two conclusions numbered I and II. You have to take the given statements to be true even if they seem to be at variance with commonly known facts. Read the conclusions and then decide which of them logically follows.

Mark answer:

(a) If only conclusion I follows

(b) If only conclusion II follows

(c) If both conclusions I and II follow

(d) If neither conclusion I nor II follows

1. **Statements:**

   Some cities are villages.

   Some towns are villages.

   Conclusions:

   I. Some cities are towns.

   II. No town is a city.

2. **Statements:**

   Some visitors are Indians.

   Some visitors are Americans.

   Conclusions:

   I. Some Indians are visitors.

   II. All Indians are visitors.

3. **Statements:**

   All books are pencils.

   Some pencils are cycles.

   Conclusions:

   I. Some cycles are pencils.

   II. Some cycles are books.

4. **Statements:**

   All pencils are pens.

   No pen is a book.

   Conclusions:

   I. No pencil is a book.

   II. Some pens are pencils.

Directions for questions 5 and 6: In the following questions, a statement is followed by two explanatory statements numbered I and II. These explanatory statements have been given to answer the question asked in the main statement.

Choose your answer as :

(a) If the data in statement I alone is sufficient to answer the question.

(b) If the data in statement II alone is sufficient to answer the question.

(c) If the data in both the statements together is not sufficient to answer the question

(d) If the data in both the statements is needed to answer the question.

5. How many girls does R have?

   I. A and B are brothers of S.

   II. H is the wife of R and mother of S.

6. Who is the tallest amongst A, B, C, D and E?

   I. C and D are taller than E but smaller than A and B.

   II. E is not the tallest

7. Mr. Ajay started from his house, walked 4 km north, then 6 km west, then 12 km south. How far away from his home was he then?

   (a) 8 km   (b) 5 km

   (c) 20 km   (d) 10 km

8. Aditya faces north and covers 24 km; turns west and covers 12 km, then turns south and covers 6 km, and turns west again and covers 12 km. In which direction is he moving?

   (a) South-east   (b) North-east

   (c) North-west   (d) South-west

9. In a certain code language EXPLOSIVE is coded as 567361945, what will be the code for COURAGE in the same code language?

   (a) 3639165   (b) 3839175

   (c) 3369175   (d) 3639175

10. In a certain code language 'cut pin luck' is coded as 'cool your temper', ' luck sick tick' is coded as 'temper is flexible' and 'cut min but' is coded as 'cool are fools', what is the code for 'is' in the same code language?

    (a) cut   (b) sick

    (c) pin   (d) Can't be determined

Directions for questions 11 to 15: Read the given information and answer the questions that follow.

I. A, B, C, D and E are five friends.

II. B earns more than E, but is as tall as C.

III. C earns less than A, but is taller than D and E.

IV. A is taller than D, but earns less than E.

V. D earns more than A, but is the shortest in the group.

11. Who among the following earns the highest?

    (a) A or B   (b) B or D

    (c) C or B   (d) D or E

12. Which of the following pair earns more than D?

    (a) BA   (b) BC

    (c) BE   (d) Can't be determined

13. Which of the following statements is/are correct about B?

    I. B is not the tallest.

    II. B is shorter to E.

    III. If they are arranged in ascending order of their heights, B will be at the centre.

    (a) Only I is correct

    (b) Only I and II are correct

    (c) All are correct

    (d) All are incorrect

14. If an another friend, F, who is taller than C, how many of them will be between F and E according to their heights?

    (a) None   (b) One

    (c) Two   (d) Can't be determined

15. Which of the following represents the correct order of earning of any four friends?

    (a) E > A > B > C   (b) A > B > E > D

    (c) B > E > A > C   (d) A > E > B > C

Directions for questions 16 and 17: Find the missing number in place of '?' from the options given in the questions.

16. 5, 10, 20, 25, 35, 40?

    (a) 45   (b) 55

    (c) 75   (d) 50

17. 1, 1.5, 2.5, 3.5, 5.5, ?

    (a) 6   (b) 6.5

    (c) 7   (d) 7.5

18. Ram and Shyam are brothers; Sita is Shyam's sister; Ajay is grandfather of Ram. What will be Ram to Sita's son Mahesh?

    (a) Father   (b) Son

    (c) Uncle   (d) Grandfather

19. If Lov's son Winnowa who has two daughters, two brothers and one sister, how many children does Lov have?

    (a) 3   (b) 4

    (c) 5   (d) Data inadequate

Directions for questions 20 to 24: In a certain code the symbol of 0 is $\otimes$ and 1 is $\oplus$. There are no other symbols for other numbers and all numbers greater than 1 are written using these two symbols only. The value of symbol $\oplus$ doubles itself every time it shifts one place to the left.

    0 is written $\otimes$,   1 is written $\oplus$

    2 is written $\oplus \otimes$,   3 is written $\oplus \oplus$

    4 is written $\oplus \otimes \otimes$

20. Which of the following represents the value of 70% of 10?

    (a) $\oplus \oplus \oplus$ (b) $\oplus \oplus \otimes \otimes$

    (c) $\oplus \oplus \otimes$ (d) None of these

21. What is the value of $\dfrac{6}{5} \times \dfrac{5}{3} \times \dfrac{2}{3} \times \dfrac{9}{2} = ?$

    (a) $\oplus \otimes \oplus$ (b) $\oplus \oplus \otimes$

    (c) $\oplus \oplus \oplus$ (d) $\oplus \otimes \otimes$

22. If $\oplus \oplus \oplus \oplus \otimes$ is divided by $\oplus \oplus \otimes$, what will be the result?

    (a) $\oplus \oplus \oplus$ (b) $\oplus \oplus \otimes$

    (c) $\oplus \otimes \oplus$ (d) None of these

23. Which of the following represents 15?

    (a) $\oplus \otimes \otimes \oplus$ (b) $\oplus \oplus \oplus \oplus$

    (c) $\oplus \oplus \oplus \otimes$ (d) $\oplus \oplus \otimes \oplus$

24. Which of the following represents 15% of 80?

    (a) $\oplus \oplus \otimes \otimes$ (b) $\oplus \oplus \oplus$

    (c) $\oplus \otimes \otimes \oplus$ (d) $\oplus \otimes \oplus \oplus$

Directions for question 25: Of the options provided, choose the one that best rearranges the letters given below to construct a meaningful word. Then indicate the first letter of the word so formed.

25. e   a   o   a   c   u   m   g   l   f

    1   2   3   4   5   6   7   8   9   10

    (a) c   (b) e

    (c) m   (d) f

Directions for questions 26 to 30: Arrange the following sentences in a logical order to form coherent paragraph.

26. A. The survey conducted by 12 consumer organisations which ordered more than 150 items from 17 countries has found that almost all consumer rights like safety and privacy have been infringed.

   B. An international comparative study of electronic commerce conducted by Consumers International, Malaysia, found that Internet shopping is more risky than the usual visit to the   market place.

   C. For even before Internet shopping can take roots and gain the acceptance of consumers, several unfair trade practices of retailers setting up shops on the world wide web have come to light.

   D. Consumers who want to shop through the Internet had better watch out.

   (a) BACD   (b) BDAC
   (c) ABCD   (d) DCBA

27. A. Currently, the term deposit rates of maturity of over three years are around 10 per cent.

   B. The continuous low inflation rates at around two per cent might prompt the RBI to take measures to reduce interest rates in the busy season credit policy to be announced on October 29.

   C. Such measures are likely to result in reduction in the term deposit rates.

   D. To this end, the Central Bank might decide to reduce the bank rates and the stipulated ratio of total deposits held by commercial banks to be maintained in the RBI.

   (a) ABCD   (b) ACDB
   (c) BDCA   (d) BCDA

28. A. And there hasn't been any drastic increase in the number of nuclear weapons recently; I think we have come far.

   B. In the earlier days, when there was a race to acquire more and more nuclear weapons, the problem was that of preventing the actual use of nuclear weapons.

   C. Pugwash was set up to encourage dialogue between the political leadership and the scientific community to prevent things from getting out of hand.

   D. It played an important part in bringing about significant reductions in the nuclear arsenal of Russia and brought about various treaties.

   (a) BCDA   (b) BDCA
   (c) CBAD   (d) CABD

29. A. The Doha experience must serve as a lesson for Indian negotiators who will have to prepare the political leadership for such an eventuality and provide escape routes.

   B. Trade analysts view the negotiations as more or less over, following the agreement between the US and the EU on farm and non-farm sector issues, and that Cancun will just be a forum seeking formal endorsement of the WTO membership on the proposals mooted by the duo.

   C. One might view this assessment as borne out of pessimism without realizing the inherent strength of the developing world.

   D. The 'eternal optimists' have cited the latest draft declaration circulated by WTO on agriculture.

   E. The draft provides for special and differential treatment to developing countries on scaling down their tariffs.

   (a) ABCDE   (b) DCABE
   (c) CDAEB   (d) BCADE

30. A. Front-ending for the US pharma lobby, the Bush administration made a serious attempt to seek 'comfort' letters from India and Brazil, the two countries with excess capacities that can provide generic versions of US patented drugs at $\frac{1}{30}$ th the cost.

   B. Both India and Brazil rejected the US demand.

   C. The argument put forth by Robert Zoellick and US negotiators was that these comfort letters were meant to prevent misuse of compulsory licences for commercial purpose, rather than for a humanitarian cause.

   (a) ABC   (b) CAB
   (c) ACB   (d) BAC

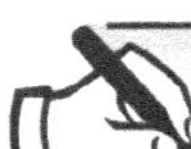

Answer Key

1. (d)	**2.** (a)	**3.** (a)	**4.** (c)	**5.** (c)	**6.** (c)	**7.** (d)	**8.** (c)	**9.** (d)	**10.** (d)
11. (b)	**12.** (d)	**13.** (a)	**14.** (d)	**15.** (c)	**16.** (d)	**17.** (b)	**18.** (c)	**19.** (b)	**20.** (a)
21. (b)	**22.** (c)	**23.** (b)	**24.** (a)	**25.** (a)	**26.** (d)	**27.** (c)	**28.** (a)	**29.** (a)	**30.** (c)

Explanations

1. d From the venn diagram we can deduce that neither I nor II follows.

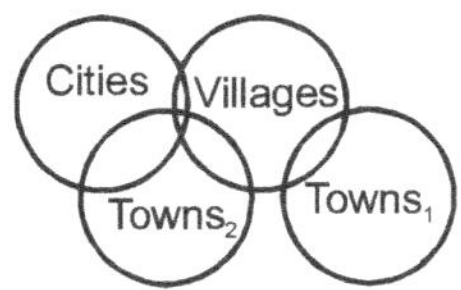

2. a

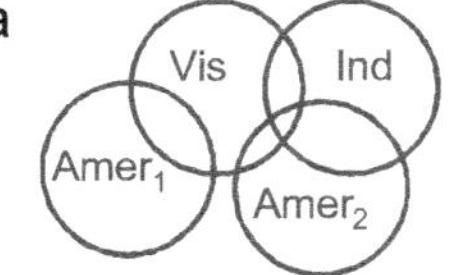

From the given venn diagram we can see only I follows.

3. a

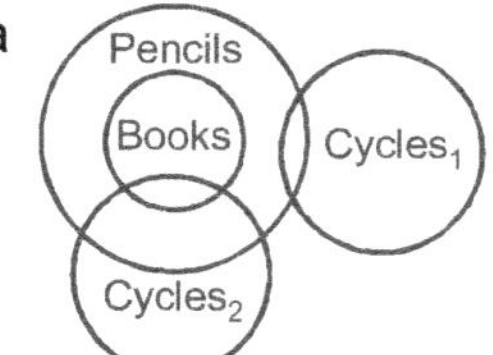

Only I definitely follows. Some cycles may or may not be books.

4. c

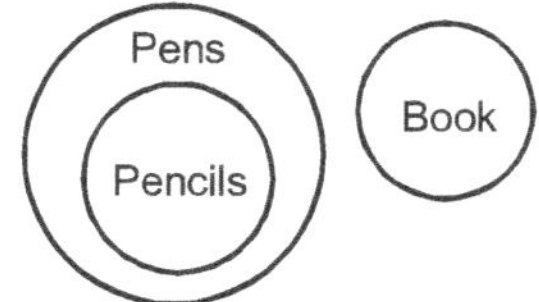

From the given venn diagram we can see that both I and II follow.

5. c Choice (c) holds good here as even after combining statements (I) and (II) we cannot conclude the number of girls that R has as the sex of S is not known.

6. c Choice (c) holds good again as, no definite conclusion can be drawn out of it.

7. d

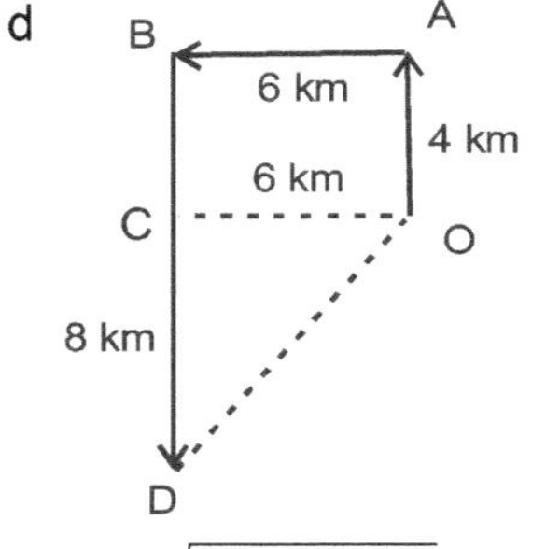

$OD = \sqrt{(OC)^2 + (CD)^2}$; $OD = \sqrt{6^2 + 8^2}$
$= \sqrt{36 + 64} = \sqrt{100} = 10$ km

8. c

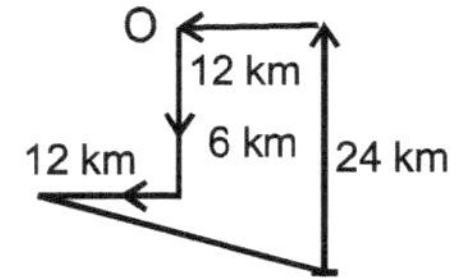

9. d Each letter is coded by the number which represents it in alphabetical sequence and if the position is in two digits, then it is represented by a single digit (which will be sum of those two digits), i.e code for S = its alphabetical position, is

$= 19 \Rightarrow 1 + 9 = 10 \Rightarrow 1 + 0 = 1.$

Hence, $S \Rightarrow 1.$

$C(3) = 3$

$O(15) = 1 + 5 = 6$

$U(21) = 2 + 1 = 3$

$R(18) = 1 + 8 = 9$

$A(1) = 1$

$G(7) = 7$

$E(5) = 5$

Hence, COURAGE would be coded as 3639175.

10. d From I and II, 'luck' = 'temper'; from I and III, 'cut' = 'cool'. But code for 'is' cannot be determined.

11. b Either B or D's earning would be highest.

12. d Again we are not certain.

13. a B is not the tallest.

14. d Since we don't know the exact sequence according to the height, we can't be sure.

15. c According to the question choice (c) is right.

16. d Multiples of 5 excluding multiples of 15.

17. b Prime number/2

18. c As Sita is sister of Ram, then Sita's son Mahesh would be the nephew of Ram or Ram will be his uncle.

19. b Lov has 4 children.

For questions 20 to 24:

$\oplus$ and $\otimes$ give the binary representation of the numbers 1 and 0. Arrange the numbers accordingly.

25. a The answer is CAMOUFLAGE.

26. d 'DC' forms a mandatory pair as in D the author states that consumers should watch out and C gives the reason behind the author's statement. Hence, 'DCBA' is the correct sequence.

27. c B is the opening sentence as it gives the subject of the passage i.e. low inflation rates and RBI's decision to take measures for the same. This is followed by D, which states the measures. C follows D as it also refers to the measures. 'CA' forms a mandatory pair as both C and A refer to 'term deposit rates'. Hence, 'BDCA' is the correct sequence.

28. a 'BC' is a mandatory pair as B gives a problem and C states its solution. D follows C as the pronoun 'it' mentioned in D refers to the 'dialogue' mentioned in C. Hence, 'BCDA' is the correct sequence.

29. a A opens the passage as it talks about the 'negotiations', which is the subject of the passage and has been discussed in sentence B as well. 'BC' forms a mandatory pair because the phrase 'this assessment' stated in C refers to B. 'DE' forms a mandatory pair as 'the draft' mentioned in E was introduced in sentence D.

30. c 'AC' is a mandatory pair as C refers to the 'comfort' letters that have been previously stated in Sentence A. B follows as it states the Indian and Brazilian response to the US's demand for 'comfort' letters. Hence, 'ACB' is the correct sequence.

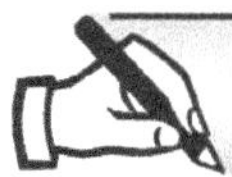

Practice Test-4

Directions for questions 1 to 5: Arrange the following sentences in a logical order to make a coherent paragraph.

1. A. Indeed, the very term would to him be most objectionable, and reeking of moral laxity.

   B. To the moralist of the Western tradition, 'business ethics' would make no sense.

   C. The authorities on ethics disagreed, of course, on what constitutes the grounds of morality — whether they be divine, human nature, or the needs of society.

   D. They equally disagreed on the specific rules of ethical behaviour.

   (a) DACB   (b) BACD
   (c) ADBC   (d) CBAD

2. A. A number of other trees exceed the largest animals in weight, and a still greater number in volume.

   B. The largest animals are whales, some of which considerably exceed one hundred tonnes in weight.

   C. They are not only the largest existing animals, but by far the largest which have ever existed.

   D. The largest trees are the big trees of California with a weight of nearly a thousand tonnes.

   (a) DABC   (b) DCAB
   (c) BADC   (d) CDAB

3. A. The answer: observe carefully how people do things.

   B. How do you get new product ideas?

   C. That is a problem that haunts many corporates.

   D. In other words, how do you get customer insight?

   (a) BADC   (b) ABDC
   (c) BDCA   (d) BACD

4. A. The liberal view grants equal rights and chances to every citizen irrespective of her caste, creed or colour.

   B. The communitarian approach is more interventionist in a manner which expects the state to safeguard the traditions and cultural forms of the minorities.

   C. The apex court's perceptions, however, give rise to two important questions relating to our political culture: By implication it asks whether the identity of an individual Indian citizen as a member of ethnic, cultural, or religious groups has any public relevance.

   D. If that is the case, how should such collective identities exist within the framework of constitutional democracy without having to suffer marginalisation?

   E. The Supreme Court's observations appear to be a kind of a combination of liberal and communitarian views.

   (a) DACBE   (b) BADCE
   (c) CDEAB   (d) ABCDE

5. A. There needs to be a political culture, which is to be shared equally by all citizens independent of their respective religious or cultural identity.

   B. The state and its legal order, however, must maintain neutrality vis-à-vis these subcultures, which are pre-political forms of life and traditions.

   C. How does this neutrality express itself? Remaining neutral means – and this is the critical edge of neutrality– decoupling the majority culture from the political culture with which it was originally fused, according to German philosopher Juergen Habermas.

   D. But this shared political culture should remain neutral and separated from all particularist cultures and collective identities, which are surely entitled to equal co-existence within society.

   (a) ABCD   (b) DACB
   (c) ADBC   (d) CADB

Directions for questions 6 and 7: Of the options provided, choose the one that best rearranges the letters given below to construct a meaningful word, and then indicate the first letter of the word so formed.

6. q   t   e   r   s   e   u
   1   2   3   4   5   6   7

   (a) r   (b) q
   (c) e   (d) u

7. t r v e e x
   1 2 3 4 5 6

   (a) v   (b) e
   (c) r   (d) t

Directions for questions 8 and 9 : Of the options provided, choose the one that best rearranges the letters given below to construct a meaningful word, and then indicate the last letter of the word so formed.

8. h n y o u i s g
   1 2 3 4 5 6 7 8

   (a) h   (b) y
   (c) u   (d) i

9. p u r c t m o e
   1 2 3 4 5 6 7 8

   (a) t   (b) p
   (c) m   (d) r

10. If it is possible to make a meaningful word with the third, sixth and ninth letters of RESTAURANT, then what will be the first letter of the word? If no such word is possible, then mark 'X' as your answer. If more than one such word is possible, then mark 'M' as your answer.

    (a) M   (b) N
    (c) S   (d) X

11. If starting from the left, the first and the seventh, the second and the eighth, the third and the ninth and so on, letters of RELATIONSHIP are interchanged; what will be the third letter from the right, if the second half of the new word thus formed is reversed?

    (a) T   (b) L
    (c) A   (d) E

12. In a certain code language FRAGMENTS is coded as STERNMFAG, what will be the code for MONITERED in the same code language?

    (a) DEEORTNMI   (b) DEOERTMNI
    (c) DEEROTMNI   (d) DEEORTMNI

13. In a certain code language MENTAL is coded as LNDFMOSUZBKM, what will be the code for TEST in the same language?

    (a) UVFGTIIV   (b) RSCDQRRS
    (c) SUDFQRSM   (d) SUDFRTSU

14. A is the son of P, while P is the daughter of R, if S is the wife of R, then how is A related to R?

    (a) Son   (b) Uncle
    (c) Grandson   (d) Brother

15. Pointing to a woman in a photograph a man says: "This woman is the mother-in-law of the only daughter of my mother-in-law." How is the man related to the woman?

    (a) Son   (b) Husband
    (c) Brother   (d) Father-in-law

16. Starting from point O, Vivek walked 40 m towards south, then he turned left and walked 60 m. He again turned left and walked 40 m. He once again turned left and walked 80 m and reached point D. How far and in which direction is D from O?

    (a) 20 m east   (b) 40 m west
    (c) 20 m west   (d) 20 m south

17. Uttam ran 40 m east; then turned right and ran 20 m; and then turned to right and ran 18 m; and again turned to left and ran 10 m; and then turned to left and ran 24 m. Finally turned to left and ran 12 m. In which direction is he running now?

    (a) West   (b) North
    (c) South   (d) East

Directions for questions 18 and 19: In each of the questions given below, find the missing number in place of '?' so as to continue the series.

18. 4, 9, 25, 49, 121, ?

    (a) 144   (b) 153
    (c) 169   (d) 199

19. 0, 3, 8, 15, ?

    (a) 18   (b) 24
    (c) 27   (d) 32

Directions for questions 20 to 24: Read the given information and answer the following questions.

Four young men Amar, Bimal, Chaman and Dinkar are friendly with four girls Anamika, Bhawna, Chetna and Deepika. Anamika and Chetna are friends. Chaman's girlfriend does not like Anamika and Chetna. Bhawna does not care for Chaman. Bimal's girlfriend is friendly with Anamika. Anamika does not like Amar.

20. Who is Amar's girlfriend?

    (a) Deepika   (b) Anamika
    (c) Chetna   (d) Bhawna

21. With whom is Anamika friendly?

    (a) Amar   (b) Bimal
    (c) Chaman   (d) Dinkar

22. Who is Deepika's boyfriend?

    (a) Amar   (b) Chaman
    (c) Bimal   (d) Chetna

23. Who does not like Anamika and Chetna?

    (a) Amar   (b) Deepika

    (c) Dinkar   (d) Chaman

24. How many pairs of boyfriend-girlfriend start their names with consecutive alphabet?

    (a) 1   (b) 0

    (c) 2   (d) 3

Directions for questions 25 and 26 : In the following questions, a statement is followed by two explanatory statements numbered I and II. These explanatory statements have been given to answer the question asked in the main statement.

Choose your answer as:

(a) If the data in statement I alone is sufficient to answer the question.

(b) If the data in statement II alone is sufficient to answer the question.

(c) If the data in both the statements together is not sufficient to answer the question

(d) If the data in both the statements is needed to answer the question.

25. Who is the sister of P?

    I. R and P are brother and sister of T.

    II. T is the youngest son of Z who is the father of R, P and T.

26. When is Manish's birthday?

    I. Manish was born between 20th of May and 22nd of May (both days being included).

    II. Manish's birthday is on an even-digit based date.

Directions for questions 27 to 30: In the following questions, there are two statements followed by two conclusions numbered I and II. You have to take the given statements to be true even if they seem to be at variance with commonly known facts. Read the conclusions and then decide which of them logically follows.

Mark answer:

(a) If only conclusion I follows

(b) If only conclusion II follows

(c) If both conclusions I and II follow

(d) If neither conclusion I nor II follows

27. **Statements:**

    All puppets are dolls.

    All dolls are toys.

    Conclusions:

    I. Some toys are puppets.

    II. All toys are puppets.

28. **Statements:**

    Some apples are oranges.

    Some oranges are bananas.

    Conclusions:

    I. Some apples are bananas.

    II. Some bananas are apples.

29. **Statements:**

    Some players are singers.

    All singers are tall.

    Conclusions:

    I. Some players are tall.

    II. All players are tall.

30. **Statements:**

    All coins are crows.

    Some crows are pens.

    Conclusions:

    I. No pen is coin.

    II. Some coins are pens.

Answer Key

1. (b)	**2.** (a)	**3.** (c)	**4.** (d)	**5.** (c)	**6.** (a)	**7.** (a)	**8.** (a)	**9.** (d)	**10.** (c)
11. (b)	**12.** (d)	**13.** (d)	**14.** (c)	**15.** (a)	**16.** (c)	**17.** (b)	**18.** (c)	**19.** (b)	**20.** (d)
21. (d)	**22.** (b)	**23.** (b)	**24.** (d)	**25.** (d)	**26.** (c)	**27.** (a)	**28.** (d)	**29.** (a)	**30.** (d)

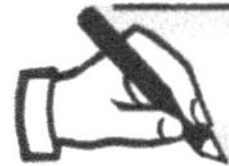

Explanations

1. b B introduces the term 'business ethics' while A explains the effect of this term. Hence, 'BA' is a mandatory pair. Also 'authorities on ethics' in C are referred to as 'they' in D. Hence, 'BACD' is the correct sequence.

2. a The 'big trees' of D is followed by 'other trees' of A and 'whales' of B are described in C. Hence, 'DABC' is the correct sequence.

3. c B starts with a question. D rephrases the question. C states that the question mentioned in D is a problem that haunts many corporates. A provides the solution and concludes. Hence, 'BDCA' is the correct sequence.

4. d A and B state two arguments, C takes its further with 'however', then D and E follow. Hence, 'ABCDE' is the correct sequence.

5. c A is the opening sentence as it states the subject of the discussion - need of a political culture. 'AD' forms a mandatory pair as 'this shared political culture' (mentioned in D) has already been stated in A. Finally 'BC' follows as the phrase 'this neutrality', mentioned in C refers to the 'neutrality' already suggested in B. Hence, 'ADBC' is the correct sequence.

6. a The answer is REQUEST.

7. a The answer is VERTEX

8. a The answer is YOUNGISH.

9. d The answer is COMPUTER.

10. c [SUN]

11. b When the 1st and 7th, 2nd and 8th, 3rd and 9th letters are interchanged the new arrangement is like ONSHIPRELATI. When the second half of the series is reversed the new arrangement will look like ONSHIPITALER. Hence, the 3rd letter from the right is L.

12. d The coding follows as

F(1) = S(9)	M(1) = D(9)
R(2) = T(8)	O(2) = E(8)
A(3) = E(6)	N(3) = E(6)
G(4) = R(2)	I(4) = O(2)
M(5) = N(7)	T(5) = R(7)
E(6) = M(5)	E(6) = T(5)
N(7) = F(1)	R(7) = M(1)
T(8) = A(3)	E(8) = N(3)
S(9) = G(4)	D(9) = I(4)

13. d The coding follows as

MENTAL is coded as **LMNDEFMNOSTUZABKLM.** Similarly, TEST would be coded as **STUDEFRSTSTU or SUDFRTSU.**

14. c With the help of this family diagram we can solve this question.

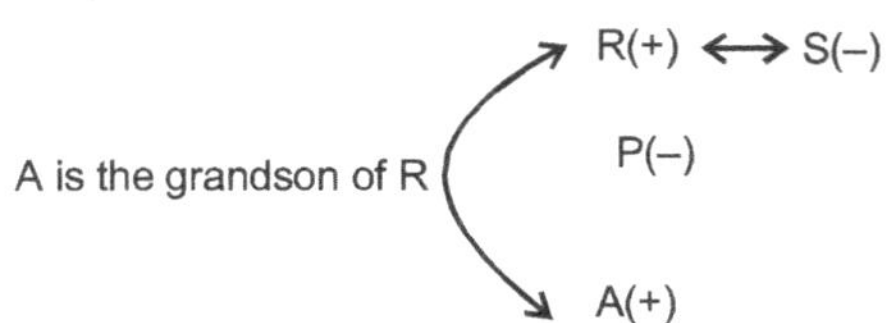

15. a [Only daughter of my mother-in-law = my wife. Mother-in-law of my wife = my mother].

16. c

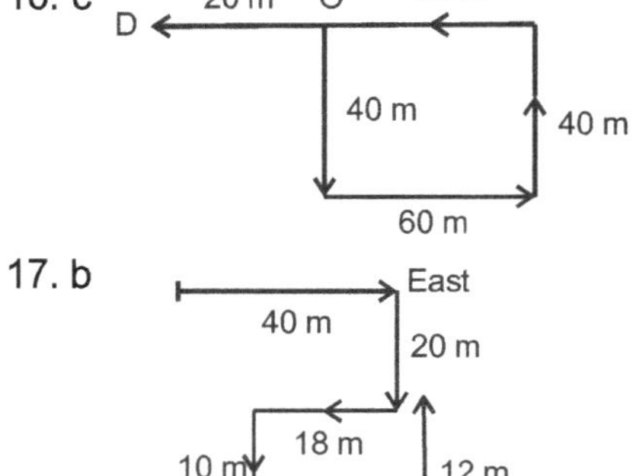

17. b

18. c Squares of prime numbers.

19. b $x^2 - 1$. The terms of the series are formed by $x^2 - 1$ where x = 1, 2, etc.

For questions 20 to 24:

Anamika and Chetna are friends and Bimal's girl friend is friendly with. Anamika. This means Bimal's girlfriend is Chetna.

Chaman's girlfriend does not like Anamika and so she is either. Bhawna or Deepika. But Bhawna does not care for Chaman. Hence Chaman's girlfriend is Deepika.

Anamika does not like. Amar. Hence.

Amar's girlfriend is Bhawna. Dinkar's girlfriend is Anamika.

The above information is shown in Tabular format as under.

Boy	Girlfriend
Dinkar	Anamika
Chaman	Deepika
Bimal	Chetnna
Amar	Bhawna

20. d Amar's girlfriend is Bhawna.

21. d Anamika is friendly with Dinkar.

22. b Deepika's boy friend is Chaman.

23. b Deepika does not like Anamika and Chetna.

24. d As seen from the table three pairs have their starting alphabets as consecutive.

25. d From I we get that R and P are the brother and sister of T.

From II, T is a male.

Since from I, R and P are brother and sister of T therefore, R has to be the brother of P. Hence, P has no sister.

26. c Choice (c) holds good as nothing conclusive can be arrived at.

27. a 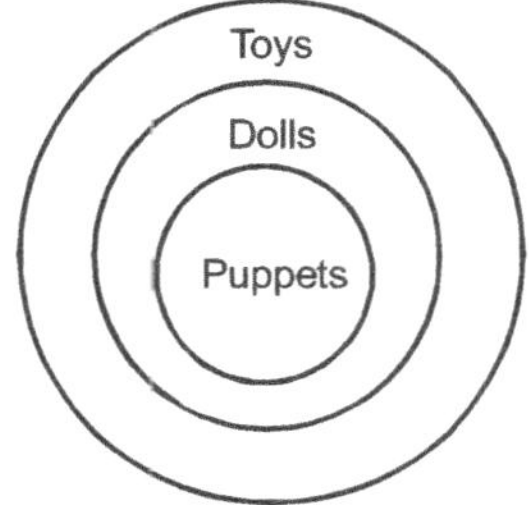

From the given venn diagram we conclude that only I follows.

28. d 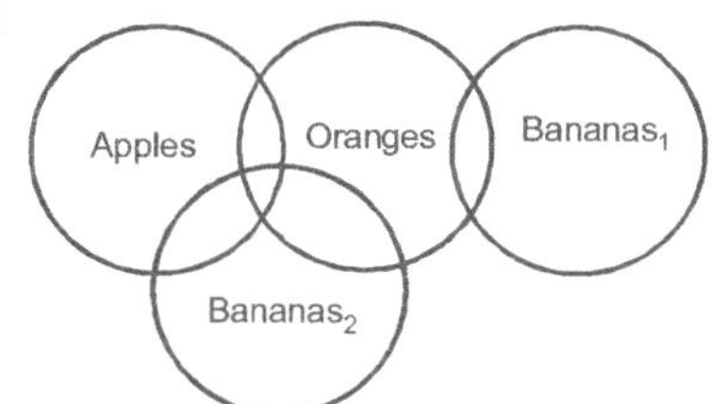

From the given venn diagram we see that both I and II cannot be definitely true. Hence, option (d) is the correct answer.

29. a 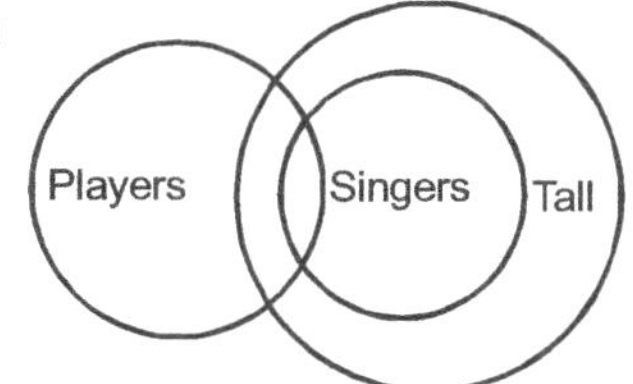

As per the venn diagram only conclusion I follows.

30. d 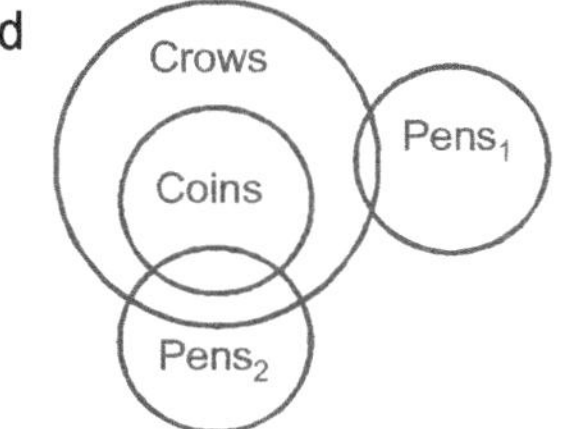

From the given venn diagram we can see that neither I nor II follows.

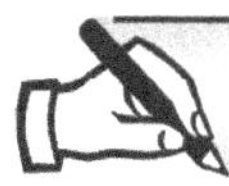

Practice Test-5

Number of questions: 30   **Time Allowed: 30 mins.**

Directions for questions 1 to 5: Answer the following questions based on the study of the following letter-number sequence.

E 7 G B D M 4 N K H 2 A C Z S V 3 F I J L O Q 5 P R

1. If every alternate letter/number is dropped starting from E onwards, which letter/number will be second to left of the tenth letter/number from your left?

    (a) V   (b) B
    (c) A   (d) Q

2. If it is possible to make a meaningful word with the first, the twelfth, the fifteenth and the twenty-first letters from left, which of the following letters will be the first letter of that word? If no such word can be made, give 'X' as the answer, and if more than one such word can be made, give 'M' as the answer.

    (a) A   (b) M
    (c) E   (d) X

3. What will come in place of the question mark (?) in the following sequence?

    GDR   BMP   D45?

    (a) 4NQ   (b) MNQ
    (c) MKO   (d) M4Q

4. If the letters/numbers only from M to L are written in the reverse order and other letters/numbers are kept unaltered, which letter/number will be third to the right of 17th letter/number from your right?

    (a) C   (b) A
    (c) S   (d) Z

5. If every third letter/number starting from your right replaces successive days of the week starting from Monday, which letter/number will replace Thursday?

    (a) A   (b) S
    (c) Z   (d) F

6. Bablu ranked sixteenth from the top and twenty-ninth from the bottom among those who passed an examination. Six boys did not participate in the competition and five failed in the examination. How many boys were there in the class?

    (a) 44   (b) 50
    (c) 55   (d) 40

7. Ram started moving towards south from his home, he moved 12 m straight and took a right turn. He moved 5 m straight and again took a right turn, and moved another 24 m. How far is he from his home?

    (a) 12 m   (b) 13 m
    (c) 17 m   (d) 29 m

8. Mandar started moving towards west from his home and took a right turn after moving 15 m straight, then he again moved to 22 m straight and took a right turn. He took 3 more right turns after that. Can you tell the direction he is travelling in with respect to his home?

    (a) East   (b) West
    (c) North-west   (d) South-east

Directions for questions 9 and 10: In each of the following questions, find the missing number in place of '?', so as to continue the series.

9. 6, 9, 14, 21, 30, ?

    (a) 32   (b) 33
    (c) 37   (d) 41

10. 2, 9, 28, 65, ?

    (a) 100   (b) 125
    (c) 126   (d) 131

Directions for questions 11 to 15: Answer the following questions based on the study of the information given below.

City High School must put together a debating team consisting of four debaters. There are candidates of equal ability: X, Y and Z who are all seniors; and A, B, C and D who are all juniors. The school requires two seniors and two juniors in the team. It is also necessary that all of the debaters of a team should be able to work with one another.

- Debaters Y and A cannot work together.
- Debaters Z and C cannot work together.
- Debaters A and B cannot work together.

11. If debater B is selected and debater Y is rejected, then which of the four debaters will form the team?

    (a) X, Z, A and B   (b) X, Z, D and B
    (c) X, Z, C and B   (d) X, D, C and B

12. If debater A is in the team, which other debaters must be in the team as well?

    (a) X, Y and B   (b) X, Z and D

    (c) X, Z and B   (d) X, Z and C

13. If both Y and Z are selected, which of the other debaters must be in the team with them?

    (a) Both C and D   (b) Only D

    (c) Both B and A   (d) Both B and D

14. Which statement(s) must be false?

    I.   Debaters Y and C are never selected together.

    II. Debaters Z and B are never selected together.

    III. Debaters Z and D are never selected together.

    (a) I only   (b) II only

    (c) I and III only   (d) All of the given

15. Which of the following statements is/are true of debater X?

    I.   Debater X must be selected as one of the seniors of the team.

    II. Debater X must be selected if debater C is selected

    III. Debater X cannot be selected if both A and C are rejected.

    (a) I only   (b) II only

    (c) III only   (d) II and III only

16. Hema, who is Sahil's daughter, says to Anjali, "Your mother Rekha is the younger sister of my father who is the third child of Captain Rathore." How is Captain Rathore related to Anjali?

    (a) Father   (b) Grandfather

    (c) Father-in-law   (d) Brother

17. Mohan said, "This girl is the wife of the grandson of my mother". What is Mohan to the girl?

    (a) Father   (b) Grandfather

    (c) Father-in-law   (d) None of these

18. In a certain code language THRICE is coded as UJUMHK, what will be the code for EQUALS in the same language?

    (a) FRVBMT   (b) FPVZMU

    (c) FSXEQY   (d) FRWDPX

19. In a certain code language, 'kew xas huma deko' means 'she is eating apples'. 'kew tepo qua' means 'she sells toys' and 'sut time deko' means 'I like apples'. Which words in the language means 'she' and 'apples'?

    (a) 'xas' and 'deko'   (b) 'deko' and 'tepo'

    (c) 'kew' and 'deko'   (d) 'xas' and 'kew'

Directions for questions 20 to 23: In the following questions, there are two statements followed by two conclusions numbered I and II. You have to take the given statements to be true even if they seem to be at variance with commonly known facts. Read the conclusions and then decide which of them logically follows.

Mark answer:

(a) If only conclusion I follows

(b) If only conclusion II follows

(c) If both conclusions I and II follow

(d) If neither conclusion I nor II follows

20. **Statements:**

    Some dogs are horses.

    No horse is black.

    Conclusions:

    I.   Some dogs are black.

    II. Some dogs are not black.

21. **Statements:**

    All poets are leaders.

    No leader is wise.

    Conclusions:

    I.   No poet is wise.

    II. All leaders are poets.

22. **Statements:**

    Some trees are houses.

    Banana is a tree.

    Conclusions:

    I.   Banana is not a tree.

    II. At least one house is tree.

23. **Statements:**

    All cows are red.

    Some buffaloes are red.

    Conclusions:

    I.   All red are not cows.

    II. Some reds are not buffaloes.

Directions for questions 24 to 28: Arrange the following sentences in a logical order to make a coherent paragraph.

24. A. However, this reasonable expectation has recently been shattered, and not for the first time.

    B. When amendments related to the law are made with the aim of providing justice to women who are victims of domestic violence, it is reasonable to expect that the law be implemented in its true spirit by lawyers, the investigating agencies and the courts.

C. The recent judgment of the Delhi High Court in the case of Savitri vs Ramesh Chand has once again revealed the shortcomings of Section 498A of the Indian Penal Code.

D. In the early 1980s, amendments were passed to make certain forms of domestic violence criminal offences.

(a) ABCD   (b) BACD
(c) DABC   (d) CABD

25. A. It is well settled that this law (498A) also covers mental cruelty, which has been recognized to cause far more injury to the health and well-being of a woman than physical battering.

B. The offence as of today, is non-bailable and cognizable.

C. According to the petitioner (the woman) in the case of Savitri Vs Ramesh Chand all the members of her husband's family should have been subjected to trial under Section 498A.

D. It is another story that establishing this aspect of domestic violence is a difficult task because of the attitudes of our investigating agencies and the judiciary.

(a) ADBC   (b) ABCD
(c) DABC   (d) CABD

26. A. Making the offence compoundable implies that the complainant may withdraw her police complaint at any point of time.

B. In the eyes of the judge, this might give the marriage another chance but it can, just as easily, make the woman even more vulnerable to exploitation.

C. In a majority of the cases, a woman filing a petition would (along with her children) be financially dependent on her husband; and she would have approached the police/courts only because of unbearable violence.

D. In all probability, the husband and the woman's in-laws would offer reconciliation so that the woman withdraws the case.

(a) CABD   (b) DBCA
(c) ABCD   (d) BDAC

27. A. Assuming for a moment (without accepting it), that 498A has been or is being misused, the larger issue is which law is not being misused?

B. And then, who is responsible?

C. And if all our laws are being used or misused, why a hue and cry only about 498A?

D. The duty, and indeed the onus, of ensuring that the law is not misused is that of the investigating and prosecuting agencies, lawyers and the courts

E. It should be considered that the women who comes out for help does not know the intricacies of the law.

(a) ABCDE   (b) DACBE
(c) ACBDE   (d) BADCE

28. A. The need at this stage is to focus on better implementation and to put things in the right perspective.

B. The Judgment blames the woman for having sought redressal for her violations in law.

C. Sensitivity is required to understand why a woman whose marriage has just broken because she has been battered physically, mentally or both, would want to rope in everyone that she can think of.

D. The nature of the law – 498A being criminal — implies that it is not meant to confer rights but to define as offences behaviour that is socially reprehensible, and to impose punishment for such offences.

(a) ABDC   (b) ACBD
(c) BADC   (d) BACD

Directions for questions 29 and 30: In the following questions, a statement is followed by two explanatory statements numbered I and II. These explanatory statements have been given to answer the question asked in the main statement.

Choose your answer as :

(a) If the data in statement I alone is sufficient to answer the question.

(b) If the data in statement II alone is sufficient to answer the question.

(c) If the data in both the statements together is not sufficient to answer the question

(d) If the data in both the statements is needed to answer the question.

29. Who is the shortest of W, X, Y and Z?

    I. Z, X and Y are not the shortest

    II. Z is taller than X.

30. What time did the flight take off today?

    I. The scheduled time of the flight is 16:30.

    II. Generally the flight leaves on time.

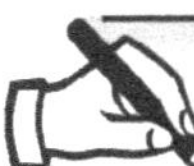

Answer Key

1. (a)	**2.** (b)	**3.** (b)	**4.** (d)	**5.** (b)	6. (c)	**7.** (b)	**8.** (c)	**9.** (d)	**10.** (c)
11. (b)	**12.** (b)	**13.** (d)	**14.** (d)	**15.** (b)	16. (b)	**17.** (c)	**18.** (c)	**19.** (c)	**20.** (d)
21. (a)	**22.** (d)	**23.** (d)	**24.** (b)	**25.** (a)	26. (c)	**27.** (c)	**28.** (d)	**29.** (a)	**30.** (c)

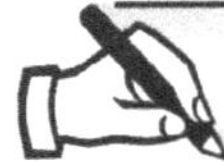

Explanations

1. a The arrangement of the series after dropping every alternate term would be like this

   7 B M N H A Z V F J O 5 R

   Hence, the second term to the left of the tenth term is V.

2. b First → E,   Twelfth → A,

   Fifteenth → S,   Twenty-first → L

   Meaningful words = SEAL and SALE

3. b $G \xrightarrow{+2} D \xrightarrow{last} R$

   $B \xrightarrow{+2} M \xrightarrow{last\ but\ 1} P$

   $D \xrightarrow{+2} 4 \xrightarrow{last\ but\ 2} 5$

   $M \xrightarrow{+2} N \xrightarrow{last\ but\ 3} Q$

   MNQ will come in place of the question mark.

4. d The arrangement of the series after reversing the series would be like this

   E 7 G B D L J I F 3 V S Z C A 2 H K N 4 M O Q 5 P R

   Hence, the term, which will be 3rd to the right of 17th tern from the right hand side, is Z.

5. b E 7 G B D M 4 N K H 2 A C Z S V 3 F I J L O Q 5 P R

                   ↑   ↑   ↑   ↑

              Thurs. Wed. Tues.   Mon.

   Hence, S will replace Thursday.

6. c Top 15th → Bablu ← 28th bottom

   ∴ No. of passed students = 28 + 15 + 1 (Bablu)

                      = 44

   ∴ Total no. of boys = 44 + 6 + 5 = 55.

7. b

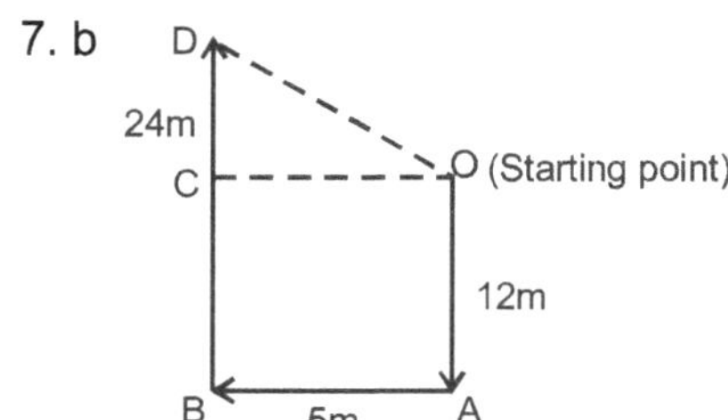

   We are to find out OD.

By Pythagoras' theorem $OD = \sqrt{OC^2 + CD^2}$

$$= \sqrt{(5)^2 + (12)^2} \quad [\because OC = AB = 5\ m$$

$$CD = DB - OA \ (as\ OA = CB)$$

$$= 24 - 12 = 12]$$

$$= \sqrt{25 + 144} = \sqrt{169} = 13\ m$$

8. c Following the directions mentioned in the question

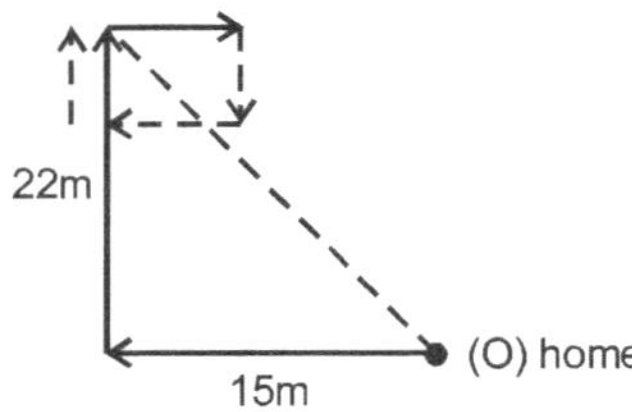

   we arrive at the diagram above with the help of which the question can be solved very easily and hence, we can say that Mandar was finally moving towards the North-west direction with respect to his home.

9. d $x^2 + 5$. The terms of the series are formed by $x^2 + 5$ where x = 1, 2 etc.

10. c $x^3 + 1$. The terms of the series are formed by $x^3 + 1$ where x = 1, 2, etc.

For questions 11 to 15: We will try to answer all the questions using options.

11. b If debater Y is rejected then it implies that the two senior debater in the team would be X and Z. If debater B is selected then it implies that we have to select two juniors among A, C and D. Now, just checking each of the options

   Option (a) can be ruled out because it is violating condition 3.

   Option (c) can be ruled out because it is violating condition 2.

   Option (d) can be ruled out because there are 3 juniors in the team.

   Only option (b) satisfies all the given condition. Hence, the correct answer is option (b).

12. b Again just go through checking the options.

Option (a) and option (c), both can be ruled out because it is violating condition 3.

Option (d) can be ruled out because it is violating condition 2. Only option (b) satisfies the given conditions. Hence, the correct answer is option (b).

13. d Option (a) and option (c) can be ruled out because they are violating condition 2 and 3 respectively. The only option satisfying the given conditions is options (d).

14. d All of the given statements are false because there is a case for each of the option.

I. X, Y, B and C

II. X, Z, B and D

III. X, Z, B and D

16. b Captain Rathore is two generations before Anjali; so from the options, answer is option b.

17. c "This girl is the wife of the grandson of my mother".

My mother in the above statement indicates Mohan's mother.

And Mohan's mother's grandson is son of Mohan. Thus Mohan's son's wife is daughter-in-law of Mohan.

Hence Mohan is father-in-law of the girl who is wife of grandson.

18. c The coding follows as

T(20) + 1 = U(21)   E(5) + 1 = F(6)

H(8) + 2 = J(10)   Q(17) + 2 = S(19)

R(18) + 3 = U(21)   U(21) + 3 = X(24)

I(9) + 4 = M(13)   A(1) + 4 = E(5)

C(3) + 5 = H(8)   L(12) + 5 = Q(17)

E(5) + 6 = K(11)   S(!9) + 6 = Y(25)

19. c From first two coded statements, kew = she and from first and last coded statements deko = apples; hence, choice (c) is the answer.

20. d 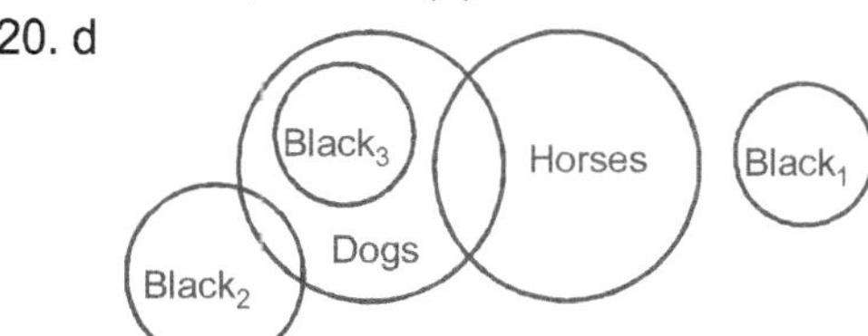

From the given venn diagram we can conclude that none of the given conclusions definitely follows.

21. a 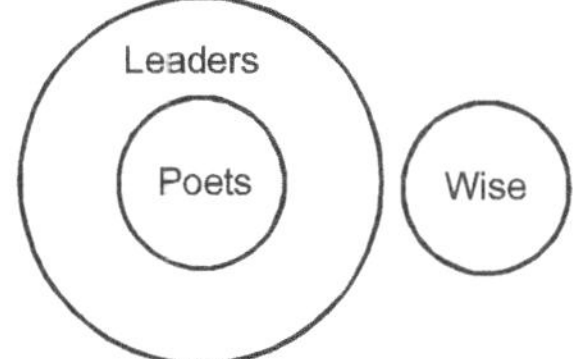

From the given venn diagram we can conclude that only conclusion I follows.

22. d 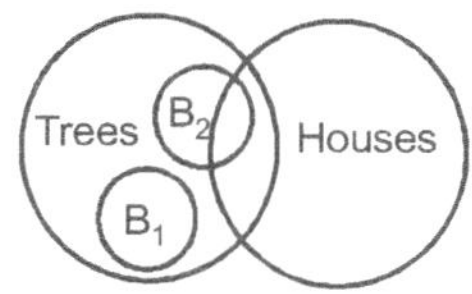

B - Banana

Both the cases B_1 and B_2 are possible as per the given venn diagram. Hence, we cannot definitely conclude that I or II is correct.

23. d 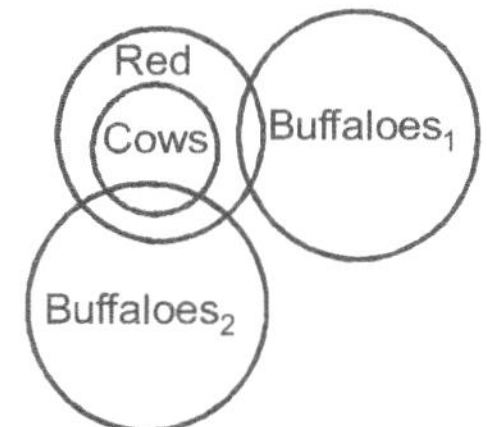

From the given venn diagram we can deduce that neither I nor II follows.

24. b The 'reasonable expectation' mentioned in A is stated in B. 'not for the first time' stated in A continues with 'once again' in C. Hence, 'BACD' is the correct sequence.

25. a 'AD' is a mandatory pair as the phrase 'it is well settled' (sentence A) is linked to the phrase 'it is another story' (sentence D). B follows D as 'the offence' stated in B refers to 'domestic violence' stated in D. Hence, 'ADBC' is the correct sequence.

26. c 'this' in B refers to the statement in A. C and D exemplify a typical outcome. Hence, 'ABCD' is the correct sequence.

27. c C follows A as they both refer to '498A'. B follows C as it also poses a question. D follows B as it answers the question asked in sentence B i.e. 'who is responsible?' Hence, 'ACBDE' is the correct sequence.

28. d 'AC' forms a mandatory pair as there is a link between 'right perspective' (mentioned in A) and 'sensitivity' (mentioned in C). This pair is there only in option (d). Hence, it is the correct answer.

29. a Choice (a) holds good as it is evident X, Y and Z are not the shortest then it is W that is left and the shortest.

From (II) it is not possible to conclude anything as nothing is said about W and Y. Hence, choice (a) holds good.

30. c Choice (c) holds good. Using both the statements together even cannot tell the exact time at which the flight took off today.

Practice Test-6

Number of questions: 30   **Time Allowed: 30 mins.**

1. In a certain code language, 'they are fools' means 'plane is risky', 'we are wise' means 'train is fast' and 'wise never fools' means 'fast always risky'. Which of the following stands for 'train'?

   (a) they   (b) we

   (c) never   (d) fools

2. In a certain code language SCIENTIST is coded as RDHFMUHTS, what will be the code for UNIQUE in the same code language?

   (a) TOHRTE   (b) TOHSTF

   (c) THORTF   (d) TOHRTF

3. Nageena is taller than Pushpa but not as tall as Manish. Rama is taller than Namita but not as tall as Pushpa. Who among them is the tallest?

   (a) Manish   (b) Pushpa

   (c) Namita   (d) Nageena

4. If it is possible to form a word with the first, fourth, seventh and eleventh letters in 'SUPERFLUOUS', then write the first letter of that word. Otherwise mark X as the answer.

   (a) S   (b) L

   (c) O   (d) X

5. In 'PARADISE', how many pairs of letters are there which have as many letters between them in the word as they have in the English alphabet?

   (a) None   (b) Three

   (c) Four   (d) Two

6. Four of the following are alike in some way and, hence, form a group. Which of these does not belong to the group?

   (a) MKL   (b) FCD

   (c) ZXY   (d) RPQ

7. Which among the following completes the series given below?

   AMU CNT EPR GSO ?

   (a) IVL   (b) IWL

   (c) IVK   (d) IWK

8. If it is possible to make a meaningful word with the 1st, 8th and 10th letters of PROPOSITIONING, which of the following will be second letter of that word? If more than one such word can be made, give 'X' as the answer. If no such word can be made, give 'M' as the answer.

   (a) M   (b) X

   (c) P   (d) T

9. Mahesh told Manish, 'Yesterday, I detected the only brother of the daughter of my grandmother'. Whom did Mahesh detect?

   (a) Son   (b) Father

   (c) Brother   (d) None of these

10. When Amir saw Monu, he recalled,' He is the son of the father of the mother of my daughter.' what is Monu to Amir?

    (a) Brother-in-law   (b) Brother

    (c) Cousin   (d) Uncle

Directions for questions 11 and 12: In each of the following questions, find the number which does not belong to the given number sequence which follows a certain pattern.

11. 11, 17, 19, 39, 41.

    (a) 41   (b) 17

    (c) 39   (d) 19

12. 14, 49, 56, 33, 63.

    (a) 49   (b) 14

    (c) 33   (d) 56

Directions for questions 13 to 17: Read the following information and answer the questions that follow.

Six persons A, B, C, D, E and F were playing a game of cards. A's father, mother and uncle were in the group. There were two women, B, the mother of A got more points than her husband. D got more points than E but less than F. Niece of E got the lowest points. Father of A got more points than F but could not win the game.

13. Who got the lowest points?

    (a) A   (b) C

    (c) E   (d) B

14. Who is the husband of B?

    (a) F   (b) E

    (c) D   (d) C

15. B was one of the ladies, who was the other lady?

    (a) C   (b) D

    (c) E   (d) A

16. Who stood second in the game?

    (a) A   (b) B

    (c) C   (d) Can't be determined

17. How is E related to A?

    (a) Uncle   (b) Sister

    (c) Husband   (d) Son

Directions for questions 18 to 21: In the following questions, there are two statements followed by two conclusions numbered I and II. You have to take the given statements to be true even if they seem to be at variance with commonly known facts. Read the conclusions and then decide which of them logically follows.

Mark answer:

(a) If only conclusion I follows

(b) If only conclusion II follows

(c) If both conclusions I and II follow

(d) If neither conclusion I nor II follows

18. **Statements:**

    All cars are expensive.

    Some expensive are cheap.

    Conclusions:

    I.   Some cars are not expensive.

    II. All expensive are cars.

19. **Statements:**

    Some balls are big.

    Some big are heavy.

    Conclusions:

    I.   Some balls are not big.

    II. Some heavy are big.

20. **Statements:**

    Some shepherds are genius.

    No genius is mad.

    Conclusions:

    I.   Some shepherds are mad.

    II. Some geniuses are not mad.

21. **Statements:**

    Some chairs are tables.

    All tables are walls.

    Conclusions:

    I.   No wall is chair.

    II. Some tables are not chairs.

22. The town of Paranda is located on Green Lake. The town of Akram is West of Paranda. Tokhada is East of Akram but West of Paranda, Kakran is East of Bopri but West of Tokhada and Akram. If they are all in the same district, which town is the farthest West?

    (a) Bopri   (b) Kakran

    (c) Akram   (d) Tokhoda

23. Starting from a point, Raju walked 12 m towards north, he turned right and walked 10 m, he again turned right and walked 12 m, then he turned left and walked 5 m. How far is he now and in which direction from the starting point?

    (a) 27 m towards east

    (b) 5 m towards east

    (c) 10 m towards west

    (d) 15 m towards east

Directions for questions 24 to 28: Arrange the following sentences in a logical order to make a coherent paragraph.

24. A. Roughly three years ago, B.M. Vyas, Managing Director of the Gujarat Cooperative Milk Marketing Federation (GCMMF) which owns the Amul brand, asked one of the cooperative's food technologists to take a course in pizza making.

    B. Once she had mastered the art, 25 more women were recruited and groomed as pizza trainers.

    C. Armed with Amul's pizza cheese, the trainers then fanned out to 200 towns across India to conduct Amul's 'Teach and Treat' classes.

    D. Soon Moitriyee Mukherjee, a food technologist, was out tasting pizzas at all the major fast- food outlets in Gujarat and learning how to prepare different kinds of the popular item.

    (a) BDCA   (b) ABCD

    (c) BACD   (d) ADBC

25. A. Launched in 25 cities in July 2001, Amul's six-inch, Rs. 20 pizza has been an instant hit.

    B. Says Vyas, 51, who stepped into the shoes of Amul's celebrated founder Verghese Kurien in 1993: "We first study the strategies of our competitors and then devise our own strategy then devise innovations before launching our product."

    C. In Delhi alone its 96 franchisee outlets are selling an average of 50 pizzas a day on weekdays and 600 a day on weekends.

    D. In two months, Amul plans to spread to 3,000 outlets across 100 cities and sell three lakh pizzas a day.

    (a) BDAC   (b) ABCD
    (c) ACDB   (d) BACD

26. A. The Rs. 2,258-crore Amul, India's largest and most successful cooperative, isn't going to stop at pizzas.

    B. It is eyeing the growing but largely under-serviced market for ready-to-eat foods for working couples and office-goers looking for cheap and healthy food.

    C. In the next six months, it plans to launch three more food products: frozen stuffed *parathas; matar paneer; and paneer pakoras.* 2

    D. Also, on the anvil are new brands of filter and instant tea and coffee.

    (a) ACBD   (b) ABCD
    (c) BACD   (d) CABD

27. A. What prompted the 55-year-old dairy cooperative to venture outside its main business of milk products?

    B. The pizza business will give a big push to its mozzarella cheese.

    C. To begin with, there is some synergy between the food products Amul is launching and its dairy business.

    D. In two months since the launch of its pizza, sales of its mozzarella cheese have doubled in cities where its pizzas are sold.

    (a) BADC   (b) ABCD
    (c) ACBD   (d) DACB

28. A. Part of Amul's aggression is driven by compulsion.

    B. The dairy sector is no longer protected.

    C. Not only are domestic companies and MNCS now allowed to enter the sector, from April this year imports of dairy products too have been freed from licensing.

    D. While that has multiplied the choice for consumers, it has intensified competition for Amul.

    E. Britannia, Le Bon and Nestle are already challenging Amul's commanding control over the butter and cheese markets.

    F. And imported brands like Laughing Cow and Kraft have hit the shelves in metros.

    (a) DABCEF   (b) ABDCEF
    (c) ABCDEF   (d) DACBEF

Directions for questions 29 and 30: In the following questions, a statement is followed by two explanatory statements numbered I and II. These explanatory statements have been given to answer the question asked in the main statement.

Choose your answer as:

(a) If the data in statement I alone is sufficient to answer the question.

(b) If the data in statement II alone is sufficient to answer the question.

(c) If the data in both the statements together is not sufficient to answer the question

(d) If the data in both the statements is needed to answer the question.

29. How is Mayank related to Kandarp?

    I. Rajesh is the brother of Mayank.

    II. Mayank is married to Poonam who is the daughter of Kandarp.

30. Among four sisters — Shanti, Kranti, Bharti and Mantri who is the most intelligent?

    I. Kranti is more intelligent than Shanti.

    II. Shanti is more intelligent than Bharti and Mantri.

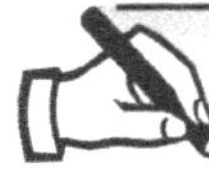

Answer Key

1. (b)	**2.** (c)	**3.** (a)	**4.** (b)	**5.** (d)	**6.** (b)	**7.** (d)	**8.** (b)	**9.** (b)	**10.** (a)
11. (c)	**12.** (c)	**13.** (a)	**14.** (d)	**15.** (d)	**16.** (c)	**17.** (a)	**18.** (d)	**19.** (b)	**20.** (a)
21. (d)	**22.** (a)	**23.** (d)	**24.** (d)	**25.** (c)	**26.** (a)	**27.** (c)	**28.** (c)	**29.** (b)	**30.** (d)

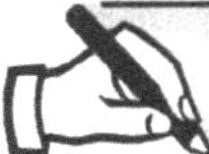

Explanations

1. b From the first two coded statements 'are' = is and from the last two coded statements 'wise' = fast; hence, code for train is 'we'.

2. c The coding follows as

$S(19) - 1 = R(18)$ $U(21) - 1 = T(20)$
$C(3) + 1 = D(4)$ $N(14) + 1 = O(15)$
$I(9) - 1 = H(8)$ $I(9) - 1 = H(8)$
$E(5) + 1 = F(6)$ $Q(17) + 1 = R(18)$
$N(14) - 1 = M(13)$ $U(21) - 1 = T(20)$
$T(20) + 1 = U(21)$ $E(5) + 1 = F(6)$
$I(9) - 1 = H(8)$
$S(19) + 1 = T(20)$
$T(20) - 1 = S(19)$
$S(19) + 1 = T(20)$

3. a Nageena > Pushpa

Nageena < Manish

Rama > Namita

Rama < Pushpa

∴ Manish > Nageena > Pushpa > Rama > Namita; Therefore, Manish is the tallest.

4. b The first, fourth, seventh and eleventh letters of the given word are S, E, L and S, respectively. The word formed is LESS.

5. d Such letter pairs are PR and AD, hence, (d) is correct.

6. b Middle, right and left letters form a continuous series. All the others follow the same pattern except (b).

7. d First letter of each group skip one letter between them. Second letter of each group skip no letter first, then one letter and then two letters and so on. Third letter of each group in the backward direction skips 2 letters first, then 1 letter and then no letter. But as it is in the reverse direction so the third letter of the fourth group will be having a difference of 3 letters in the reverse direction, i.e. it will be K. Following this rule, choice (d) is the answer.

8. b TOP, POT, OPT.

9. b He is detected to his father.

10. a Monu is the brother in-law of Sonu.

11. c All the terms except 39 are prime numbers.

12. c All the terms except 33 are multiples of 7.

For questions 13 to 17:

This will be the order according to points

B > C > F > D > E > A

C → Father

B → Mother

A → Daughter of B and C.

A → Niece of E.

18. d

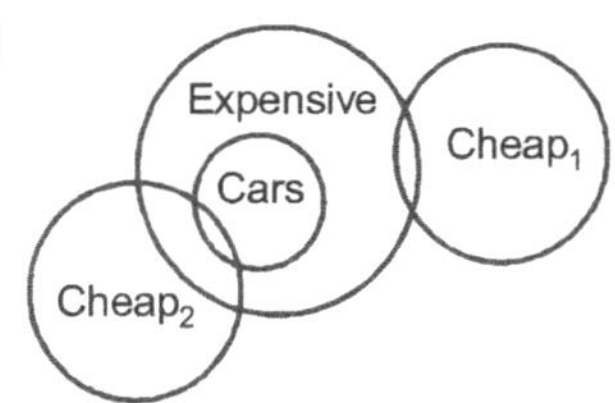

As per the venn diagram none of the given conclusions follows.

19. b

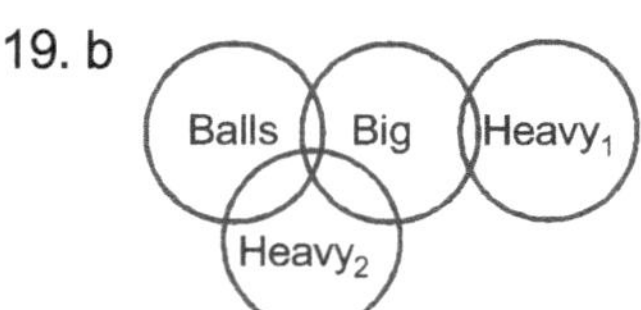

Only conclusion II definitely follows.

20. a

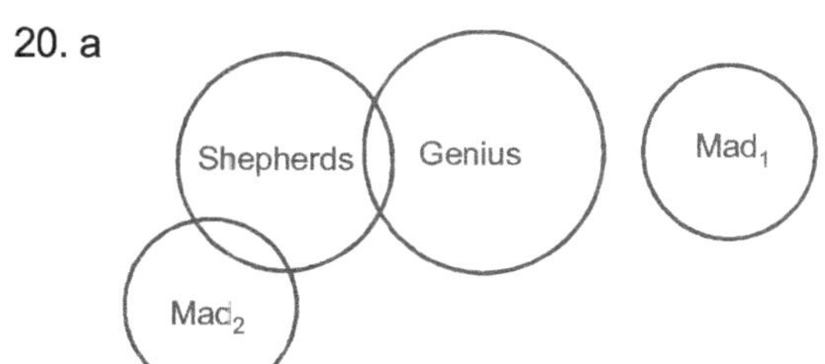

As per the given venn diagram we can conclude that neither I nor II definitely follows.

21. d

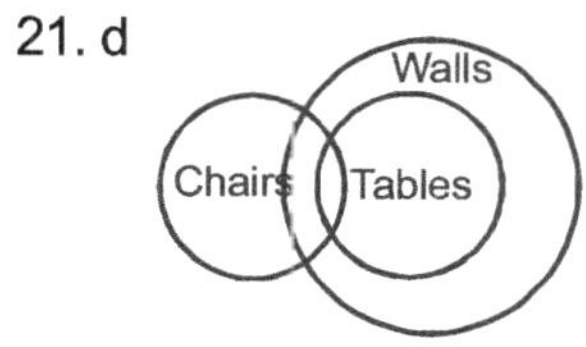

As per the given venn diagram none of the two conclusions follows.

22. a The location of the towns from west to east is in the following order:

Bopri-Kakran-Akram-Takhoda-Paranda.

23. d

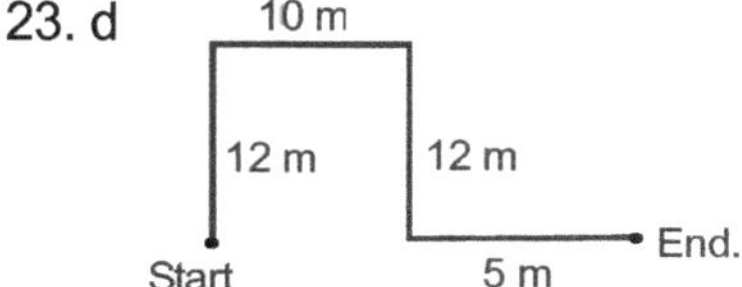

24. d 'she' in B refers to the name in D. 'trainers' link B to C.

Hence, 'ADBC' is the correct sequence.

25. c The pronoun 'its' in C refers to the 'Rs. 20 pizza' in A. The statistics stated in D will logically follow sentence C. Hence, 'ACDB' is the correct sequence.

26. a 'not going to stop' and 'three more food products' make a link in 'AC'. B is the target for the food in C. Hence, 'ACBD' is the correct sequence.

27. c The answer to the question in A begins in C. D follows B as it continues talking about the 'mozzarella cheese' already stated in B.

28. c B follows A as it states the reason behind Amul's compulsion. C elaborates on what is stated in B. D states the consequence of what has been stated in C and E and F elaborate on the *competition* mentioned in D. Hence, 'ABCDEF' is the correct answer.

29. b From statement I any conclusive relationship between Kandarp and Mayank cannot be established, while statement II clearly establishes that Kandarp is the father-in-law of Mayank. Hence, Mayank is the son-in-law of Kandarp.

30. d From (I) we get

Kranti > Shanti and from (II) we get   … (A)

Shanti > Bharti and Mantri   … (B)

Obviously combining (A) and (B) we get Kranti the most intelligent of all.

Practice Test-7

Number of questions: 30   **Time Allowed: 30 mins.**

Directions for questions 1 to 5: Read the information given carefully and answer the questions that follow.

Amit, Bharati, Cheryl, Deepak and Eric are five friends sitting in a restaurant. They are wearing caps of five different colours — yellow, blue, green, white and red. Also they are eating five different snacks — burgers, sandwiches, ice cream, pastries and pizza.

I.   The person wearing a red cap is eating pastries.

II. Amit does not eat ice cream and Cheryl is eating sandwiches.

III. Bharati is wearing a yellow cap and Amit wearing a blue cap.

IV. Eric is eating pizza and is not wearing a green cap.

1. What is Amit eating?
   (a) Burgers   (b) Sandwiches
   (c) Ice cream   (d) Pastries

2. Who among the following friends is wearing the green cap?
   (a) Amit   (b) Bharati
   (c) Cheryl   (d) Deepak

3. Who among the following friends is having ice cream?
   (a) Amit   (b) Bharati
   (c) Cheryl   (d) Deepak

4. What is the colour of the cap Eric is wearing?
   (a) Yellow   (b) Blue
   (c) Green   (d) White

5. Which of the following combinations is not correct?
   (a) Yellow + ice cream
   (b) Red + pastries
   (c) White + pizza
   (d) Green + burger

6. Sapna started moving towards west from her home, she travelled 25 m and took a left turn. She travelled another 10 m and took a right turn and moved another 50 m, she took a left turn and moved another 25 m. How far is she from home?
   (a) 25.32 m   (b) 27.84 m
   (c) 29.15 m   (d) 29.86 m

7. If Sanjay, facing east, takes 24 right turns consecutively and then takes 45 left turns consecutively — after moving some equal distance before each turn which direction does he finally face?
   (a) North   (b) South
   (c) East   (d) West

Directions for questions 8 to 12: In the following questions, find the missing number in place of '?'.

8.

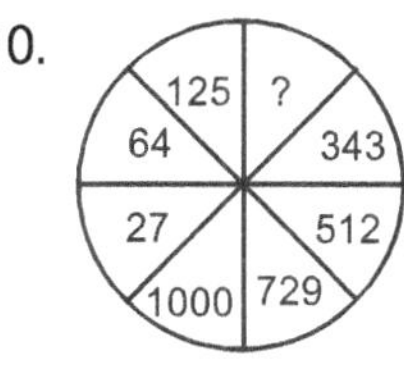

   (a) 65   (b) 69
   (c) 71   (d) 73

9.

   (a) 13   (b) 11
   (c) 9   (d) 6

10.

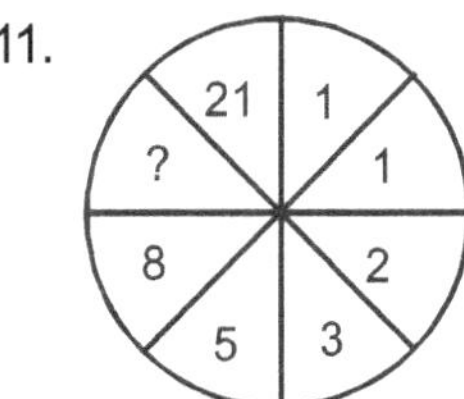

   (a) 224   (b) 246
   (c) 216   (d) 288

11.

   (a) 13   (b) 14
   (c) 15   (d) 16

12.

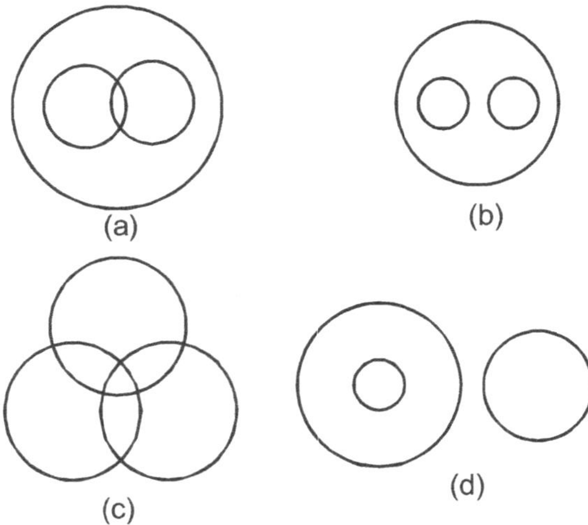

(a) 874 (b) 3

(c) 784 (d) 4

Directions for question 13: In the following question, three classes are given. Out of the four given figures, you are to indicate the figure which best represents the relationship with the three classes.

(a)

(b)

(c)

(d)

13. Musician, Magician, Artist.

Directions for questions 14 and 15: Each question is followed by two statements, I and II. Answer the questions using the following instructions. Choose the answer as

(a) If the question can be answered by one of the statements alone, but cannot be answered by using the other statement alone.

(b) If the question can be answered by using either statement alone.

(c) If the question can be answered by using both the statements together, but cannot be answered by using either statement alone.

(d) If the question cannot be answered even by using both the statements together.

14. Is x greater than y?

    I. $x + y = 6$

    II. $x + 2k = 15$, $y + k = 10$

15. Of the 100 employees of a Swedish company, how many know both English and French?

    I. 60 people know English, 50 people know French.

    II. 10 people know German.

Directions for questions 16 to 20: Arrange the following sentences in a logical order to make a coherent paragraph.

16. A. In his letter inviting General Pervez Musharraf for talks last week, the Prime Minister wrote, "Our common enemy is poverty. For the welfare of our peoples, there is no other recourse but a pursuit of the path of reconciliation." True.

    B. The vast majority of Indians and Pakistanis do without these things because we spend more on soldiers than on doctors, more on bombs and guns than on schools and roads.

    C. The result in both countries is a standard of living so abysmal that it is not considered a standard of living outside South Asia.

    D. Despite our vaunted nuclear capabilities and our vainglory, India and Pakistan are among the few countries left in the world in which the average citizen still has no access to the most basic requirements of modern life: clean water, education, reliable supply of electricity; roads; public transport; and healthcare.

    (a) BCDA (b) ADBC

    (c) ABCD (d) DACB

17. A. Is there anything else to cheer about?

    B. We have gone through the motions many times before.

    C. Amid much fanfare and excitement our representatives meet in Islamabad or Delhi and sit across tables looking self-important and purposeful.

    D. A difficult question to answer because we do not yet know if either India or Pakistan really want to talk or simply go through the motions of doing so.

    E. To show how secular we are, our lot usually throws in a few pieces of bad Urdu poetry while their lot responds with similar tawdry verse.

    F. Then they return home empty handed and sullen.

    (a) ADBCEF (b) BADCEF

    (c) DCABEF (d) ACDBEF

18. A. Our attempts at dialogue usually fail because India refuses to discuss Kashmir — we consider it a domestic problem — while Pakistan insists that unless we talk about Kashmir it is not worth talking.

    B. So are things going to be different this time?

C. It is for Pakistan, as Musharraf often repeats, the core issue.

D. They could be if the A.B. Vajpayee government sets itself a clear agenda that unambiguously states what we can do and what we cannot do about Kashmir.

(a) ABCD   (b) ACBD

(c) DACB   (d) CABD

19. A. Dealing with Pakistan has not been easy.

B. The Lahore bus trip was a sincere attempt at friendship and the General gave us Kargil.

C. After that, he has whined on about being ready to talk to us anywhere at any time and at any place without understanding that we saw no reason to talk to him.

D. In the words of a senior South Block bureaucrat, "We wanted them to stew a little. Why should we talk to them anyway?"

(a) ABCD   (b) BACD

(c) DABC   (d) CDAB

20. A. But what can he talk to us about?

B. If he is going to stick to the Pakistani position of a referendum under those ancient UN resolutions, which even the UN Secretary General has described as unenforceable, then there is nothing to talk about.

C. If, on the other hand, he is prepared to consider peace without Kashmir being handed to him like some trophy, then there is a possibility of a dialogue.

D. If he continues to deny that it is Pakistani terrorists who are killing innocent people on our side of the border then again we face a dialogue of the deaf.

(a) ADCB   (b) ABDC

(c) BACD   (d) CADB

Directions for questions 21 to 24: In the following questions, there are two statements followed by two conclusions numbered I and II. You have to take the given statements to be true even if they seem to be at variance with commonly known facts. Read the conclusions and then decide which of them logically follows.

Mark answer:

(a) If only conclusion I follows

(b) If only conclusion II follows

(c) If both conclusions I and II follow

(d) If neither conclusion I nor II follows

21. **Statements:**

All cycles are cars.

Some cars are not aeroplanes.

Conclusions:

I. Some cars are not aeroplanes.

II. All cars are not cycles.

22. **Statements:**

All bags are boxes.

No box is a purse.

Conclusions:

I. Some purses are not boxes.

II. Some boxes are not bags.

23. **Statements:**

All males are players.

All players are tall.

Conclusions:

I. All males are tall.

II. Some talls are males.

24. **Statements:**

Some boys are honest.

No honest is a fool.

Conclusions:

I. Some honest are not fools.

II. No boy is a fool.

25. In a certain code language ORIGINAL is coded as PTLKNTHT, what will be the code for REMARKS in the same code language?

(a) SGPFWQZ   (b) SGPEWRZ

(c) SGPEWQZ   (d) SGEPWQZ

26. In a certain code language JAPAN is coded as KCSES, what will be the code for CASTLE in the same code language?

(a) WTKKBU   (b) WTKKAT

(c) WTKLBT   (d) WTKKBT

27. Find the wrong term in the series.

51, 119, 153, 187, 223

(a) 187   (b) 119

(c) 223   (d) 51

28. Find the missing term in the series.

2, 7, 18, 41, 88, 183, ?

(a) 356   (b) 360

(c) 366   (d) 374

29. Pointing to a man in the photograph, Asha said, "His mother's only daughter is my mother." How is Asha related to that man?

    (a) nephew

    (b) sister

    (c) wife

    (d) niece

30. P is the brother of D, X is the sister of P. A is the brother of F. F is the daughter of D. M is the father of X. Who is the uncle of A?

    (a) X

    (b) P

    (c) F

    (d) M

Answer Key

1. (a)	2. (c)	3. (b)	4. (d)	5. (d)	6. (c)	7. (a)	8. (c)	9. (d)	10. (c)
11. (a)	12. (b)	13. (b)	14. (c)	15. (d)	16. (b)	17. (a)	18. (b)	19. (a)	20. (b)
21. (d)	22. (a)	23. (c)	24. (a)	25. (c)	26. (d)	27. (c)	28. (d)	29. (d)	30. (b)

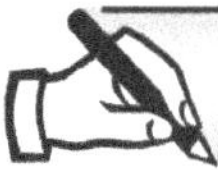 # Explanations

For questions 1 to 5: Fill up all the absolute data given. You will get the following table.

	Caps	Snacks
Amit	Blue	
Bharati	Yellow	
Cheryl		Sandwich
Deepak		
Eric		Pizz

Now from I, red cap and pastries have to be a combination. This cannot fit in anywhere but for Deepak since parts of the other combinations have filled. That leaves us with two colours of caps — green and white and two snacks ice cream and burgers. For caps, Eric does not wear green cap, hence out of the colours left, he has to wear the white cap. Again, Amit does not eat ice cream, therefore he has to eat burgers from the choices of snacks left. So we get

	Caps	**Snacks**
Amit	Blue	Burgers
Bharati	Yellow	Ice cream
Cheryl	Green	Sandwich
Deepak	Red	Pastries
Eric	White	Pizz

6. c Based on the direction given in the question we draw the following diagram with the help of which we can solve the question very easily:

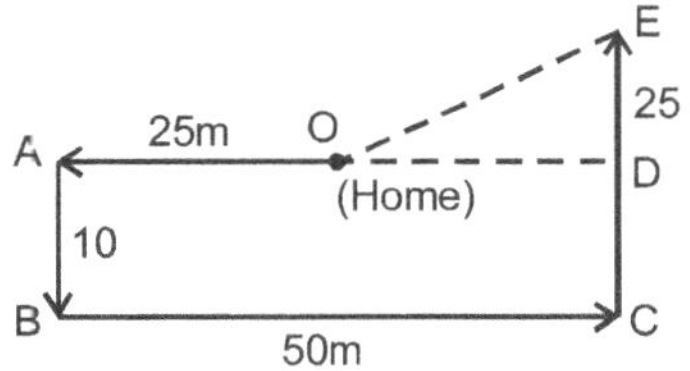

we have to figure out OE.

By Pythagoras' theorem we get,

$$OE^2 = OD^2 + DE^2$$

OR $OE = \sqrt{OD^2 + DE^2}$

$\Rightarrow OD = BC - AO \Rightarrow 50m - 25m = 25m$

$DE = CE - AB \Rightarrow 25 - 10 = 15\ m$

Putting the values of OD and DE in (A) we get

$OE = \sqrt{25^2 + 15^2} = \sqrt{625 + 225} = \sqrt{850} = 29.15\ m.$

7. a After each consecutive four turns, the person is at the similar position from where he started. This holds true for both the right and left consecutive turns. as both 24 and 44 both are multiples of 4.

Therefore, after the 44th turn he is at the similar position from where he started. Obviously after the next left turn he will be facing north.

8. c Starting from 13, the next term in the upward direction is after +29 and +29 is added to the next terms.

9. d Two alternate series are moving, i.e.: 3, 4, 5, 6 and 6, 7, 8, 9. But these digits occupy the alternate sectors. As, 3, 4, 5 is there, the next term would be 6.

10. c All are perfect cubes of 3, 4, 5, 6, 7, 8, 9, 10, i.e.: 27, 64 and so on. Therefore, ? mark would be replaced by cube of 6 = 216. Hence, choice (c) is the answer.

11. a Sum of the numbers in two slices is equal to the number in the third slice, i.e.: 1 + 1 = 2 and 2 + 3 = 5, hence, 5 + 8 = 13. Therefore, choice (a) is correct.

12. b Each number is double of its previous number, i.e., 2 is double of 1 and 96 is double of 48. Similarly, 6 will be double of 3. Hence, choice (b) is the answer.

13. b Relation (b) i.e.

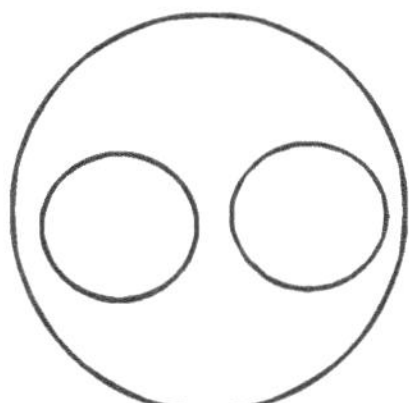

represents the relationship of the three classes. The relation says that

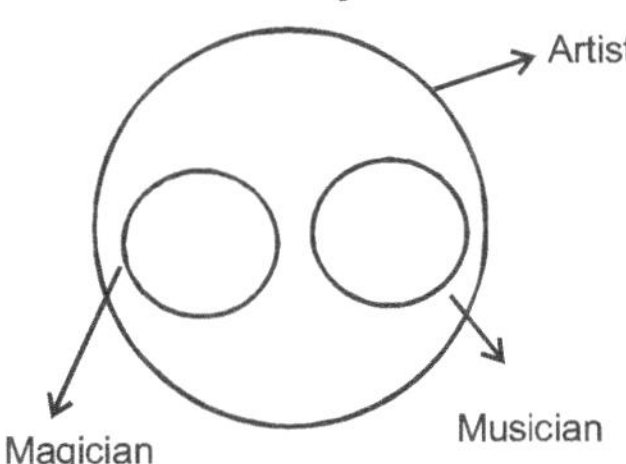

14. c (i) $x + y = 6$

(ii) $x + 2k = 15,\ y + k = 10$

$\Rightarrow x + 2(10 - y) = 15$

$\Rightarrow 2y - x = 5$

Solving $x + y = 6$ and $2y - x = 5$

We get $x = \dfrac{11}{3}$ and $y = \dfrac{7}{3}$

So x is greater than y.

15. d Total number of languages spoken by the 100 employees is not given.

16. b These things in B refer to the list given towards the end of D. C concludes with the results. Hence, 'ADBC' is the correct sequence.

17. a The answer to the question in A is given in D. B follows D because of the reference to 'motions'. Thus 'ADB' is a mandatory sequence. This sequence is seen only in option (a), which is the correct answer.

18. b 'It' in C refers to Kashmir in A. The answer to B is given in D. Hence, 'ACBD' is the correct answer.

19. a A begins the paragraph by putting forward the topic of discussion, which is 'dealing with Pakistan'. 'BC' forms a mandatory pair as the phrase 'after that' in C refers to 'the Lahore bus trip' stated in B. Hence, 'ABCD' is the correct sequence.

20. b The negative aspects in B and D are discussed first in continuation with A. C looks at the positive side with 'on the other hand.' Hence, option (b) is the correct answer.

21. d

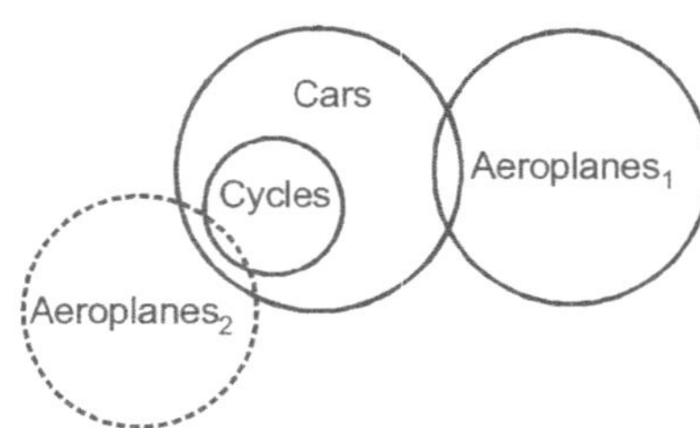

From the given venn diagram we can see that neither I nor II can be concluded.

22. a

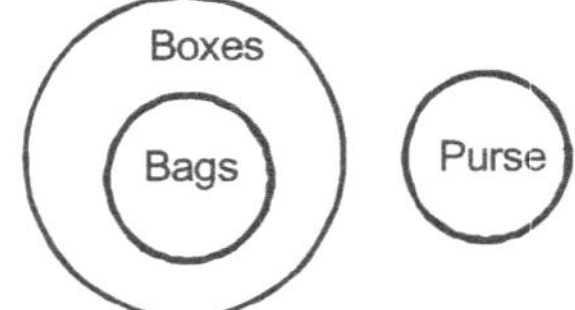

Only conclusion I follows.

23. c

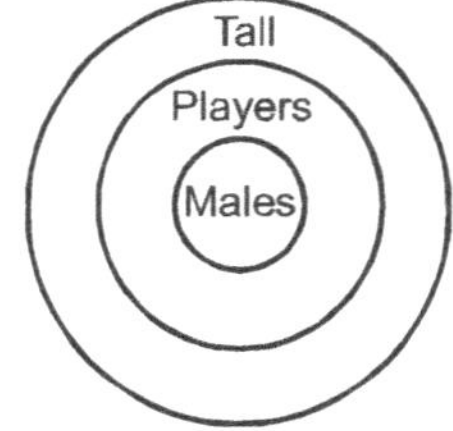

From the given venn diagram, both conclusions I and II follow.

24. a

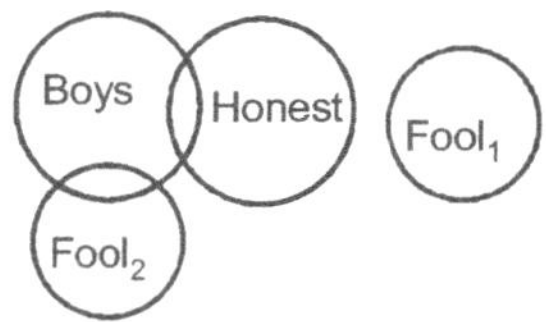

As per the given venn diagram, only conclusion I definitely follows.

25. c The coding follows as

O(15) + 1 = P(16)	R(18) + 1 = S(19)
R(18) + 2 = T(20)	E(5) + 2 = G(7)
I(9) + 3 = L(12)	M(13) + 3 = P(16)
G(7) + 4 = K(11)	A(1) + 4 = E(5)
I(9) + 5 = N(14)	R(18) + 5 = W(23)
N(14) + 6 = T(20)	K(11) + 6 = Q(17)
A(1) + 7 = H(8)	S(19) + 7 = Z(26)
L(12) + 8 = T(20)	

26. d The coding follows as

J(10) − 6 = D(4)	C(3) − 6 = W(23)
A(1) − 7 = T(20)	A(1) − 7 = T(20)
P(16) − 8 = H(8)	S(19) − 8 = K(11)
A(1) − 9 = R(18)	T(20) − 9 = K(11)
N(14) − 10 = D(4)	L(12) − 10 = B(2)
	E(5) − 11 = T(20)

27. c All the terms are multiples of 17.

28. d The term of the series are × 2 + 3, × 2 + 4, × 2 + 5, × 2 + 6, etc. Hence, the answer would be 183 × 2 + 8 = 374.

29. d "His mother's only daughter is my mother".

'His mother's' in the statement indicates that **'His'** is the son. Now **'Mother's only daughter'** indicates that **'His'** and **'only daughter'** both are brother sister. Now **'only daughter is my mother'** indicates that only daughter is Asha's mother. Now, Brother of Asha's brother is uncle of Asha and, thus, Asha is Niece of that man.

30. b

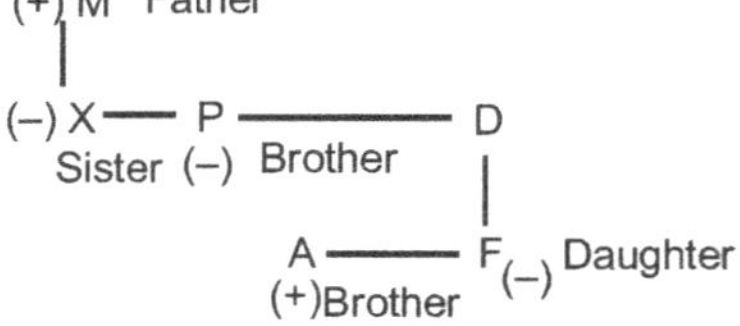

From the above relation,

X, P and D have the relation of brother and sister among them. M is father of X, P and D. D has a daughter F and son A. Now P is the brother of D.

∴ A's uncle is P.

Number of questions: 30　　　　　　　　　**Time Allowed: 30 mins.**

Directions for questions 1 to 6: Choose the Venn diagram which best illustrates the relationship between three given classes in each of the following questions :

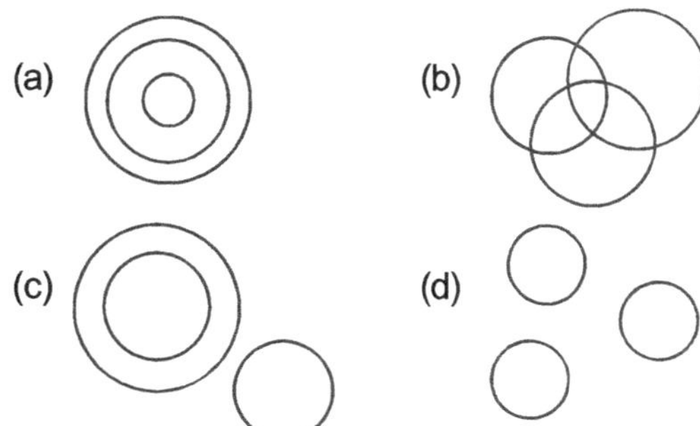

(a)　(b)

(c)　(d)

1. Son, Father, Grandfather
2. Car, Train, Aeroplane
3. Males, Father, Mother
4. Birds, Feathers, Cows
5. Mothers, Widows, Doctors
6. Flowers, Petals, Fruits.

Directions for questions 7 and 8: In each of the following questions, find the number which does not belong to the given number sequence which follows a certain pattern.

7. 91, 27, 36, 18, 54.
   (a) 91　　　　　(b) 36
   (c) 18　　　　　(d) 27
8. 25, 15, 85, 58, 65.
   (a) 58　　　　　(b) 15
   (c) 65　　　　　(d) 85

9. Ajay started moving facing east. He travelled 10m and took a left turn. After that, he moved another 15m and took a right turn. He moved another 50m and took a right turn. He moved another 25m and took a left turn then he moved again 20m and took another right turn before stopping. Which direction is he facing now?
   (a) South east　　　(b) North west
   (c) South　　　　　(d) South west

10. Pawan facing north moved 15 m straight, then he took a left turn and moved another 20 m. After that he took a left turn and moved another 25 m. After that he took a right turn and moved another 30 m and stopped. He is presently in which direction with respect to the starting point?

    (a) North-East　　　(b) South-West
    (c) North-West　　　(d) South-East

11. A is the Grandfather of P. Q is the wife of D whereas D is the brother of X. D and P are brother and sister. How is A related to X?
    (a) Father　　　　(b) Uncle
    (c) Grandfather　　(d) Son

12. Seeta said, "Mohan's father is the only son of my father." How is Seeta related to Mohan?
    (a) Sister　　　　(b) Mother
    (c) Brother　　　　(d) Aunt

Directions for questions 13 and 14: Some relationships have been expressed through symbols which are explained below.

'÷' Stands for 'equal to'

'×' Stands for 'not greater than'

'+' Stands for 'less than'

'∅' Stands for 'not less than'

'o' Stands for 'greater than'

Bearing the symbolic representation in mind pick the correct answer for each of the following questions.

13. If a ∅ b o c + d , then which of the following conclusion is true?
    (a) a o c　　　　　(b) b ÷ d
    (c) d + a　　　　　(d) b o d

14. If d × c + b and a ∅ b , then which of the following conclusion is true?
    (a) c o d　　　　　(b) a ∅ d
    (c) d + a　　　　　(d) a ÷ b

Directions for questions 15 to 19: Arrange the following sentences in a logical order to make a coherent paragraph.

15. A. Fusion, you would say, is a relatively new term.

    B. Amassed by Sheikha Hussah and Sheikh Naser-al-Sabah of Kuwait over a period of 25 years, the 297 fine art pieces on view since May 18 depict the cultural, political and religious influences of society at an important time in history.

C. Most of the pieces date back to the 17th century.

D. But when you walk into the British Museum and saunter through the collection of jewels and jewelled artifacts from Islamic India, you know the phenomenon could not be all that new.

(a) ADBC   (b) ABCD

(c) BACD   (d) CADB

16. A. It is a perfect showcase of the fusion of Islamic and Indian creative ideas along with the European artistic influences that shaped Mughal art as we know it today.

    B. The exhibition, 'Treasury of the World', put together by curator Manuel Keene is on till September 2.

    C. The art objects on display underline how flexible Indian craftsmen were in the 17th century in adapting and using foreign techniques.

    D. At the same time, however, they had the creativity to move beyond imitation and develop their own, unique style.

(a) ABCD   (b) ADCB

(c) BACD   (d) ACDB

17. A. The exhibition begins by laying out the various types of stone settings.

    B. The naturally lit line within the agate creates a border around the large agate in the center of the ornament.

    C. The 'channel settings' are remarkable as they allow the gemstones to retain their natural lines without breaking the pattern.

    D. An example of how the natural beauty of the stones has been enhanced is an elegant diamond and agate upper armband made of gold and worked in the *kundan* technique.

(a) ABCD   (b) DACB

(c) BCDA   (d) ACDB

18. A. A considerable number of European jewellers may have been employed in India during the Mughal period especially under the rule of Emperor Aurangzeb (1658 – 1707).

    B. A large section of the current exhibition is devoted to the influence of enamel on Mughal art.

    C. And they may have been instrumental in the development of the enamel work technique.

D. Enamel was used extensively from the 16th century till the 19th century.

(a) BADC   (b) ABCD

(c) DABC   (d) ACBD

19. A. The East-West blend in jewellery cannot be missed.

    B. Rings with gold linear designs connect to white enamel shapes.

    C. Without a doubt, they are Indian, but their decoration is distinctly European.

    D. Even in the early Mughal period, thumb-protecting archery rings in India sported definite European features.

    E. But Indians turned the technique to their own use for making dagger handles out of jade with enamel, for instance.

(a) DCABE   (b) ABCDE

(c) CADBE   (d) BDACE

Directions for questions 20 and 21: Each question is followed by two statements, I and II. Answer the questions using the following instructions:

(a) If the question can be answered by one of the statements alone, but cannot be answered by using the other statement alone.

(b) If the question can be answered by using either statement alone.

(c) If the question can be answered by using both the statements together, but cannot be answered by using either statement alone.

(d) If the question cannot be answered even by using both the statements together.

20. A, B and C are points on a circle. What is the angle ACB?

    I.   Segment AB divides the circle into two equal halves.

    II. $\angle ABC = 35°$

21. What is the distance of the point (x, y) from the origin?

    I. $x^2 + y^2 = 9$

    II. $x = 3, y = 0$

Directions for questions 22 to 25: In the following questions, there are two statements followed by two conclusions numbered I and II. You have to take the given statements to be true even if they seem to be at variance with commonly known facts. Read the conclusions and then decide which of them logically follows.

Mark answer:

(a) If only conclusion I follows

(b) If only conclusion II follows

(c) If both conclusions I and II follow

(d) If neither conclusion I nor II follows

22. **Statements:**

All hard workers are fools.

Some fools are brilliant.

Conclusions:

I. Some fools are not brilliant.

II. Some fools are hard workers.

23. **Statements:**

No champion is healthy.

All healthy are obese.

Conclusions:

I. Some obese are not champions.

II. Some healthy are not champions.

24. **Statements:**

Some seniors are juniors.

No junior is bad.

Conclusions:

I. Some seniors are bad.

II. Some seniors are not bad.

25. **Statements:**

No boy is girl.

Some girls are cultured.

Conclusions:

I. Some cultured are not boys.

II. No girl is a boy.

Directions for questions 26 to 30: Answer the questions based on the information given below.

On rolling 6 dice, it is found that:

I. three of the dice show the same number. The rest show different numbers.

II. only one die shows 6.

III. not more than 3 dice show 4 or more.

26. What is the minimum possible total of numbers on the faces if the three dice having same number show 2?

(a) 14   (b) 21

(c) 16   (d) 9

27. What is the maximum total if 4 of the dice show less than 4?

(a) 29   (b) 23

(c) 17   (d) 22

28. What would be the maximum total if 3 dice are faulty and have only 5 on all faces? (Condition III is waived.)

(a) 31   (b) 28

(c) 34   (d) 44

29. If only 1 die shows 1, what is the maximum number of dice with numbers greater than 4?

(a) 3   (b) 1

(c) 2   (d) 4

30. What is the maximum number that can be on the face of the 3 dice which show the same number?

(a) 2   (b) 4

(c) 3   (d) 5

Answer Key

1. (a)	**2.** (d)	**3.** (c)	**4.** (c)	**5.** (b)	**6.** (c)	**7.** (a)	**8.** (a)	**9.** (a)	**10.** (b)
11. (c)	**12.** (d)	**13.** (a)	**14.** (c)	**15.** (a)	**16.** (c)	**17.** (d)	**18.** (d)	**19.** (b)	**20.** (b)
21. (a)	**22.** (b)	**23.** (c)	**24.** (b)	**25.** (c)	**26.** (b)	**27.** (d)	**28.** (a)	**29.** (b)	**30.** (c)

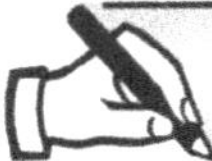

Explanations

1. a Here we have the relation.

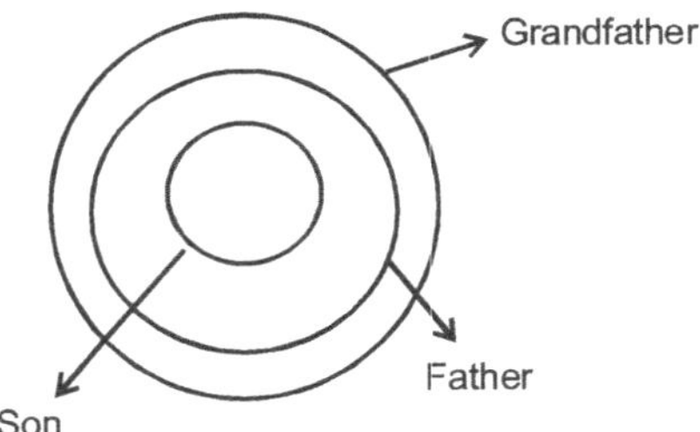

2. d All three are of different categories.

Car runs on road.

Train runs on rail.

Aeroplane flies.

Thus, the best diagramatic relationship is

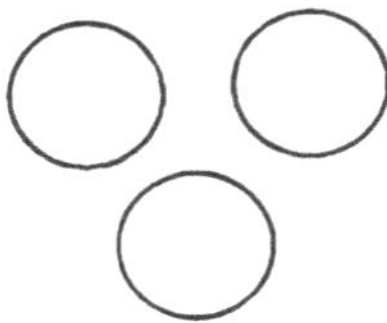

3. c Father comes under male gender. Mother comes under female gender which is not given. Thus, the best Venn diagram is

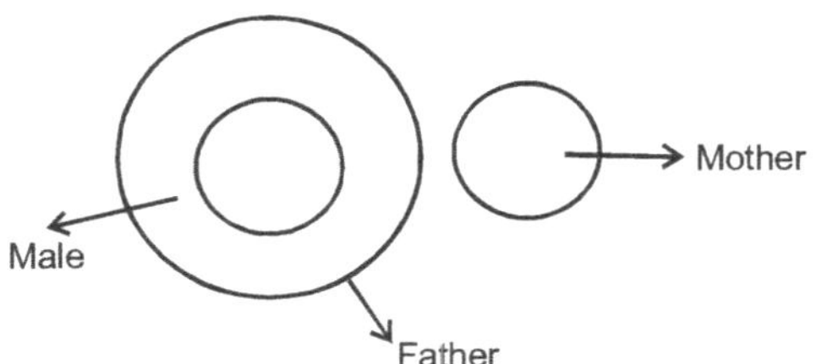

4. c Birds is a common category.

Feathers are related to birds but cow comes under animal category.

∴ The best venn diagram is

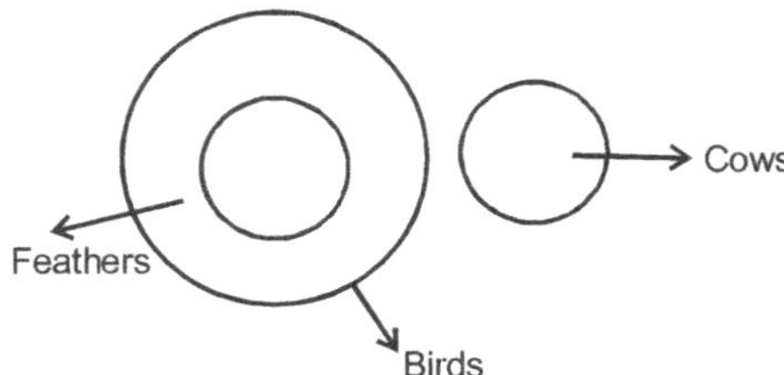

5. b Mother can be widow, a widow can be a doctor. Also, a mother can be a doctor. And a widow mother can be a doctor. Thus, the best Venn diagram is

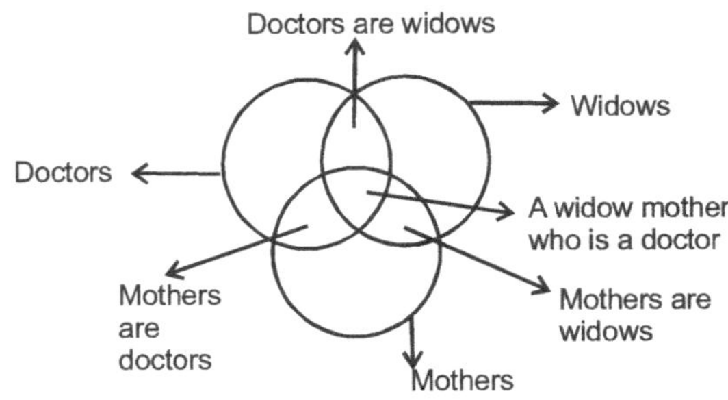

6. c Flowers have petals, thus considering flower as a wider category, petals are the parts of flower. The Venn diagram that represents best is

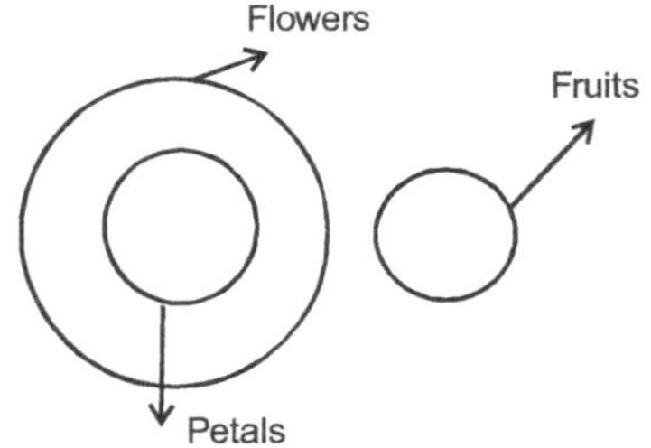

7. a All the terms are multiples of 3 except 91.

8. a All the terms are multiples of 5 except 58.

9. a

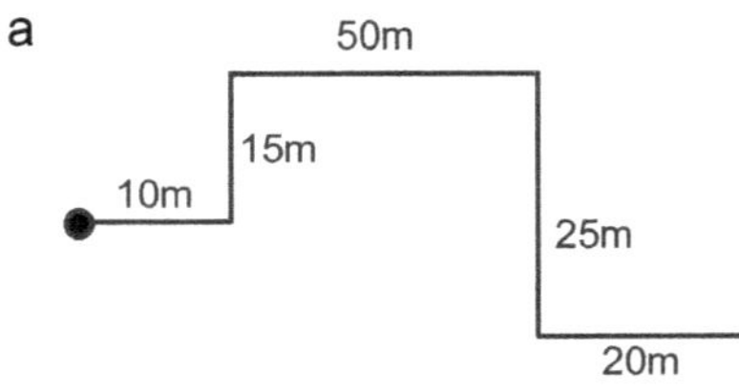

10. b On the basis of the directions given in the question, we arrive at the following diagram with the help of which the question can be solved easily.

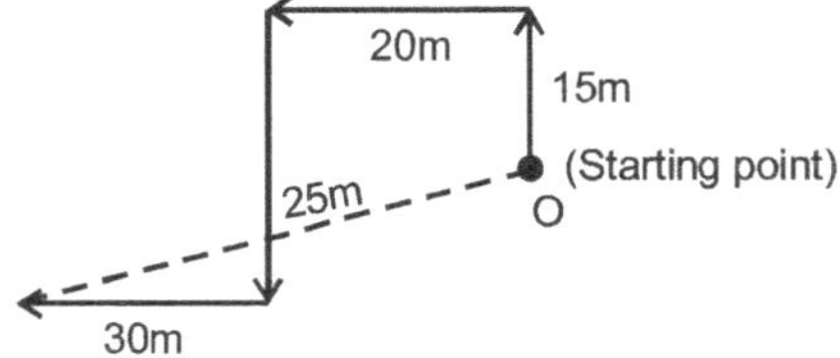

As per the diagram, Pawan is in the South-West direction with respect to the starting point.

11. c

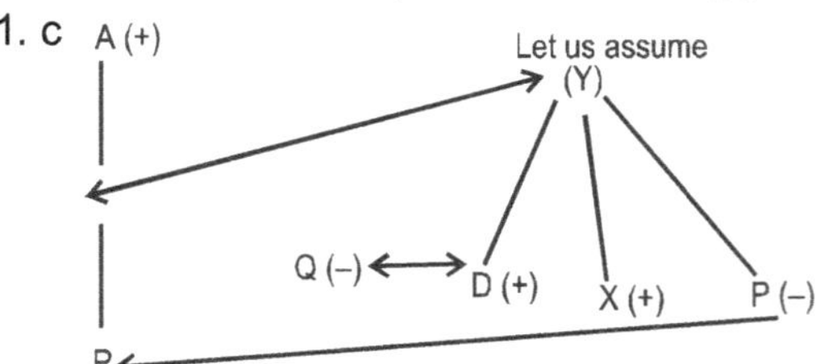

Obviously from the diagram it is clear that A is the grandfather of x.

12. d From the question, only son of Seeta's father is Seeta's brother, therefore son of Seeta's brother. Mohan is Seeta's nephew or Seeta is aunt of Mohan.

13. a After changing the given symbols to their appropriate meaning we get $a \geq b > c$ and $d > c$. Among the given options only option (a) is true.

14. c After changing the given symbols to their appropriate meaning we get $a \geq b > c \geq d$. Among the given options only option (c) is true.

15. a 'new' connects A to D. 'pieces' connect B to C. Hence, 'ADBC' is the correct sequence.

16. c 'It' in A refers to 'exhibition' in B. C provides reference to 'foreign' techniques, while D refers to 'unique styles'. Hence, 'BACD' is the correct sequence.

17. d Th word 'settings' links A to C. And 'agate' links D to B.

18. d 'they' in C refer to 'jewellers' in A. enamel connects B to D. Hence, 'ACBD' is the correct answer.

19. b 'they' in C refer to the 'rings' in B. 'European' in D links to 'Indians… own use' in E.

20. b Angle in a semicircle is right angle.

21. a (i) $x^2 + y^2 = 3^2$

   The circle is equidistant from the origin (0, 0), so the radius will be 3.

   So distance of point (x, y) from origin is 3.

   (ii) Distance of point (x, y) = (3, 0) from origin is 3.

For questions 22 to 25 :

22. b

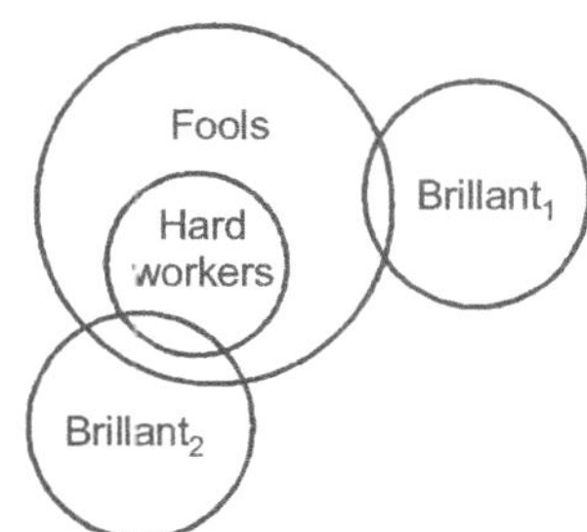

Only conclusion II follows.

23. c

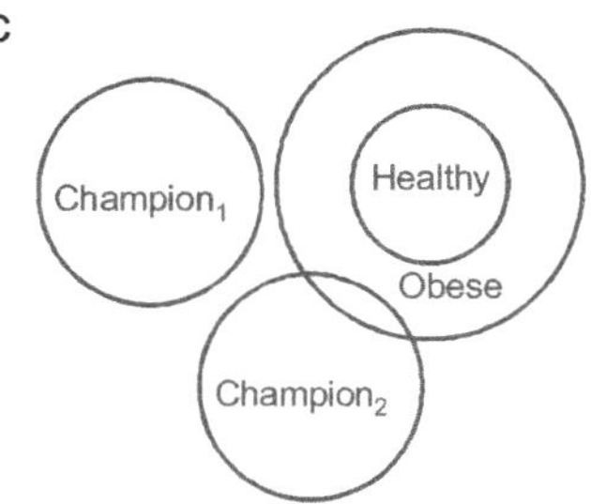

From the given venn diagram we can conclude that both I and II follow.

24. d

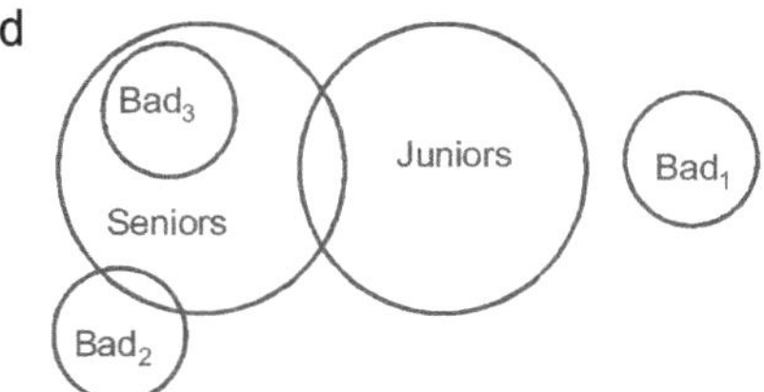

Neither conclusion I nor II definitely follow.

25. c

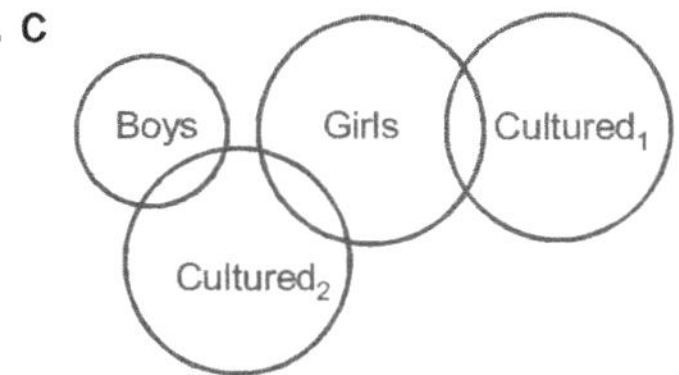

Both conclusion I and II follow.

For questions 26 to 30: Based on rules II and III, we can say that the 3 dice with the same number either show 1 or 2 or 3.

26. b $2 + 2 + 2 + 6 + 5 + 4 = 21$

27. d $3 + 3 + 3 + 6 + 2 + 5 = 22$

28. a $5 + 5 + 5 + 6 + 5 + 5 = 31$

29. b 2 because 1 die shows 6, one shows 1 and 3 are ≤ 3. Hence, one more can be greater than 4.

30. c One die should show 6. But there cannot be more than 3 dice showing 4 or more than 4. The maximum number that 3 dice can show is 3.

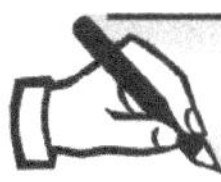

Practice Test-9

Number of questions: 30   **Time Allowed: 30 mins.**

Directions for questions 1 to 6: Choose the Venn diagram which best illustrates the relationship between three given classes in each of the following questions:

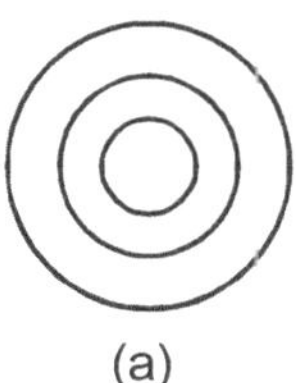

(a)

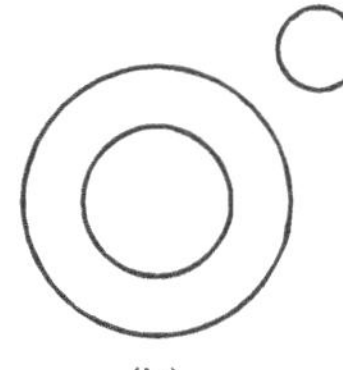

(b)

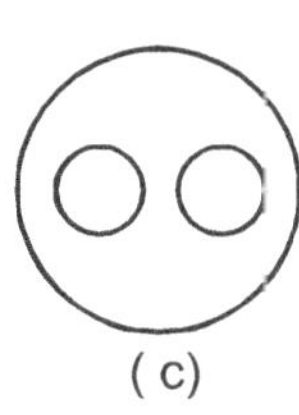

(c)

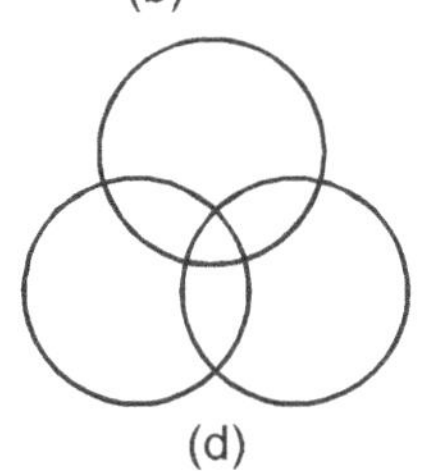

(d)

1. Stationery, Pen, Bat
2. Vehicle, Car, Scooter
3. Eatables, Vegetables, Brinjal
4. Graduate, Writer, Teacher
5. Uttar Pradesh, Rajasthan, India.
6. Doctor, Writer, Cook
7. If 'A + B' means 'A is the brother of B'. 'A – B' means 'A is sister of B'. 'A × B' means 'A is the mother of B' and ' A ÷ B ' means 'A is the father of B'. Which of the following would mean X is the grandfather of Y?

    (a) X × Z × Y + W   (b) Y + X ÷ Z ÷ W

    (c) X ÷ Z ÷ Y + W   (d) X + Y ÷ Z × W

8. Pointing to a photograph, Pawan said, "she is the mother of the wife of my brother's father." How is Pawan related to the lady in the photograph?

    (a) Mother   (b) Sister

    (c) Grandson   (d) Grandmother

9. Aditya left his house facing opposite to the sun in the morning at 6.45 a.m. He moved 50 m and took a left turn. Then he moved another 40 m and took a right turn. Then he moved 20 m and took a right turn, and after moving 25 m he stopped. Which direction is he facing now?

    (a) North   (b) South

    (c) East   (d) West

Directions for questions 10 and 11: Each question is followed by two statements, I and II. Answer the questions using the following instructions:

(a) If the question can be answered by one of the statements alone, but cannot be answered by using the other statement alone.

(b) If the question can be answered by using either statement alone.

(c) If the question can be answered by using both the statements together, but cannot be answered by using either statement alone.

(d) If the question cannot be answered even by using both the statements together.

10. The average age of the three people in the car is 30. Is any one of them above 40?

    I. The driver is 31 years old.

    II. All the three are past their teens.

11. What is the value of the prime number?

    I. The number is not divisible by any other prime number.

    II. When 6 is added to the number, the resultant is divisible by 2.

Directions for questions 12 to 15: In the following questions, there are two statements followed by two conclusions numbered I and II. You have to take the given statements to be true even if they seem to be at variance with commonly known facts. Read the conclusions and then decide which of them logically follows.

Mark answer:

(a) If only conclusion I follows

(b) If only conclusion II follows

(c) If both conclusions I and II follow

(d) If neither conclusion I nor II follows

12. **Statements:**

    Some books are magazines.

    Some magazines are thesauruses.

    Conclusions:

    I. Some books are thesauruses.

    II. Some thesauruses are not magazines.

13. **Statements:**

   All stars are bright.

   Some moons are bright.

   Conclusions:

   I. Some brights are moons.

   II. Some brights are stars.

14. **Statements:**

   No pant is a shirt.

   No shirt is a kurta.

   Conclusions:

   I. Some shirts are not pants.

   II. No kurta is shirt.

15. **Statements:**

   Some pens are pencils.

   No pencil is fan.

   Conclusions:

   I. Some pencils are not fans.

   II. Some pencil is a fan.

Directions for questions 16 to 20: Arrange the following sentences in a logical order to make a coherent paragraph.

16. A. It's called the gentle giant of the sea.

   B. The mindless slaughter on the shores of Gujarat in recent years, in particular, has gradually diminished its numbers.

   C. Yet, the mammoth whale shark — a docile warm-water creature, has received anything but gentle treatment along India's picturesque western coastline.

   D. Rhincodon typus, the world's largest fish, has obviously been in need of help.

   (a) ACBD   (b) BADC

   (c) ABCD   (d) CABD

17. A. The whale shark has now been added to Schedule 1 of the Wildlife Protection Act, making it the first fish on the list.

   B. So starting May 28, 2001, hunting whale sharks is an offence that could invite imprisonment.

   C. Not that whale shark fishing has stopped yet.

   (a) ABC   (b) BAC

   (c) CAB   (d) CBA

18. A. These individual trees are competing for the privilege of surviving in their descendants.

   B. The species could certainly perpetuate itself with a much more modest expenditure of living material.

   C. In flowering plants, the struggle for reproduction between different individuals often produces results which, if not directly harmful to the species, are at least incredibly wasteful.

   D. We need only think of the fantastic profusion of bloom on flowering trees like dogwood or Catalpa, or the still more fantastic profusion of pollen in trees which rely on fertilization by the wind, like pine and fir.

   (a) BDCA   (b) ADCB

   (c) ACBD   (d) CDAB

19. A. Much of the anxiety and negative attitudes that individuals may be feeling about the future, is undoubtedly due to the many pressures and uncertainties of the changing work environment.

   B. Rapid changes in business are making many workers vulnerable to pink slips, stagnation, and total disruption of their careers and financial lives.

   C. Fear of job security has become rampant in both the government and the private sector.

   D. Many employees have been left in a state of shock as they have watched many of their colleagues terminated and discarded.

   (a) DCBA   (b) CBAD

   (c) CDBA   (d) BCAD

20. A. It earned him a banishment from the sport for a year; much else has happened to Tyson since.

   B. When Tyson and Holyfield met to fight for the world heavyweight boxing crown the last time, Tyson did not tell his rival "I will enchant thine ear", but bit it all the same.

   C. It gives his promoters much to talk about and the spectators the thrill to watch in action someone who is both a hero and a villain rolled into one.

   D. He spent several years in prison for assault and rape, and has acquired a bad boy image which, in boxing, is not a hindrance but a help.

   (a) BADC   (b) BDCA

   (c) BDAC   (d) CBDA

21. Ramesh started moving to the right hand side while facing the sunset. He moved 25 m, took a left turn and moved another 20 m. After that he took a right turn and moved another 25 m. How far is he from the starting point?

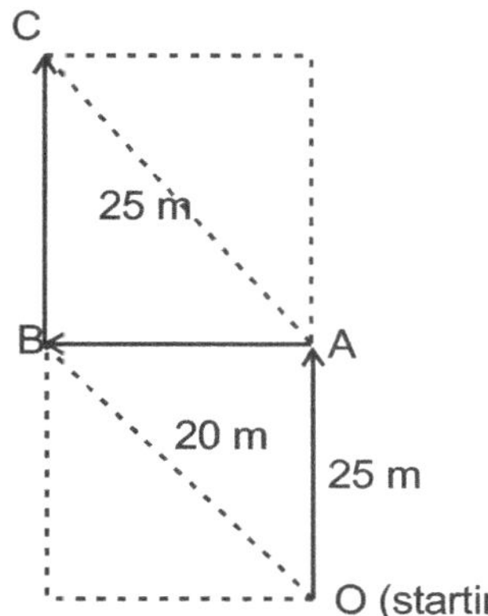

   (a) 45.28 m   (b) 48.36 m
   (c) 52.34 m   (d) 53.85 m

Directions for questions 22 and 23: In each of the following questions given below, which of the answer choices would replace the question marks '?'.

22. 4, 16, 36, 64, 100, ?
   (a) 144   (b) 121
   (c) 169   (d) 196

23. 1, 2, 3, 5, 8, 13, 21, ?
   (a) 31   (b) 33
   (c) 34   (d) 36

24. In a certain code language JAISALMER is coded as 11913459, what will be the code for ACCENTUATION in the same code language?

   (a) 133562312865   (b) 133552412956
   (c) 133543212965   (d) 133552312965

25. In a certain code language ELEPHANT is coded as UOBIQFMF, what will be the code for COCKROACH in the same code language?
   (a) IDBPRLDQD   (b) IDBPSLDPD
   (c) IDPBSLEPD   (d) IDPBSLFPD

Directions for questions 26 to 30: Answer the questions based on the following statement. A cube is coloured black on all the faces. It is cut into 64 smaller cubes of equal sizes.

26. How many cubes have two black opposite faces?
   (a) 8   (b) 16
   (c) 0   (d) 3

27. How many cubes are not coloured on any face?
   (a) 4   (b) 8
   (c) 16   (d) 0

28. How many cubes are coloured on three faces?
   (a) 20   (b) 0
   (c) 8   (d) 4

29. How many total number of cubes are there?
   (a) 64   (b) 24
   (c) 32   (d) 16

30. How many cubes are coloured on one face only?
   (a) 24   (b) 18
   (c) 32   (d) 16

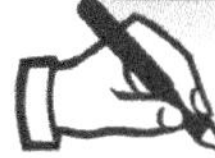

Answer Key

1. (b)	2. (c)	3. (a)	4. (d)	5. (c)	6. (d)	7. (c)	8. (c)	9. (a)	10. (c)
11. (a)	12. (d)	13. (c)	14. (c)	15. (a)	16. (a)	17. (a)	18. (d)	19. (d)	20. (a)
21. (d)	22. (a)	23. (c)	24. (d)	25. (b)	26. (c)	27. (b)	28. (c)	29. (a)	30. (a)

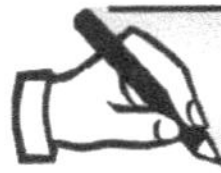

Explanations

1. b Pen is a stationery but bat is a sports equipment. Thus the best Venn diagram is

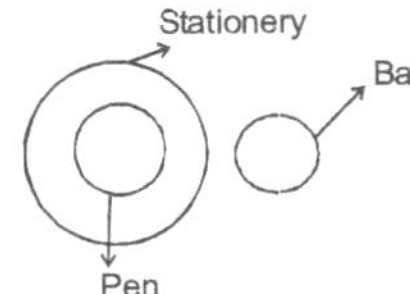

2. c Car is a four-wheeler vehicle. Scooter is a two-wheeler vehicle. Thus, the best Venn diagram is

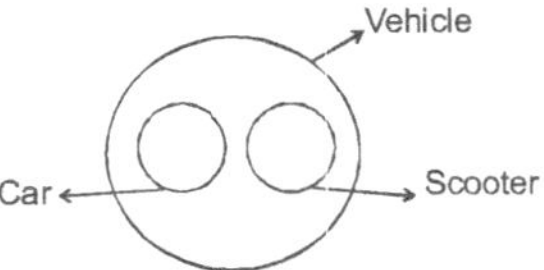

3. a Bringal is a vegetable. All vegetables are eatables. Thus, the best Venn diagram is

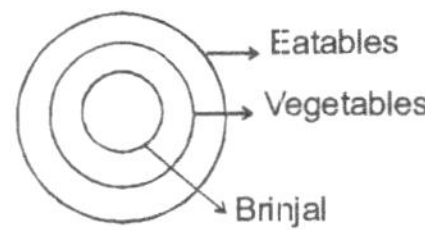

4. d Graduate can be a writer, writer can be a teacher, a teacher can be a graduate and vice-versa can also be true. Also, a graduate writer can be a teacher.

Thus, the best Venn diagram is

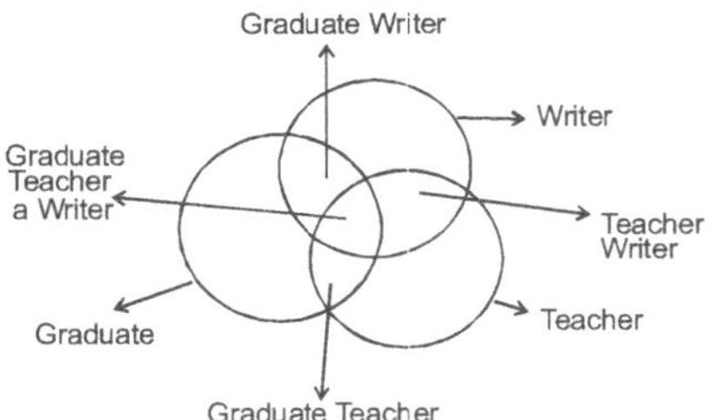

5. c Uttar Pradesh and Rajasthan are the states of India. Thus, the best diagram is

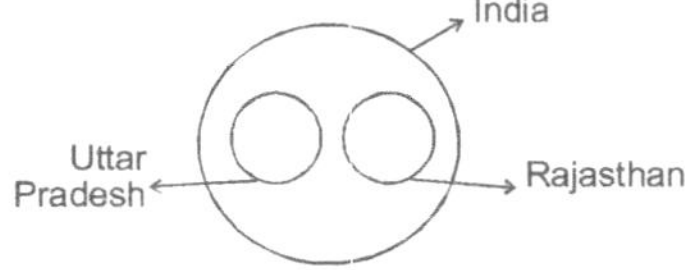

6. d Doctor, writer and cook is represented by the following Venn diagram.

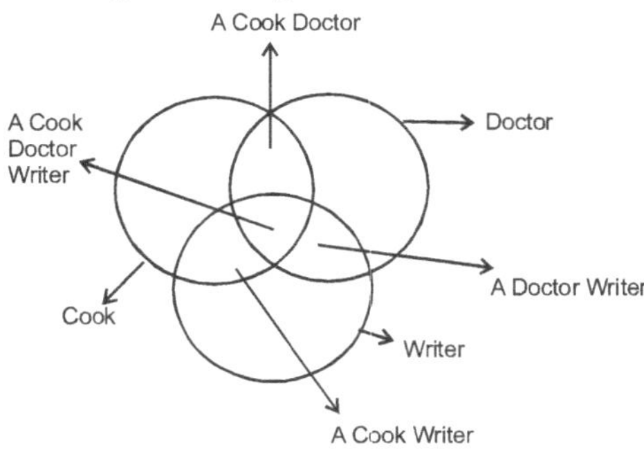

7. c Obviously, choice (c) holds good here. It says that X is the father of Z who is the father of Y and W, where Y and W are brothers.

8. c

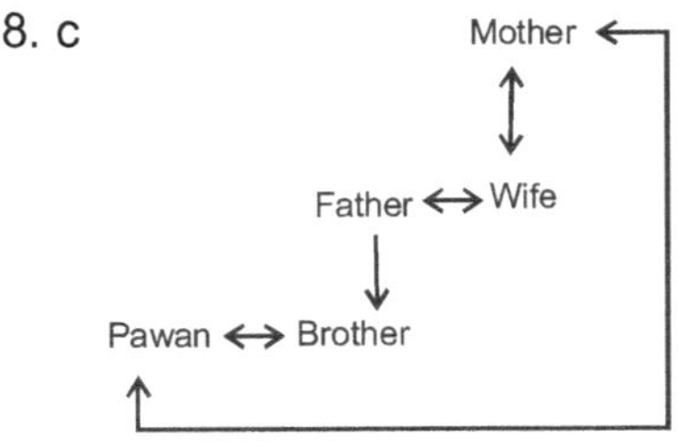

Pawan is the grandson of the lady in the photograph.

9. a From the given direction in the question, we draw the following diagram which helps us in solving the question.

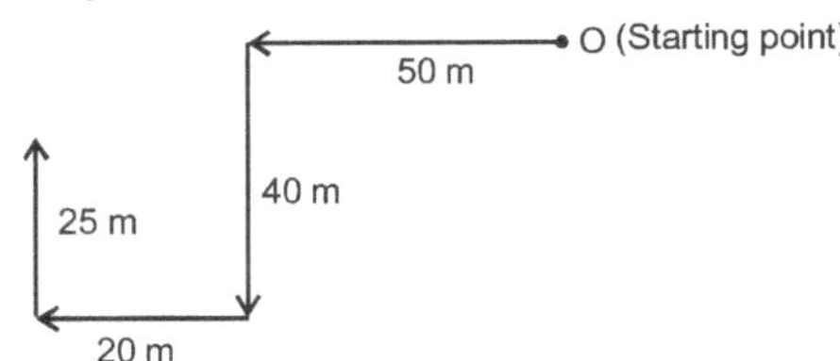

So obviously from the diagram above finally he is facing north.

10. c Combining statements I and II

Average age of 3 people = 30

Total age = 90

Age of other 2 people = 90 − 31 = 59

Since all of them are past their teens, there is none with age above 40.

11. a Statement I is redundant

Statement II gives the answer = 2

2 + 6 = 8; is divisible by 2

12. d

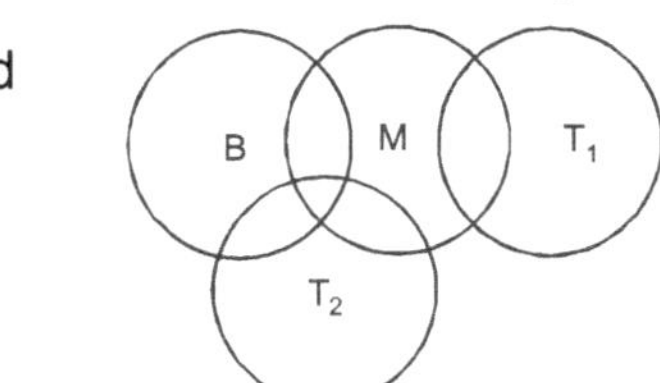

B - books   M - magazines   T - thesauruses

Neither conclusion I nor II follows.

13. c As per the given venn diagram, both conclusions I and II follow.

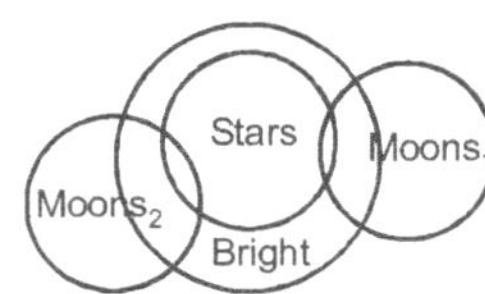

14. c

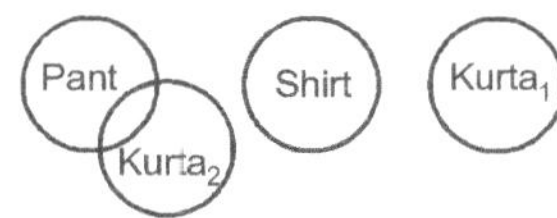

Both I and II follow.

15. a

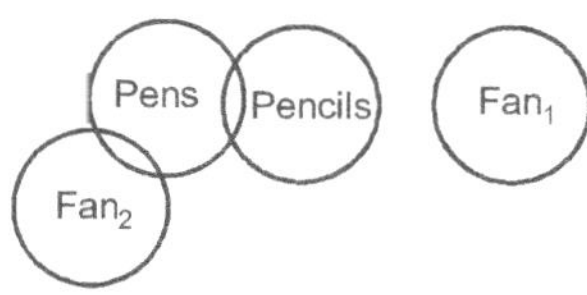

As per the given venn diagram, only conclusion I follows.

16. a The word 'gentle' links A to C. 'its' in B refers to 'whale shark' in C. Hence, 'ACBD' is the correct sequence.

17. a 'So' in B refers to the action in A. C provides contrast to B. Hence, 'ABC' is the correct sequence.

18. d The phrase, 'these trees' in A refers to pine, fir, dogwood and catalpa of D. The examples of flowering plants of C are given in D. Hence, option (d) is the correct sequence.

19. d B introduces the main idea of the passage i.e. vulnerability of workers. 'CA' is a mandatory pair as the words 'fear' and 'anxiety' denote thought continuation. Statement D gives the conclusion that employees have been left in a state of shock.

20. a 'BA' is thought continuation, as biting Holyfield's ear earned Tyson banishment. D follows by stating that his 'bad boy image' has helped him. C states 'how' it has helped him. Hence, 'BADC' is the correct sequence.

21. d

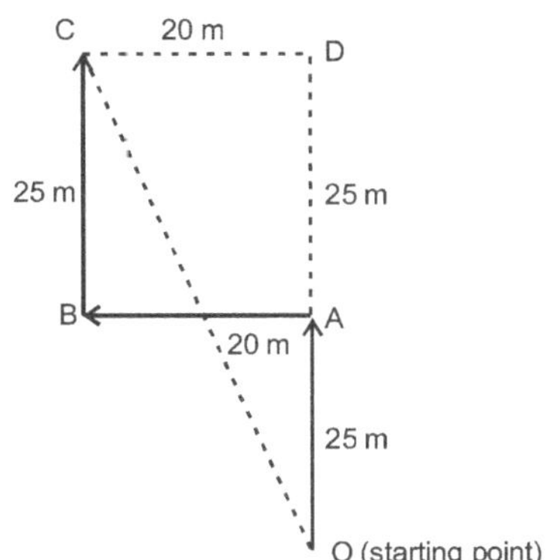

From the figure above that shows the movement of Ramesh, we are to figure out OC.

By Pythagoras' theorem $OC^2 = OD^2 + DC^2$

Or

$OC = \sqrt{OD^2 + OC^2}$ = OD = OA + AD

= OA + BC (as AD = BC)= 25 + 25

OD = 50 m and DC = AB = 20 m

So $OC = \sqrt{50^2 + 20^2}$

$= \sqrt{2500 + 400} = \sqrt{2900} = 53.85$ m

22. a The series is formed by the square of even numbers, starting with 2.

23. c A number is obtained as the sum of the previous two numbers.

24. d The numeral value of alphabets is coded. In case the alphabet has double digit value then they are added to result in a single digit. For example: JAISALMER

Alphabet		Numeral value	Code
J	→	10	1 + 0 = 1
A	→	1	1
I	→	9	9
S	→	19	1 + 9 = 10 = 1 + 0 = 1
A	→	1	1
L	→	12	1 + 2 = 3
M	→	13	1 + 3 = 4
E	→	5	5
R	→	18	1 + 8 = 9

Hence JAISALMER = 119113459, similarly ACCENATION can be coded to arrive at 133552312965.

25. b The letters of the word are reversed and the subsequent letter is written as its code, i.e.

ELEPHANT → TNAHPELE → UOBIQFMF

Similarly

COCKROACH → HCAORKCOC → IDBPSLDPD

Hence, choice (b) holds good.

26. c A small cube would have to be on two opposite faces of the larger cube at the same time; for this to be true.

27. b The dimensions of a larger cube = $4 \times 4 \times 4$ times the edge of the smaller cube. Since all the small cubes that are exposed are painted, only the ones that are inside will have no paint. Hence, the dimension of the unpainted centre will be $(4 - 2) \times (4 - 2) \times (4 - 2) = 8$.

28. c The cubes in each corner are coloured on three faces. Thus, 4 such cubes on the top surface and 4 on the bottom surface, thus, altogether 8.

29. a The question states, clearly, that there are 64 cubes altogether.

30. a On any one surface, there are four cubes that are coloured on one face only. Thus, altogether there are $6 \times 4 = 24$ such cubes.

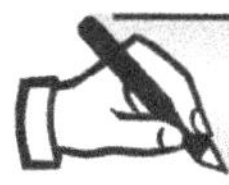

Practice Test-10

Number of questions: 30 **Time Allowed: 30 mins.**

Directions for questions 1 and 2: In each of the following questions, find the term that can replace the questions mark.

1. AD, EI, JO, PV, ?
   (a) VD
   (b) WC
   (c) WD
   (d) VE

2. XYQ, ZAR, BCS, DET, ?
   (a) GFU
   (b) FUG
   (c) FZU
   (d) FGU

3. If 'P + Q' means 'P is the mother of Q',
   'P ÷ Q' means 'P is the daughter of Q' and
   'P – Q' means 'P is the sister of Q',
   then which of the following represents 'A is the husband of B'?
   (a) B + A – N
   (b) B ÷ A + N
   (c) B + N ÷ A
   (d) B ÷ A ÷ R

4. In the question 3, which of the following represents 'B is the son of F'?
   (a) B + C ÷ F – D
   (b) F – C + D ÷ B
   (c) F + B ÷ C
   (d) None of these

5. In a certain code language 'rain' is coded as 'water' 'water', is coded as 'air', 'air' is coded as 'food' and 'food' is coded as 'computer', then what will be the code for the thing that satiates our hunger?
   (a) air
   (b) water
   (c) food
   (d) computer

6. In a certain code language TRACTOR is coded as VTCEVQT, what will be the code for GENUINE in that code language?
   (a) IGPWKPH
   (b) IGPXKPG
   (c) IGPWKPG
   (d) IGPWLPG

Directions for questions 7 to 11: Answer the questions on the basis of the following letter series:

A	B	C	D	5	F	G	H	9	J	K	L	M
N	15	P	Q	R	16	T	U	22	W	X	Z	

7. If the above letters are written in the reverse order, which letter will be the 16th letter from the left?
   (a) K
   (b) L
   (c) M
   (d) J

8. Which letter/number is 5th to the left of the 19th letter from the right of A?
   (a) N
   (b) P
   (c) Q
   (d) 15

9. Which letter/number is 9th to the left of the 14th letter from your left?
   (a) 5
   (b) C
   (c) T
   (d) R

10. Which of the following would replace the ? mark?
    AC5   G9K   M15Q   ?
    (a) Q16U
    (b) RT22
    (c) 16UW
    (d) 16TU

11. Which letter is between the 7th letter from left and the 11th letter from right?
    (a) K
    (b) L
    (c) M
    (d) J

Directions for question 12: Choose the Venn diagram which best illustrates the relationship between the three given classes.

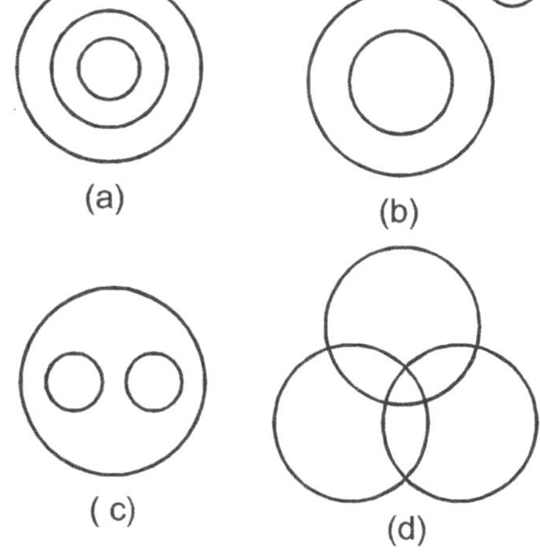

12. Banana, Mango, Fruits

Directions for questions 13 to 16: In the following questions, there are two statements followed by two conclusions numbered I and II. You have to take the given statements to be true even if they seem to be at variance with commonly known facts. Read the conclusions and then decide which of them logically follows.

Mark answer:

(a) If only conclusion I follows

(b) If only conclusion II follows

(c) If both conclusions I and II follow

(d) If neither conclusion I nor II follows

13. **Statements:**

    All paintings are beautiful.

    All photos are paintings.

    Conclusions:

    I.   All beautiful are paintings.

    II. All paintings are photos.

14. **Statements:**

    Some cats are rats.

    No rat is a bat.

    Conclusions:

    I.   Some bats are not cats.

    II. Some rats are not cats.

15. **Statements:**

    Some whites are black.

    No whites are green.

    Conclusions:

    I.   Some whites are green.

    II. Some whites are not green.

16. **Statements:**

    All flowers are stems.

    All stems are roots.

    Conclusions:

    I.   All roots are flowers.

    II. All stems are flowers.

Directions for questions 17 and 18: Each question is followed by two statements, I and II. Answer the questions using the following instructions. Choose the answer as:

(a) If the question can be answered by one of the statements alone, but cannot be answered by using the other statement alone.

(b) If the question can be answered by using either statement alone.

(c) If the question can be answered by using both the statements together, but cannot be answered by using either statement alone.

(d) If the question cannot be answered even by using both the statements together.

17. What sum did Raman keep in his savings bank account ?

    I.   The interest for the first year was Rs. 600 and for the second year was Rs. 672.

    II. Raman never withdrew any money from the account within two years.

18. A plane, starting from London at 9 a.m. local time, reached New York at 9 a.m. local time. How long did the flight last ?

    I.   The plane spent half hour in mid-air refuelling.

    II. When the plane landed at New York, it was 3 p.m. London time

Directions for questions 19 to 23: Arrange the following sentences in a logical order to make a coherent paragraph.

19. A. Shastry is not the lone one to adopt the mantle of a crusading apostle for Sanskrit.

    B. Prima facie their efforts are noble – some would say native, given that Sanskrit in its classical sense existed only as an exclusive preserve of the learned, never as an item of mass currency.

    C. But it's in the note of alacrity and urgency with which such efforts are being espoused and patronised, with eyes firmly set on its attendant emotive baggage, that is cause for worry.

    D. Pandit Sadanand Dikshit, a scholar from the Kendriya Sanskrit Vidyapeeth, Tirupati, runs a similar campaign called the Lok Bhasha Prachar Samiti in Puri, Orissa.

    (a) ABCD   (b) DABC

    (c) ADBC   (d) BDCA

20. A. There's an inbuilt subtlety here, for political projects often come encased in declarations of good intent.

    B. To illustrate, look no further than Union HRD Minister Murli Manohar Joshi. "Sanskrit and the study of its literature would be a great help in bringing about a renaissance of values in our modern strife-ridden society," says Sanskrit's chief patron in the government.

    C. The symbolic value of Sanskrit is ideal fodder for the BJP's dream project of shaping a *'Hindu rashtra'*.

    D. The intimate relationship between power and knowledge has never been more fully revealed than here.

    (a) ADCB   (b) CDBA

    (c) DABC   (d) ABCD

21. A. A new UGC course in astrology and Vedic rituals and an ISRO project on ancient Indian astronomy, go along with the creation of a string of new Sanskrit departments and universities.

    B. The handsome boost that the languishing language and its practitioners have received – its annual budget having gone up by seven times in the past five years – should have been worthy of praise, but for the zealous overdrive that marks it.

    C. The controversial NCERT proposal to make Sanskrit compulsory in schools from class 3 to 10 bears out this intent.

    D. Lamenting the deteriorating quality of techniques of imparting it, an overhaul is suggested – by teaching Sanskrit in Sanskrit, instead of the in-vogue grammar-translation method, so that students are "able to understand properly and utilise the wealth of knowledge, both spiritual and scientific, contained in Sanskrit literature for human welfare".

    (a) ADCB   (b) ABCD

    (c) DCBA   (d) BADC

22. A. A pilot project is under way in about 100 CBSE schools in the country.

    B. The NCERT would assess the project, make the necessary revisions and then move to "universalise it".

    C. Students in many Delhi schools – Modern, St Columba's Ramjas and Mother's International – are being taught Sanskrit in Sanskrit.

    D. But the apologists, despite their reformist tilt towards Sanskrit pedagogy, fall prey to a greater danger – that of trivialising and reducing to kitsch what they hope to resurrect.

    (a) BDCA   (b) ACBD

    (c) DBCA   (d) CADB

23. A. The attempt to foist Sanskrit on the nation, on the pretext of popularising it, has reignited the potentially explosive politics of language – simmering ever since Hindi as the national language ran up against riots in Tamil Nadu in the '60s.

    B. The fear, well justified, therefore is that the attempt to turn Sanskrit into a revivalist symbol might similarly backfire, Says Mishra: "I hope the government takes a lesson from what happened to Hindi."

    C. A recent book by Bangalore-based computer scientist N.S. Rajaram and Bengal Vedic scholar Natwar Jha argues that the lineage of Vedic Sanskrit can be traced back to the Indus civilisation.

    D. Francois Gautier, South Asia correspondent of French daily *Le Figaro*, writes: "Let the scholars begin now to revive and modernise the Sanskrit language. It would be a sure sign of the dawning of the Indian Renaissance."

    (a) CDAB   (b) DACB

    (c) ABCD   (d) BDCA

Directions for questions 24 to 28: Answer the questions based on the following information.

- Each radio station transmits on a frequency that is at least 10 cycles more or less than that of another station.

- Station A is 10 cycles lower than station B.

- Station B is 20 cycles lower than station C.

- Station D is 50 cycles higher than station E.

- Station E is 10 cycles higher than station F.

- Station F is 30 cycles lower than station B.

24. Which of the statements about an additional station R could be true?

    (a) Station R operates on a frequency between A and B.

    (b) Station R operates on a frequency between B and C.

    (c) Both (a) and (b).

    (d) Station R operates on a frequency between C and D.

25. What is the order of stations from the highest frequency to the lowest?

    (a) D C B A F E   (b) A B F E D C

    (c) F E A B C D   (d) D C B A E F

26. If A were to reduce by 10 cycles, it would overlap with
    - (a) E
    - (b) D
    - (c) C
    - (d) B

27. The difference between the frequencies of A and F is ___ cycles.
    - (a) 40
    - (b) 30
    - (c) 20
    - (d) 10

28. Which station is 10 cycles higher than station F?
    - (a) A
    - (b) B
    - (c) C
    - (d) E

29. The door of my house faces east. I walk 100m from my back door, then turn right and walk 100 m and turn left and walk 50 m and reach a point X. In which direction am I from the starting point?
    - (a) North-West
    - (b) South-West
    - (c) North
    - (d) North-East

30. If P is to the south of Q and R is to the east of Q, in what direction is P with respect to R?
    - (a) South-West
    - (b) South
    - (c) North-East
    - (d) North

Answer Key

1. (c)	2. (d)	3. (c)	4. (d)	5. (d)	6. (c)	7. (d)	8. (d)	9. (a)	10. (c)
11. (a)	12. (c)	13. (d)	14. (d)	15. (b)	16. (d)	17. (c)	18. (c)	19. (c)	20. (d)
21. (b)	22. (b)	23. (a)	24. (b)	25. (d)	26. (a)	27. (b)	28. (d)	29. (a)	30. (a)

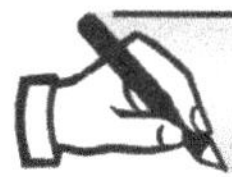

Explanations

1. c The first letter of subsequent groups have a difference of 4, 5 and 6 places respectively, whereas the second letter of the subsequent groups has a difference of 5, 6 and 7 places, respectively. Therefore, on following the same pattern, we get 'WD' as the next term which would replace the question mark. Hence, choice (c) is the answer.

2. d Here, first two terms of every group of letters are in continuation, like XY, ZA, BC, DE, and the third letter of each group is again in forward continuation, i.e., Q, R, S, T. Hence, the term replacing the question mark would be FGU. Hence, choice (d) is the answer.

3. c From the question, A must be male and B must be female. Going by options, we get choice (c) as the answer, i.e. B + N ÷ A means B is the mother of N and N is the daughter of A, therefore A and B are father and mother of N respectively.

4. d While reading the question, we can conclude that B is a male. And after going through the choices, we find that in none of the choices (a) or (c), B is a male. And in choice (b), B turns out to be the brother-in-law of F.

5. d It is food that satiates our hunger and as food is coded as 'computer', choice (d) is the correct option.

6. c Each letter of the word is coded by the second letter next to it in the forward direction. Hence, choice (c) will be the code for GENUINE.

7. d Reverse order of series will be

   Z X W 22 U T 16 R Q P 15 N M L K J 9 H G F 5 D C B A
   ↑ 16th letter

8. d A B C D 5 F G H 9 J K L M N 15 P Q R 16 T U 22 W X Z
   ↑ 5th   ↑ 19th letter

9. a A B C D 5 F G H 9 J K L M N 15 P Q R 16 T U 22 W X Z
   ↑ 9th   ↑ 14th letter

10. c Each group is made by leaving one letter/number between two terms. Hence the next term would be 16UW.

11. a A B C D 5 F G H 9 J K L M N 15 P Q R 16 T U 22 W X Z
    ↑ 7th ↑ middle ↑ 11th from right

12. c Banana and mango are two different types of fruits. Thus, the best Venn-diagram is

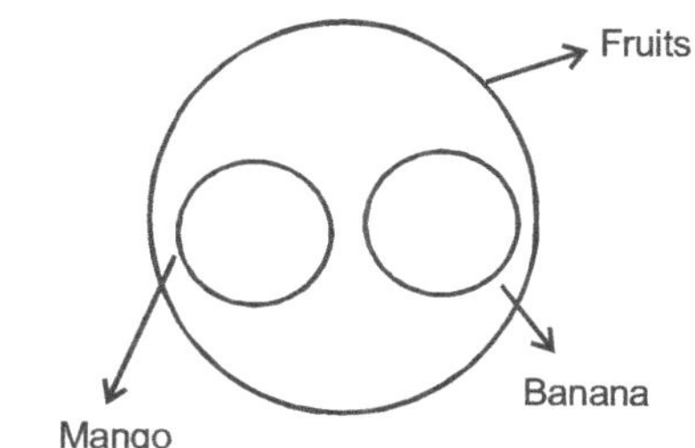

13. d

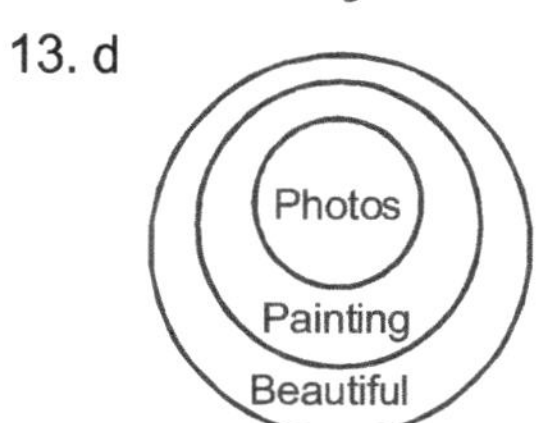

Neither I nor II follows.

14. d

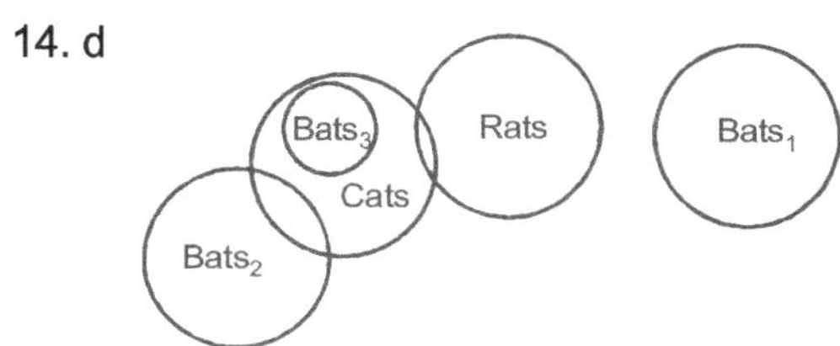

As per the given venn diagram neither of the two conclusions follows.

15. b

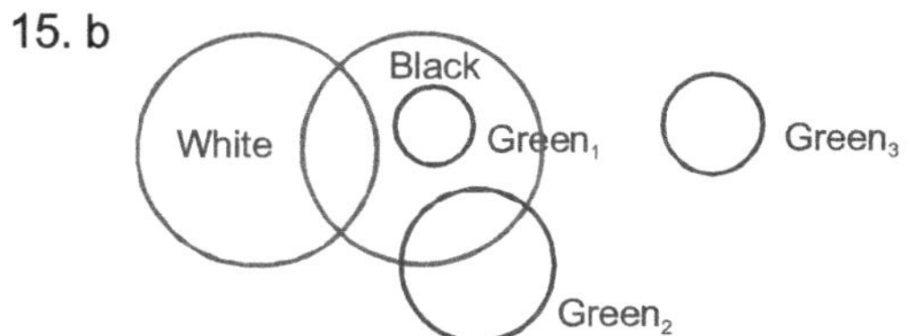

Only conclusion II follows.

16. d

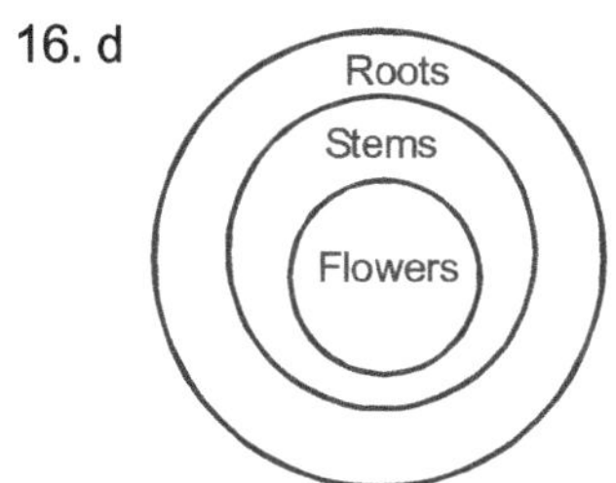

As per the given venn diagram neither conclusion I nor II follows.

17. c Both the statements are required to answer the question.

18. c Combining statements I and II, we get that the flight lasted for $5\frac{1}{2}$ hr.

19. c 'Shastry is not the only one' in A and 'Pandit Sadanand Dikshit' in D make a link. 'Efforts' are noble in B and a cause for worry in C. Hence, 'BC' forms a mandatory pair. So, 'ADBC' is the correct sequence.

20. d 'Political' in A can be directly related to 'HRD Minister' in B. 'Sanskrit' and 'BJP' in C can be related to 'power' and 'knowledge' in D. Hence, option (d) is the correct answer.

21. b The 'language' mentioned in B refers to 'Sanskrit' already stated in A. Also, the phrase 'bears out this intent' in C refers to 'zealous overdrive' in B. Hence, 'ABCD' is the correct sequence.

22. b C is more directly related to A as schools are exemplified. B and D discuss the operational aspects and the limitations. Hence, 'ACBD' is the correct sequence.

23. a 'CD' talks about the history of Sanskrit. 'AB' talks about the negative aspects. Hence, 'CDAB' is the answer.

For questions 24 to 28: All of the given information can be represented as

$A = B - 10$, $B = C - 20$, $D = E + 50$, $E = 10 + F$ and $F + 30 = B$

Let the frequency of A = 100 cycles. Now, the frequency of the other stations can be taken as

B = 110 cycles, C = 130 cycles, D = 140 cycles, E = 90 cycles and F = 80 cycles

Now, the answer of each question can be determined easily.

29. a The movement is:

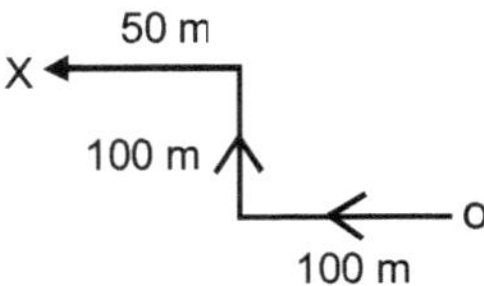

We have to assume that the back door faces the west.

30. a

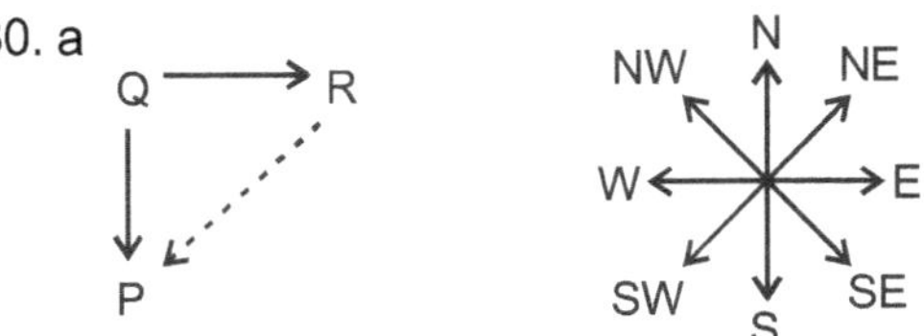

It is clear that P is to the South-West of R.

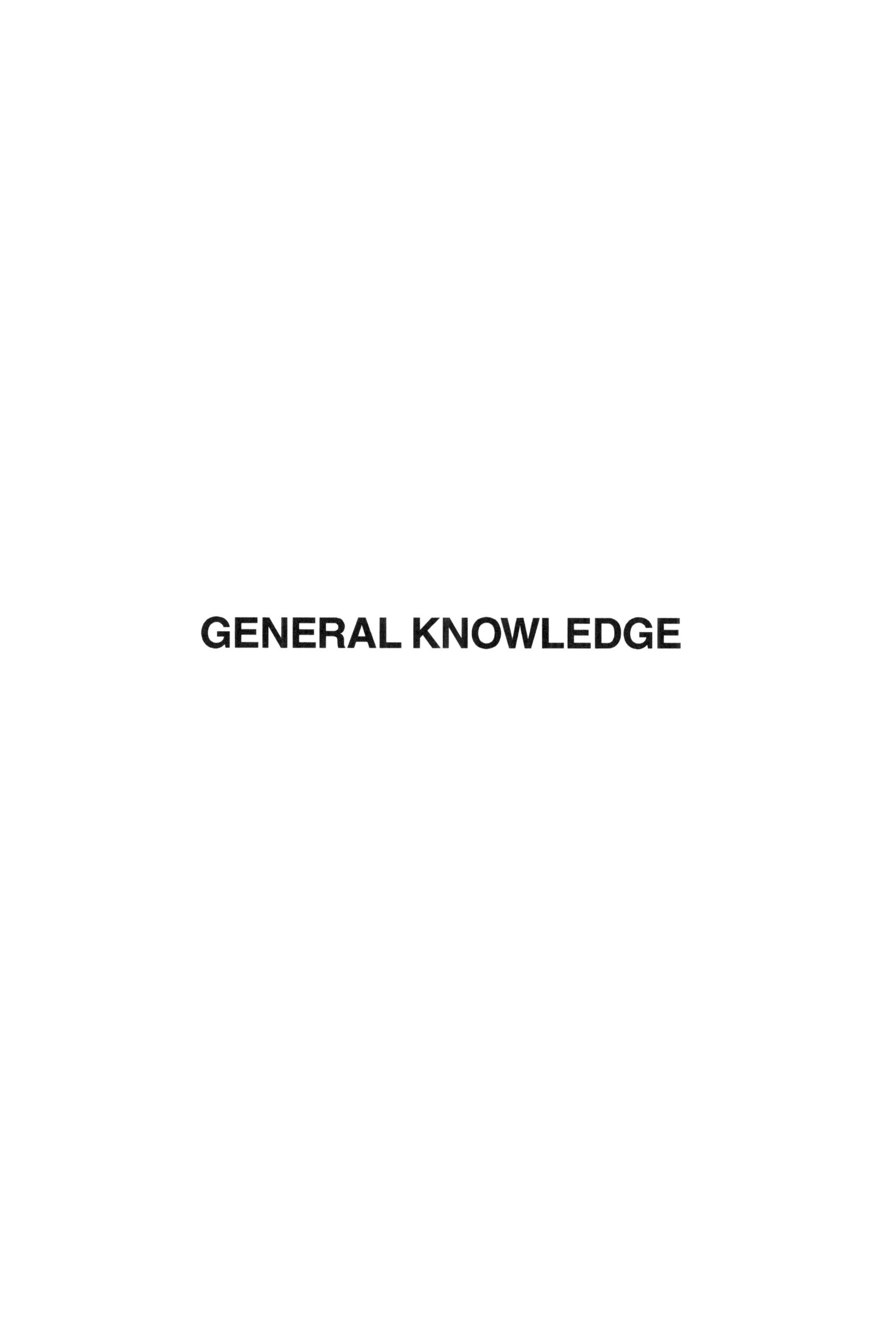

GENERAL KNOWLEDGE

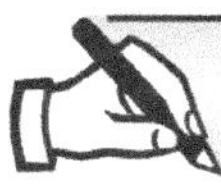# Practice Test-1

1. Who was the person behind the 'Kuka movement'?
   (a) Kunwar Singh   (b) V. B. Phadke
   (c) Guru Ram Singh   (d) Sir Syed Ahmad Khan

2. In the 552 — strong Lok Sabha, how many members are there from the Union Territories?
   (a) 10   (b) 20
   (c) 30   (d) 40

3. Which of the following personalities gave 'The Laws of Heredity'?
   (a) Robert Hook   (b) G. J. Mendel
   (c) Chearles Darwin   (d) William Harvey

4. Name the personality who was also known as Deshbandhu.
   (a) S. Radhakrishanan (b) G. K. Gokhale
   (c) Chittaranjan Das (d) Madan Mohan Malviya

5. Which of the following is NOT the language enshrined in the eighth schedule of the Indian Constitution, as the language of the state?
   (a) Nepali   (b) Kashmiri
   (c) English   (d) Konkani

6. The capital of Uttarakhand is
   (a) Masoorie   (b) Dehra Dun
   (c) Nainital   (d) None of these

7. *Geet Govind* is a famous creation of
   (a) Banabhatt   (b) Kalidas
   (c) Jayadev   (d) Bharat Muni

8. Which of the following represents the Finance Commissions that have been set-up so far?
   (a) 10   (b) 11
   (c) 12   (d) 15

9. World Trade Organization came into existence in
   (a) 1992   (b) 1993
   (c) 1994   (d) 1995

10. According to the Constitution of India, which of the following is NOT one of the main organs of the Government?
    (a) Legislature   (b) Bureaucracy
    (c) Executive   (d) Judiciary

11. In which year did the Cabinet Mission arrive in India?
    (a) 1942   (b) 1943
    (c) 1945   (d) 1946

12. Panchayati Raj comes under
    (a) Residual list   (b) Concurrent list
    (c) State list   (d) Union list

13. Which of the following constitutional amendments was responsible for deleting the right to property from the list of fundamentals rights?
    (a) 43rd amendment (b) 44th amendment
    (c) 48th amendment (d) 52nd amendment

14. *Harshcharita* and *Kadambari* are the works of
    (a) Kalhan   (b) Panini
    (c) Banabhatta   (d) Patanjali

15. When did the war of Americans Independence take place?
    (a) 1770   (b) 1772
    (c) 1774   (d) 1776

16. Which of the following countries is NOT a member of SAARC?
    (a) Maldives   (b) Bhutan
    (c) Malaysia   (d) Nepal

17. Bloemfontein is the judicial capital of
    (a) South Africa   (b) Denmark
    (c) Columbia   (d) The Netherlands

18. Which of the following planets is NOT a terrestrial planet?
    (a) Mercury   (b) Venus
    (c) Earth   (d) Saturn

19. What is the minimum age required to become the President, Vice-President of India or Governor of Indian state?
    (a) 21 years   (b) 25 years
    (c) 30 years   (d) 35 years

20. The Treaty of Versailles was signed in
    (a) 1914   (b) 1916
    (c) 1919   (d) 1923

21. Which of the following personalities was the first to climb Mount Everest twice?
    (a) Tenzing Norway   (b) Tamba Tsheri
    (c) Nawang Gombu   (d) Phu Dorjee

22. The controversial Tehri Dam was built over
    (a) Ganga   (b) Godavari
    (c) Bhagirathi   (d) Narmada

23. Which of the following constitutional amendments was responsible for the inclusion of Konkani, Manipuri and Nepali languages in the eighth schedule of the Constitution?
    (a) 68th amendment   (b) 70th amendment
    (c) 71st amendment   (d) 76th amendment

24. Vincent van Gogh was a
    (a) German poet   (b) Dutch painter
    (c) Polish scientist (d) French musician

25. Who was the first premier of Pakistan?
    (a) Liaquat Ali Khan
    (b) Mohammad Ali Jinnah
    (c) Ali Mohammad Khusro
    (d) Mohammed Ayub Khan

26. Telephone was invented by
    (a) J. L. Baird   (b) Alexander Graham Bell
    (c) K. Macmillan   (d) None of them

27. The famous Chinese traveller Fa-hien came to India during the reign of
    (a) Harshvardhan   (b) Chandragupta II
    (c) Kanishka   (d) Samudragupta

28. Name the Governor-General and the first Viceroy of India during whose tenure the 1857 revolt took place.
    (a) Lord Rippon   (b) Lord Curzon
    (c) Lord Canning   (d) Lord Hardinge

29. The absorption of ink by a blotting paper is based on
    (a) Newton third law of motion
    (b) Bernoulli's theorem
    (c) Pascal's law
    (d) Capillary action

30. The point in the orbit of any artificial satellite of earth which is at the maximum distance from the earth is known as
    (a) Perigee   (b) Aphelion
    (c) Antipodes   (d) Apogee

31. Mother Teresa won the Nobel Prize of peace in
    (a) 1977   (b) 1979
    (c) 1982   (d) 1984

32. Topographical map of India is approved by
    (a) Archaeological Survey of India
    (b) Geographical Survey of India
    (c) Surveyor General of India
    (d) None of these

33. This country is known as the 'Sugar Bowl of the World'. Identify it from the given options.
    (a) Brazil   (b) Cuba
    (c) Mexico   (d) Algeria

34. The North-East Frontier Agency became the Union Territory of Arunachal Pradesh in
    (a) 1947   (b) 1950
    (c) 1963   (d) 1972

35. Maastricht Treaty is related to
    (a) environment pollution
    (b) European unification
    (c) landmines
    (d) biological weapons

36. National Science Day is observed on
    (a) January 4   (b) February 28
    (c) March 11   (d) August 5

37. Capital of East Timor is
    (a) Kiev   (b) Dili
    (c) Grozny   (d) Bratislava

38. Can you identify this bowler who is the first in the history of the world cricket to have claimed 500 wickets in the One day Internationals?
    (a) Shane Warne   (b) Wasim Akram
    (c) Courtney Walsh   (d) Muttiah Muralitharan

39. The first woman Chief Minister of an Indian state is
    (a) Sarojini Naidu   (b) Indira Gandhi
    (c) Sucheta Kripalani (d) Rajkumari Amrita Kaur

40. This organelle of the human body is known as the 'powerhouse of the cell'. Name it from the given options.
    (a) Golgi bodies   (b) Mitochondria
    (c) Lysosomes   (d) Chloroplasm

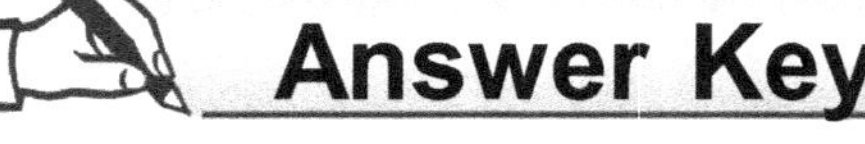

Answer Key

1. (c)	2. (b)	3. (b)	4. (c)	5. (c)	6. (b)	7. (c)	8. (d)	9. (d)	10. (b)
11. (d)	12. (c)	13. (b)	14. (c)	15. (d)	16. (c)	17. (a)	18. (d)	19. (d)	20. (c)
21. (c)	22. (c)	23. (c)	24. (b)	25. (a)	26. (b)	27. (b)	28. (c)	29. (d)	30. (d)
31. (b)	32. (c)	33. (b)	34. (d)	35. (b)	36. (b)	37. (b)	38. (b)	39. (c)	40. (b)

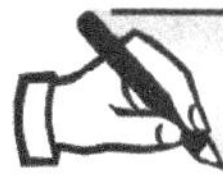

Practice Test-2

Number of questions: 40   **Time Allowed: 20 mins.**

1. This disease is caused by the deficiency of protein. Can you identify it from the given options?
   - (a) Goitre
   - (b) Kwashiorkar
   - (c) Hypokalemia
   - (d) Dermatosis

2. We all know very well that the Pacific Ocean is the earth's largest ocean. Which of the following represents the percentage area (approximately) of the earth covered by it?
   - (a) 25%
   - (b) 35%
   - (c) 40%
   - (d) 45%

3. This place is the wettest place on earth. Can you identify it from the given options?
   - (a) Mount Waialeale
   - (b) Cherapoonji
   - (c) Mawsynram
   - (d) None of these

4. The number of non-permanent members of the UN Security Council is
   - (a) 5
   - (b) 10
   - (c) 15
   - (d) 20

5. According to the latest population Census, the state with the least population density is
   - (a) Sikkim
   - (b) Mizoram
   - (c) Andaman & Nicobar Islands
   - (d) Arunachal Pradesh

6. The number of Union Territories in India is
   - (a) 5
   - (b) 6
   - (c) 7
   - (d) 8

7. The maximum duration for which the President's office can remain vacant is
   - (a) 1 month
   - (b) 2 months
   - (c) 3 months
   - (d) 6 months

8. Which of the following represents the minimum age required to become the member of the Rajya Sabha?
   - (a) 25 years
   - (b) 30 years
   - (c) 35 years
   - (d) There is no age limit as such

9. As per the Constitution of India, the fundamental rights are _______ in number.
   - (a) 5
   - (b) 6
   - (c) 7
   - (d) 8

10. Sakyamuni is another name of
    - (a) Mahavir
    - (b) Buddha
    - (c) Lord Shiva
    - (d) Lord Vishnu

11. *The Maratha* and *The Kesari* were the two main newspapers started by
    - (a) Lala Lajpat Rai
    - (b) Gopal Krishna Gokhale
    - (c) Bal Gangadhar Tilak
    - (d) Madan Mohan Malviya

12. National emergency arising out of war, armed rebellion or external aggression is dealt under
    - (a) Article 280
    - (b) Article 352
    - (c) Article 356
    - (d) Article 370

13. Which of the following personalities is considered to be the originator of Sankhya philosophy?
    - (a) Bharat Muni
    - (b) Kapila Muni
    - (c) Adi Shankaracharya
    - (d) Agatsya Rishi

14. Which of the following personalities from India is the only winner of Special Oscar in the history of Indian Cinema so far?
    - (a) Mrinal Sen
    - (b) Shyam Benegal
    - (c) Satyajit Ray
    - (d) Mira Nair

15. Mahatma Gandhi founded the ___ newspaper in 1903 at South Africa.
    - (a) Indian Opinion
    - (b) Harijan
    - (c) Indian Speaker
    - (d) India News

16. Who wrote *Arthashastra*?
    - (a) Kalhana
    - (b) Vishakhadutta
    - (c) Banabhatta
    - (d) Chanakya

17. Chauri Chaura incident, which took place in 1922, find prominence in the India's national movement. Can you identify the state in which Chauri Chaura is located?

    (a) Maharashtra   (b) Uttar Pradesh

    (c) Rajasthan   (d) Uttar Pradesh

18. H. J. Kania was the first

    (a) Chief Justice of the Supreme Court of India

    (b) Attorney-General of India

    (c) Solicitor-General of India

    (d) None of them

19. Who among the following is known as 'The Saint of Gutters'?

    (a) Baba Amte   (b) Mother Teresa

    (c) Anna Hazare   (d) None of them

20. The capital of Ethiopia is

    (a) Abuja   (b) Dar-es-salaam

    (c) Adis Ababa   (d) Harare

21. World Human Rights Day is celebrated every year on

    (a) December 1   (b) December 3

    (c) December 10   (d) December 22

22. Which of the following represents the year in which NABARD was established?

    (a) 1976   (b) 1982

    (c) 1988   (d) 1992

23. Mesopotamia is the former name of

    (a) Tanzania   (b) Iran

    (c) Iraq   (d) Zambia

24. We All know very well that Gujarat has the longest coastline amongst all. Which of the following represents the length of the coastline of Gujarat?

    (a) 1200 km   (b) 1400 km

    (c) 1600 km   (d) 1800 km

25. This personality was also known as 'Blood and Iron Man of Germany'. Can you identify him from the given options?

    (a) Mustafa Kamal Ataturk

    (b) Benito Mussolini

    (c) Bismarck

    (d) Hitler

26. *Gulliver's Travels* is a famous work of

    (a) James Joyce   (b) Jonathan Swift

    (c) James Hilton   (d) Ernest Hemingway

27. Which of the following represents the original number of officially recognized languages enshrined in the Indian Constitution?

    (a) 14   (b) 16

    (c) 18   (d) 22

28. The first Battle of Panipat took place in

    (a) 1498   (b) 1516

    (c) 1526   (d) 1532

29. Sukumar Sen was

    (a) the first Chief Justice of the Supreme Court of India

    (b) the first Chief Election Commissioner of India

    (c) the first Speaker of the Lok Sabha

    (d) the first Governor of an Indian state

30. Lal Krishna Advani was the ___ Deputy Prime Minister of India.

    (a) fourth   (b) fifth

    (c) sixth   (d) seventh

31. Which of the following heads the table of Precedence of the Government of India?

    (a) Vice-President (b) Prime Minister

    (c) President   (d) Chief Justice of India

32. Which of the following cricketer holds the world record for being the captain of a team for maximum number of times?

    (a) Allan Border   (b) Alec Stewart

    (c) Sunil Gavaskar (d) Steve Waugh

33. Which among the following is the oldest High Courts in India?

    (a) Bombay   (b) Madras

    (c) Calcutta   (d) Delhi

34. Wightman Cup is associated with

    (a) table tennis   (b) lawn tennis

    (c) badminton   (d) volleyball

35. Netaji Subhash Institute of National Sports is situated at

    (a) Gwalior   (b) Patiala

    (c) New Delhi   (d) Bangalore

36. This personality is the winner of the maximum number of World Billiards Championship titles from India. Can you identify him from the given options?

    (a) Michael Ferrara (b) Geet Sethi

    (c) Wilson Jones   (d) Manoj Kothari

37. The Sardar Sarovar Project is based on river
    - (a) Godavari
    - (b) Tapti
    - (c) Narmada
    - (d) Krishna

38. Jyotiba Phule was founder of
    - (a) Servants of India society
    - (b) Satya Sodhak Samaj
    - (c) Home rule movement
    - (d) Tatva Bodhini Sabha

39. The height of the tallest mountain of the world — Mount Everest is
    - (a) 8,834 metres
    - (b) 8,838 metres
    - (c) 8,842 metres
    - (d) 8,848 metres

40. He is known as the 'Builder of Modern Turkey'. Can you name him from the given options?
    - (a) Marshal Tito
    - (b) Anwar Sadat
    - (c) Mustafa Kamal Ataturk
    - (d) Benito Mussolini

Answer Key

1. (b)	**2.** (b)	**3.** (c)	**4.** (b)	**5.** (d)	**6.** (c)	**7.** (d)	**8.** (b)	**9.** (b)	**10.** (b)
11. (c)	**12.** (b)	**13.** (b)	**14.** (c)	**15.** (a)	**16.** (d)	**17.** (b)	**18.** (a)	**19.** (b)	**20.** (c)
21. (c)	**22.** (b)	**23.** (c)	**24.** (c)	**25.** (c)	**26.** (b)	**27.** (d)	**28.** (c)	**29.** (b)	**30.** (d)
31. (c)	**32.** (d)	**33.** (c)	**34.** (b)	**35.** (b)	**36.** (b)	**37.** (c)	**38.** (b)	**39.** (d)	**40.** (c)

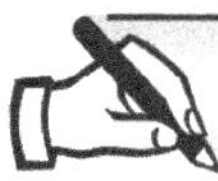

Practice Test-3

Number of questions: 40 **Time Allowed: 20 mins.**

1. 'AFP', is the news agency of
   (a) UK   (b) USA
   (c) Germany   (d) None of these

2. Which of the following represents the year in which Alexander invaded India?
   (a) 323 BC   (b) 324 BC
   (c) 326 BC   (d) 328 BC

3. Khyber Pass is in
   (a) Pakistan   (b) India
   (c) Myanmar   (d) Afghanistan

4. The first secretary-general of the United Nations was
   (a) U. Thant
   (b) Trygve Lie
   (c) Boutros-Boutros Ghali
   (d) Javier Perez de Cuellar

5. Southern Railway is headquartered at
   (a) Hyderabad   (b) Bangalore
   (c) Secunderabad (d) Chennai

6. First ministerial meeting of World Trade Organization (WTO) took place at
   (a) Washington   (b) New York
   (c) Geneva   (d) Singapore

7. The highest producer of milk in world is
   (a) USA   (b) China
   (c) India   (d) Germany

8. The first woman chief justice of high court of India was
   (a) Fatima Biwi
   (b) Ruma Pal
   (c) Leila Seth
   (d) None of these

9. Identify the correct match:

Date		Celebrated as
(a) May 8	-	World Health Day
(b) May 1	-	World Literacy Day
(c) May 17	-	World Telecommunication Day
(d) June 5	-	World Ozone Day

10. The world record for the fastest double century in tests is held by
    (a) Sanath Jaisurya   (b) Nathan Astle
    (c) Adam Gilchrist   (d) Saeed Anwar

11. The first speaker of the Lok Sabha was
    (a) K.M. Munshi   (b) C.D.Deshmukh
    (c) G.V. Mavalankar   (d) H.J.Kania

12. Which of the following represents the number of member nations of the Non-Aligned Movement?
    (a) 54   (b) 75
    (c) 93   (d) 118

13. This personality is known as the Father of Economics. Can you identify him from the given options?
    (a) J.M.Keyens   (b) Adam Smith
    (c) Abraham Maslow   (d) J.K. Galbraith

14. Mount Etna is a famous volcano located in
    (a) Argentina   (b) Italy
    (c) Mexico   (d) Phillipines

15. Where is the Tungabhadra sanctuary located?
    (a) Madhya Pradesh
    (b) Uttar Pradesh
    (c) Karnataka
    (d) West Bengal

16. The agency of United Nations that was set up to strengthen the international cooperation in the field of education and improve the standards of education is
    (a) UNEP   (b) UNCTAD
    (c) UNESCO   (d) UNDP

17. Reserve Bank of India is headquarted at
    (a) Kolkata   (b) New Delhi
    (c) Mumbai   (d) Chennai

18. *Jana Gana Mana*, was accepted as the National Anthem of India by the Constituent Assembly of India in which of the following years?
    (a) 1950   (b) 1949
    (c) 1948   (d) 1947

19. The person who has climbed Mount Everest the most — 17 times — is
    (a) Babu Chheri   (b) Appa Sherpa
    (c) Peter Hillary   (d) T. W. Tenzing

20. Which Indian state has its maximum area under the forest cover?
    (a) Maharashtra
    (b) Madhya Pradesh
    (c) Arunachal Pradesh
    (d) Kerala

21. This personality is known as *The Father of Geometry*. Identify him from the given option.
    (a) Euclid   (b) Pythagoras
    (c) Newton   (d) Laplace

22. The biggest producers of oil within the members of Organization of Petroleum Exporting Countries (OPEC)   is
    (a) Iraq   (b) Iran
    (c) Saudi Arabia   (d) Kuwait

23. The first Indian animation film was produced by
    (a) H. S. Bhatwadekar
    (b) Dada Saheb Phalke
    (c) Hiralal Sen
    (d) J. F. Madan

24. Who is the founder of the World Economic Forum?
    (a) George McDonald
    (b) Jack Barry
    (c) Robert Allen
    (d) Klaus Schwab

25. Who among the following is the author of *Meghdoot*?
    (a) Bana Bhatta   (b) Kalhana
    (c) Kalidas   (d) Tulsidas

26. Under whose presidentship, the first session of Indian National Congress took place in Bombay?
    (a) A. O. Hume
    (b) Dadabhai Naoroji
    (c) G. K. Gokhale
    (d) W. C. Bannerjee

27. How many members are there in the Rajya Sabha?
    (a) 238   (b) 242
    (c) 246   (d) 250

28. Panama Canal links which of the following water resources?
    (a) Pacific Ocean and Atlantic Ocean
    (b) Red Sea and Mediterranean Sea
    (c) Red Sea and Caspian Sea
    (d) Atlantic Ocean and Arctic Ocean

29. Which of the following rays is NOT harmful?
    (a) Ultraviolet rays
    (b) X-rays
    (c) Infrared rays
    (d) Short radio waves

30. Who is considered as the *Father of History*?
    (a) Aristotle   (b) Herodotus
    (c) Socrates   (d) Plato

31. Who among the following Indian President has also been the speaker of the Lok Sabha?
    (a) N. Sanjiva Reddy
    (b) R. Venkatraman
    (c) Dr. Shankar Dayal Sharma
    (d) Giani Zail Singh

32. Over which of the following rivers, the Bhakhra Nangal dam is built?
    (a) Ravi   (b) Chenab
    (c) Sutluj   (d) Beas

33. The Ottawa process negotiations are related to
    (a) environmental pollution
    (b) ozone layer's depletion
    (c) nuclear weapons
    (d) banning of landmines

34. What percentage of the world area is occupied by India?
    (a) 1.3%   (b) 2.4%
    (c) 4.5%   (d) 5.7%

35. In which of the following years, the General Agreement on Tariffs and Trade (GATT) came into existence?
    (a) 1947   (b) 1948
    (c) 1969   (d) 1984

36. In a normal healthy man, the quantity of blood is about
    (a) 3 litres   (b) 4 litres
    (c) 5 litres   (d) 6 litres

37. The credit for the classification of the blood groups goes to
    (a) William Harvey
    (b) K. Landsteiner
    (c) Robert Hook
    (d) Z. Janssen

38. Which part of the body gets affected in Pleurisy?
    (a) Joints
    (b) Lungs
    (c) Liver
    (d) Throat

39. *Unhappy India* is the name of the book written by
    (a) Bal Gangadhar Tilak
    (b) Lala Lajpat Rai
    (c) Gopal Krishna Gokhale
    (d) Dr Rajendra Prasad

40. The venue of the first Asian Games that took place in 1951 was
    (a) Bangkok
    (b) New Delhi
    (c) Tokyo
    (d) Manila

Answer Key

1. (d)	**2.** (c)	**3.** (d)	**4.** (b)	**5.** (d)	**6.** (d)	**7.** (c)	**8.** (c)	**9.** (c)	**10.** (b)
11. (c)	**12.** (d)	**13.** (b)	**14.** (b)	**15.** (c)	**16.** (c)	**17.** (c)	**18.** (a)	**19.** (b)	**20.** (c)
21. (a)	**22.** (c)	**23.** (b)	**24.** (d)	**25.** (c)	**26.** (d)	**27.** (d)	**28.** (a)	**29.** (d)	**30.** (b)
31. (a)	**32.** (c)	**33.** (d)	**34.** (b)	**35.** (b)	**36.** (c)	**37.** (b)	**38.** (b)	**39.** (b)	**40.** (b)

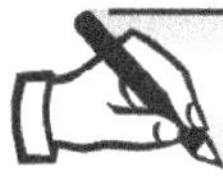

Number of questions: 40   **Time Allowed: 20 mins.**

1. International Rice Research Institute is based at
   - (a) Bangkok
   - (b) Manila
   - (c) Kuala Lumpur
   - (d) Tokyo

2. What is the effect on the density of a gas if it is heated under constant pressure?
   - (a) It will decrease
   - (b) It will increase
   - (c) Remains constant
   - (d) First it will increase and then decrease

3. The Life Insurance Corporation of India (LIC) came into being in which of the following years?
   - (a) 1952
   - (b) 1954
   - (c) 1956
   - (d) 1958

4. This person has written National Anthem for two nations. Who is he?
   - (a) Iqbal
   - (b) Bankim Chandra Chatterjee
   - (c) Rabindra Nath Tagore
   - (d) Sharat Chandra Chatterjee

5. Milk is basically a type of
   - (a) emulsion
   - (b) solvent
   - (c) suspension
   - (d) gel

6. Scientific principle of electric motor was discovered by which of the following scientists?
   - (a) Michael Faraday
   - (b) B. Franklin
   - (c) T. A. Edison
   - (d) Enrico Fermi

7. World Consumer Rights Day is observed on which of the following days?
   - (a) March 4
   - (b) March 15
   - (c) March 30
   - (d) April 7

8. The maximum contribution to the tax revenue collection of the government comes through
   - (a) income tax
   - (b) customs duty
   - (c) excise duty
   - (d) service tax

9. The capital of Portugal is
   - (a) Algiers
   - (b) Lisbon
   - (c) Brussels
   - (d) Madrid

10. Where is the headquarters of world's foremost Human Right's Organization, Amnesty International?
    - (a) Berlin
    - (b) New York
    - (c) London
    - (d) Geneva

11. During whose reign did Huen Tsang visited India?
    - (a) Kanishka
    - (b) Chandragupta
    - (c) Ashok
    - (d) Harsha

12. Which of the following is not an official language of the United Nations?
    - (a) Chinese
    - (b) French
    - (c) German
    - (d) Arabic

13. In which of the following years was the name of G-7 changed to G-8?
    - (a) 1994
    - (b) 1996
    - (c) 1998
    - (d) 1999

14. Where are the headquarters of the World Trade Orgnaization (WTO)?
    - (a) Brussels
    - (b) Geneva
    - (c) London
    - (d) Rome

15. 'White Revolution' is related to
    - (a) flood control
    - (b) fish production
    - (c) wheat production
    - (d) milk production

16. Which of the following days is celebrated as the International Labour Day throughout the world?
    - (a) April 1
    - (b) May 1
    - (c) June 1
    - (d) July 1

17. Brass is an alloy which consists of
    - (a) Zinc and Sulphur
    - (b) Sulphur and Copper
    - (c) Copper and Zinc
    - (d) Zinc and Magnesium

18. The youngest mountaineer to have scaled Mount Everest is
    - (a) Temba Tsheri
    - (b) Ang Rita
    - (c) Nawang Gombu
    - (d) Fu Dorjee

19. The World Tourism Day is celebrated on
    - (a) August 16
    - (b) September 3
    - (c) September 27
    - (d) October 7

20. India's first steel plant was set-up at
    - (a) Rourkela
    - (b) Bhilai
    - (c) Durgapur
    - (d) Jamshedpur

21. LIBOR stands for
    - (a) Long Island Borrowing Offer Rate
    - (b) London Inter Bank Offer Rate
    - (c) Luxemburg International Banks Organization Regime
    - (d) None of the above

22. When was the rupee devalued for the first time after independence?
    - (a) 1948
    - (b) 1949
    - (c) 1952
    - (d) 1954

23. Central Drug Research Institute (CDRI) is based at
    - (a) Jabalpur
    - (b) Pune
    - (c) Lucknow
    - (d) Hyderabad

24. The nature of Indian Economy can best be described as
    - (a) socialist
    - (b) mixed
    - (c) capitalist
    - (d) None of these

25. 'Cue' is a term used in which of the following sports disciplines?
    - (a) Billiards
    - (b) Football
    - (c) Hockey
    - (d) Chess

26. Word 'secular', was inserted into the Constitution of India with the help of which of the following constitutional amendments?
    - (a) 38th
    - (b) 36th
    - (c) 44th
    - (d) 42nd

27. The year in which the first train from Thane to Mumbai started in India was
    - (a) 1843
    - (b) 1848
    - (c) 1851
    - (d) 1853

28. A person bends forward to
    - (a) reduce atmospheric pressure
    - (b) decrease friction
    - (c) increase stability
    - (d) avoid slip-ups

29. 'Tripitakas', are the sacred text of
    - (a) Jainism
    - (b) Buddhism
    - (c) Hinduism
    - (d) Sikhism

30. Sanjukta Panigrahi is a famous dancer of
    - (a) Bharat Natyam
    - (b) Kathak
    - (c) Odissi
    - (d) Mohini Attam

31. Indian Agriculture Research Institute (IARI) is headquartered at
    - (a) New Delhi
    - (b) Mumbai
    - (c) Lucknow
    - (d) Bhopal

32. The name of the first cloned horse is
    - (a) Ponny
    - (b) Prometea
    - (c) Proteas
    - (d) Prozac

33. Brahmos is a/an
    - (a) Supersonic Cruise Missile
    - (b) Tank
    - (c) Submarine
    - (d) Fighter plane

34. Lucknow is situated on the banks of which of the following rivers?
    - (a) Gomti
    - (b) Godavari
    - (c) Narmada
    - (d) Ganga

35. 'Sugar Bowl of India', is
    - (a) Madhya Pradesh
    - (b) Uttar Pradesh
    - (c) Kerala
    - (d) Karnataka

36. Who among the following is credited with the invention of polio vaccine?
    - (a) Louis Pasteur
    - (b) Albert Sabin
    - (c) Jonas Salk
    - (d) Alexander Fleming

37. Which of the following countries is also known as 'Dairy of Northern Europe'?
    - (a) Switzerland
    - (b) Finland
    - (c) Denmark
    - (d) Belgium

38. Currency of Denmark is
    - (a) Rand
    - (b) Krone
    - (c) Pound
    - (d) Peseta

39. Which of the following is a Central Government tax?
    - (a) Income tax
    - (b) Corporation tax
    - (c) Sales tax
    - (d) Octroi

40. English education in India was introduced by
    - (a) Lord Dalhousie
    - (b) Lord Curzon
    - (c) Lord Macaulay
    - (d) Lord Rippon

Answer Key

1. (b)	**2.** (a)	**3.** (c)	**4.** (c)	**5.** (c)	**6.** (a)	**7.** (b)	**8.** (c)	**9.** (b)	**10.** (c)
11. (d)	**12.** (c)	**13.** (c)	**14.** (b)	**15.** (d)	**16.** (b)	**17.** (c)	**18.** (a)	**19.** (c)	**20.** (d)
21. (b)	**22.** (b)	**23.** (c)	**24.** (b)	**25.** (a)	**26.** (d)	**27.** (d)	**28.** (c)	**29.** (b)	**30.** (c)
31. (a)	**32.** (b)	**33.** (a)	**34.** (a)	**35.** (b)	**36.** (c)	**37.** (c)	**38.** (b)	**39.** (a)	**40.** (c)

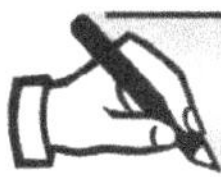

Practice Test-5

Number of questions: 40   **Time Allowed: 20 mins.**

1. Governor is appointed by the
   (a) Prime Minister
   (b) President
   (c) Chief Justice of India
   (d) Chief Justice of the concerned state high court

2. Find the odd one out.
   (a) A. Ramaswamy
   (b) Pankaj Advani
   (c) P. Harikrishna
   (d) S. S. Ganguly

3. *My Passage from India*, is a book authored by
   (a) E. M. Foster
   (b) Ismail Merchant
   (c) Mulk Raj Anand
   (d) Nirad C. Choudhary

4. *Coolie*, is a famous work of...
   (a) Khushwant Singh
   (b) V. S. Naipaul
   (c) Mulk Raj Anand
   (d) R. K. Narayan

5. This personality is credited with the invention of e-mail. Can you identify him from the given options?
   (a) T. Lee Burns
   (b) Larry Page
   (c) Ray Tomlinson
   (d) None of these

6. When did the Second Round Table conference took place?
   (a) 1915   (b) 1922
   (c) 1928   (d) 1931

7. 'Ansett' is the name of the domestic airline of which of the following countries?
   (a) New Zealand   (b) Germany
   (c) The Netherlands (d) Australia

8. Metals which chemically behave both as metals and non-metals is called
   (a) alloys   (b) metalloids
   (c) halogens   (d) chalkogens

9. Which of the following articles of the Constitution deals with financial emergency?
   (a) Article 352   (b) Article 356
   (c) Article 360   (d) Article 370

10. The largest river (in terms of volume of water it carries) is
    (a) Nile   (b) Mississippi Missourie
    (c) Amazon   (d) Yangtze

11. The World Environment Day is celebrated thought the world on______ every year.
    (a) May 8   (b) June 5
    (c) July 11   (d) August 27

12. FICCI expands to
    (a) Federation of Indian Companies of Commerce and Instrumentation
    (b) Federation of Indian Chambers of Commerce and Industries
    (c) Federation of International Chambers of Commerce and Industries
    (d) Federation of Indian Conglomerate of Commerce and Industries

13. This place is also known as the 'Manchester of South India'. Identify it from the given options.
    (a) Madurai
    (b) Coimbatore
    (c) Bangalore
    (d) Thiruvananthapuram

14. Approximately what portion of the world's population reside in India?
    (a) One-third   (b) One-fourth
    (c) One-fifth   (d) One-sixth

15. Decibel is the unit of
    (a) frequency   (b) wavelength
    (c) sound   (d) luminous intensity

16. Which of the following trains is India's first certified ISO-9001 train?
    (a) Mumbai-Delhi Shatabdi Express
    (b) Magadh Express
    (c) Bhopal Express
    (d) AP Express

17. Central Leather Research Institute (CLRI) is based at
    (a) Varanasi   (b) Chennai
    (c) Hyderabad   (d) Kanpur

18. December 1 is celebrated as the ___ throughout the world.
    (a) World Health Day
    (b) World AIDS Day
    (c) World Human Rights Day
    (d) World Habitat Day

19. Who wrote the book *The Algebra of Infinite Justice*?
    (a) Vikram seth   (b) Rohington Mistry
    (c) Anurag Mathur   (d) Arundhati Roy

20. 'Manas Tiger Sanctuary', is in
    (a) Uttar Pradesh   (b) Assam
    (c) West Bengal   (d) Rajasthan

21. Panini was
    (a) a Greek philosopher
    (b) an Indian astronomer and famous mathematician
    (c) a sanskrit grammarian of vedic times
    (d) great poet of ancient times

22. *Mein Kempf* is authored by
    (a) Karl Marx   (b) Napoleon Bonaparte
    (c) Adolf Hitler   (d) Benito Mussolini

23. Which of the following is the largest and the deepest ocean of the world?
    (a) Arctic   (b) Atlantic
    (c) Pacific   (d) Indian

24. The literacy rate of India is
    (a) 57.86%   (b) 61.34%
    (c) 63.98%   (d) 74.04%

25. Which Indian state has the least literacy rate?
    (a) Bihar   (b) Arunachal Pradesh
    (c) Rajasthan   (d) Orissa

26. SAARC was formed in
    (a) 1982   (b) 1984
    (c) 1985   (d) 1986

27. Which of the following is NOT the member of the European Union?
    (a) Greece   (b) Finland
    (c) Norway   (d) United Kingdom

28. ASEAN is headquartered at
    (a) Male   (b) Kathamandu
    (c) Jakarta   (d) Kuala Lumpur

29. This river was also called as the Ganges of the South. Name the river from the given options.
    (a) Godavari   (b) Krishna
    (c) Cauvery   (d) None of these

30. Which Indian state is inhabited by 'Jaintiya tribes'?
    (a) Arunachal Pradesh   (b) Mizoram
    (c) Manipur   (d) Meghalaya

31. The capital of Greece is
    (a) Warsaw   (b) Athens
    (c) Oslo   (d) Ottawa

32. This country is known as the cockpit of Europe. Identify it from the given options.
    (a) Poland   (b) Belgium
    (c) Turkey   (d) Sweden

33. *Natyashastra* is a famous work of
    (a) Banabhatta   (b) Bharatmuni
    (c) Kalhana   (d) Kalidas

34. In which of the following years did United Nations (UN) come into existence?
    (a) 1941   (b) 1943
    (c) 1944   (d) 1945

35. Eduskusta is the name of the Parliament of
    (a) Norway   (b) Finland
    (c) Austria   (d) Italy

36. The line that demarcates the boundary between India and Pakistan is
    (a) MacMahon Line   (b) Durand Line
    (c) Radcliffe Line   (d) None of these

37. Which of the following represents the number of judges in The International Court of Justice?
    (a) 12   (b) 15
    (c) 18   (d) 21

38. Obstetrics is
    (a) a branch of medicine that deals with pregnancy, labour and child birth
    (b) a branch of medicine that deals with child diseases
    (c) a branch of medicine that deals with eye related diseases
    (d) a branch of medicine that deals with kidney diseases

39. Which of the following years you would associate with the foundation of Indian National Congress (INC)?
    (a) 1875
    (b) 1881
    (c) 1883
    (d) 1885

40. The weight of the man will be ____ on the surface of the moon of his actual weight.
    (a) one-third
    (b) one-fourth
    (c) one-fifth
    (d) one-sixth

Answer Key

1. (b)	**2.** (b)	**3.** (b)	**4.** (c)	**5.** (c)	**6.** (d)	**7.** (d)	**8.** (b)	**9.** (c)	**10.** (c)
11. (b)	**12.** (b)	**13.** (b)	**14.** (d)	**15.** (c)	**16.** (c)	**17.** (b)	**18.** (b)	**19.** (d)	**20.** (b)
21. (c)	**22.** (c)	**23.** (c)	**24.** (d)	**25.** (a)	**26.** (c)	**27.** (c)	**28.** (c)	**29.** (c)	**30.** (d)
31. (b)	**32.** (b)	**33.** (b)	**34.** (d)	**35.** (b)	**36.** (c)	**37.** (b)	**38.** (a)	**39.** (d)	**40.** (d)

9 789392 837470